Letters from Ireland during the Famine of 1847

Alexander Somerville

Letters from Ireland during the Famine of 1847

ALEXANDER SOMERVILLE

Edited, with an introduction by
K.D.M. SNELL

IRISH ACADEMIC PRESS

This book was typeset
in 11 on 12.5 Ehrhardt by
Koinonia, Bury
and first published in 1994 by
IRISH ACADEMIC PRESS
Kill Lane, Blackrock Co. Dublin, Ireland,

and in North America by
IRISH ACADEMIC PRESS
c/o International Specialized Book Services,
5804 NE Hassalo Street, Portland, OR 97213.

A catalogue record for this title
is available from the British Library.

ISBN 0-7165-2530-5
0-7165-2545-3 (pbk)

First published in August 1994
Reprinted in November 1994

Printed in Ireland by
Colour Books Ltd.

CONTENTS

Places mentioned in *Letters from Ireland during the Famine of 1847*

INTRODUCTION

At an early point in his investigation of Ireland during the great famine, Alexander Somerville found himself one morning in Clonmel, on the 29th January, 1847. He had decided to accompany a convoy about to set off towards Waterford, to distribute Indian corn to the starving population. It was half past five and still dark, the morning was stormy, rain poured from a blackened and sullen sky, and there was a strong but increasingly saturated military escort gathering to accompany the laden carts.

Somerville waited. And as he surveyed the drenched scene, he commented on how few travellers stirred anywhere without fortifying themselves with weapons. Apparently the state of the country was such that pay clerks at public works were often attacked and robbed; land stewards and agents also never felt themselves to be safe. Such people, like commercial travellers, merchants, property owners and many others, went everywhere heavily armed. Somerville described how men came into hotels, and in taking off their coats, relieved themselves of a heavy burden of guns and pistols, which they carried or secreted in various parts of their clothing. He said that he had himself been warned that if he was to travel through the Irish country he had better arm himself in a similar fashion. Accordingly, he wrote, 'as arming seemed the order of the day, I armed myself ... I took one of my carpet bags and emptied everything of luggage kind out; took it to a baker's shop and purchased several shillings' worth of loaves of bread, and to a general dealer's shop, and purchased a piece of cheese. I put them in the bag, put the bag on the car by my side, ready, if any hungry Tipperarian or dweller on the Waterford mountains should present a blunderbuss at me, to put my hand into the bag, pull out, present, and throw to him a bullet of bread; not fearing but that this style of defence would be more effective than a defence by powder and lead.'[1] This passage reveals much about Somerville, about his abhorrence of repression and of his deeply sympathetic attitude towards the starving people of Ireland during the famine.

Alexander Somerville, known as 'The Whistler at the Plough', had himself been born into deep poverty in 1811, the eleventh child of a

---

1 *Letters from Ireland during the Famine of 1847*, p. 449 (hereafter *Letters*). On people arming themselves, see C. Woodham-Smith, *The Great Hunger: Ireland, 1845-9* (1962), pp. 150-1.

family living in a one-roomed, tiled hovel in Oldhamstocks, East Lothian. The hovel was windowless, except for a single pane of glass, owned and treasured by his farm labouring father, who moved it with him every time he changed his residence. His father had been born in Nether-aichlin-Sky, Perthshire, and his mother came from Ayton in Berwickshire. Both his parents were from very poor Scottish labouring families. Alexander himself had worked in his youth as a farm helper, ploughboy, sawyer, limekiln labourer, stone breaker, sheep shearer, itinerant harvester, drainer, quarryman, and dock labourer. This was not a promising start in life for a man of letters – a man whose voluminous writings included this forceful and very humane account of Ireland during the famine, first published as newspaper reports in the *Manchester Examiner*, and subsequently as part of his *The Whistler at the Plough* in 1852.[2] It is now reprinted under the title Somerville himself gave it.

One can best understand the sympathetic position he took during the Irish famine by appreciating the poverty he experienced as a farm worker, and the injustice he suffered at the hands of the British army. Much is known about him, for he was the author of a very readable nineteenth-century working-class autobiography, *The Autobiography of a Working Man* (1848).[3] In this he describes his childhood. 'I came into the family at a time when I could have been very well spared', he wrote, referring to the famine prices of 1811-13 and the poverty in which he grew up. His mother worked in the fields. His schooling had to be delayed because his parents could not find adequate clothing for him, other than the rags he normally wore. He was accordingly mistreated by the other children at school on account of his raggedness. His fondness for history – he was to write a history of the British Legion and the 1835-7 war in Spain, and a history of free trade and the Anti-Corn Law League[4] – began when he befriended an old blind shepherd, who held

2 The original pp. 433-624 of *The Whistler at the Plough* (Manchester, 1852) are reprinted here, using the title *Letters from Ireland During the Famine of 1847* which Somerville gave them. His 'Extracts from Irish *Letters*', on the state of Ireland in 1843, are included at the end, just as he published them. There is a further discussion of Irish rural conditions in 1843 in *The Whistler at the Plough* (1852 ed.), pp. 185-192, entitled 'Journey from Navan to Trim. Visit to the birthplace of the Duke of Wellington in 1843'. This has been reprinted here as an Appendix. The English and Scottish part of *The Whistler at the Plough* has been reprinted as a separate book, under that title, by Merlin Press, 1989, edited by K.D.M. Snell.

3 Alexander Somerville, *The Autobiography of a Working Man* (1848, 1951 ed.). This autobiography provided the basis for the summary of the life of 'a peasant, bred and nurtured under the most disadvantageous circumstances' in Scotland, in R.M. Garnier, *Annals of the British Peasantry* (1895), pp. 321-8.

4 A. Somerville, *History of the British Legion and War in Spain* (1839); and his *Free Trade and the League: a Biographical History* (1852), the latter originally published with *The Whistler at the Plough*.

imaginary conversations with Elizabethan courtiers. At an young age he began his miscellany of employments in agriculture and other labouring work. The early pages of his *Autobiography* tell much about working conditions in his region of Scotland at the time. On harvest migration for example, such a prevalent feature of nineteenth-century Irish life, he wrote that 'To us who went from Lothian to the Merse, the higher wages was always the ruling cause of our migration, and no amount of work ... deterred us.'[5] But it was a difficult time, with many men facing unemployment, and there was much political agitation to improve miserable living standards. Somerville seems to have joined in some of the activity in Edinburgh in support of political reform. After failing to find employment as a librarian (he was considered socially too inferior for such a job), and being unsuccessful in trying to attract subscriptions for a newspaper, Somerville himself enlisted in the Scots Greys.

In doing this, he set in train the tragic and brutal course of events which made him celebrated among the public, and which had a major influence on his later development and attitudes. The harrowing story is told in considerable detail in his *Autobiography*. He first served in Brighton, and was then marched to Birmingham, through the rural areas affected by the 'Captain Swing' unrest of 1830-1. Birmingham on the eve of the Reform Act was regarded as a danger to the political establishment, a hotbed of radical reformist ideas, one of the main venues for Reform riots. The Scots Greys were ordered to sharpen their swords to prepare to deal with crowd trouble. It was only a decade or so since the Peterloo Massacre of innocent civilians.

It was then that Somerville wrote a letter to the editor of the *Weekly Dispatch*. He said that while the Scots Greys could be relied upon to put down disorderly conduct, they should never be ordered to lift up arms against the liberties of the country and peaceful demonstrations of the people. The inexperienced officer in charge, Major Wyndham, saw fit to take this as a libel on the regiment. Accordingly, Somerville was then charged at an informal and very hastily convened 'court martial' with a trumped up offence, and was sentenced to a military flogging of two hundred lashes. He refused to grovel before Major Wyndham in the anticipated manner, refused to accept rum from the other soldiers before the flogging, and bore the flogging in silence in front of the regiment on parade. The relentlessly detailed pages telling of it in his *Autobiography* provide a harrowing and enduring castigation on the British army at this time. 'I put my tongue between my teeth, held it there, and bit it almost in two pieces. What with the blood from my tongue, and my lips, which I had also bitten, and the blood from my lungs, or some other internal

5 *Autobiography*, p. 107.

part ruptured by the writhing agony, I was almost choked, and became black in the face ... Only fifty had been inflicted, and the time since they began was like a long period of life: I felt as if I had lived all the time of my real life in pain and torture, and that the time when existence had pleasure in it was a dream, long, long gone by.'[6] Finally, after a hundred lashes, he was taken down in case he died – and in the hospital afterwards said, 'This shall be heard of, yet; I shall make it as public over England as newspapers can make it.'[7]

His case became front-page news, discussed in Parliament, referred to the King. The incident was officially investigated, and the regiment's officers were execrated in public by indignant crowds. There were large popular demonstrations against flogging in the army. The English rural labouring poor were as sympathetic to his case as were workers in the towns. Major Wyndham received an official reprimand. Somerville became a hero of the reform movement, used for political ends, in many cases against his inclinations. A public subscription was started for him. He met and was befriended by William Cobbett, a man who also had considerable experience of the army, who had made his voice heard against military flogging, and who had written at length on conditions in Ireland, often in a similar tone to that later adopted by Somerville.[8] Cobbett offered him advice on a career as a writer. Somerville was able in August 1832 to purchase his release from the army, and he returned to Scotland, where he went back to work as a wood sawyer in Edinburgh. His efforts to start a paper and then a shop were unsuccessful. So he joined the so-called 'British Legion', serving with it for two years in Spain, involved in the very grim warfare of 1835-7 on behalf of Queen Isabella against her uncle, Don Carlos. He received special commendations and was promoted to lieutenant, before being invalided out in 1837 with a bullet in his arm which he carried with him to the grave.

His politics were not of the more radical kind, and he became increasingly 'conservative' during his life – although his conservatism was of an idiosnycratic, humane and economically liberal kind, informed also by his Scottish covenanting background. In the 1830s he supported the transported Tolpuddle Martyrs, but berated trade-union leaders for seizing on the Martyrs' cause in an opportunistic way, which was not primarily concerned with the plight of the persecuted Dorset labourers. He condemned anti-combination laws, but criticised restrictions on entry practised by trade unions via apprenticeship, and the unions' secrecy. In 1837 he published his *Narrative of the British Legion in Spain*, an account

6 *Autobiography*, p. 189.
7 *Autobiography*, p. 190
8 See D. Knight (ed), *Cobbett in Ireland; a Warning to England* (1984).

of his military experience of the Spanish Civil War of 1835-7.

This was followed by his *Warnings to the People on Street Warfare*, attacking the 'instructions' issued by the revolutionary Colonel Francis Maceroni to the people on street warfare. Somerville argued for the futility of using violence in England to achieve political ends.[9] He had returned in the autumn of 1837 with first-hand experience of the brutal savagery of war in Spain; and he was soon introduced to two members of a Chartist 'Secret Committee of War', as an experienced soldier 'who could give a practical opinion of the feasibility of their intended insurrection'. Somerville, a huge and powerfully built man himself told the secret committee that he had seen, besides the horrors of bloodshed and death in battle, 'fertile fields trodden under the hoofs and wheels of the artillery ... vines cut down ... the houses of rich and poor ... of political and non-political inhabitants, battered to atoms.'[10] In particular, he attacked what he called the 'absurd ... dangerous, warlike notions' of the Chartist Peter McDouall, pointing out that, unlike continental soldiers, British troops were unlikely to go over to the side of crowds, and that the army was a formidable force for civilians to confront.[11]

He wrote to similar effect, in his *Public and Personal Affairs*, of how 'the agitation in the manufacturing districts is high enough for immediate action, and from a too well grounded discontent – but that agitation is not yet national, nor from the mingled indifference and opposition of the middle classes will it soon become general – therefore an armed movement must be defeated.'[12] There were some who tried to persuade him to join the 'Welsh insurrection of 1839' – the Newport Rising – but he refused to become involved.[13] He also wrote critically of the Chartist

---

9 *Narrative of the British Legion in Spain* (1837); *Warnings to the People on Street Warfare. A Series of Weekly Letters* (1839). Francis Maceroni's instructions were issued in his *Defensive Instructions for the People in Street Warfare* (1832, 1834). Somerville also wrote *Public and Personal Affairs. Being an Enquiry into the Physical Strength of the People, in which the Value of their Pikes and Rifles is compared with that of the Grape Shot ... of the Woolwich Artillery* (1839). For brief discussions of Somerville's role in the controversy over Chartist physical force tactics, see W.T. Ward, *Chartism* (1973), p. 262; F.C. Mather (ed), *Chartism and Society: an Anthology of Documents* (1980), pp. 37, 139, 246; M. Hovell, *The Chartist Movement* (Manchester, 1918, 1970 ed.); H. Weisser, *British Working-Class Movements and Europe, 1815-48* (Manchester, 1975), p. 100; A. Plummer, *Bronterre: A Political Biography of Bronterre O'Brien, 1804-1864* (1971), pp. 107-9, 137; and see Somerville's *Autobiography*.

10 Plummer, *Bronterre*, pp. 107-8.

11 Weisser, *British Working-Class Movements and Europe*, p. 100. On McDouall, see for example J. Epstein, *The Lion of Freedom; Feargus O'Connor and the Chartist Movement, 1832-1842* (1982), eg. pp. 197, 221, 271-2, 295-7.

12 Plummer, *Bronterre*, p. 109.

13 Plummer, *Bronterre*, p. 137.

Land Plan in the *Manchester Examiner*, as he does on occasion in the *Letters from Ireland*, basing his view on an assessment of the questionable viability of extremely small-scale peasant holdings, as found in many parts of northern and western pre-famine Ireland.[14] Indeed, his criticism was such that two historians have since referred to him as 'the vitriolic anti-Land Plan propagandist.'[15]

It is for the part Somerville played in the troubles of these years that he has been remembered, mainly by historians of Chartism. Yet it is probable that his best literary work was his subsequent rural commentaries on Ireland, Scotland and England: devoting himself largely to social and economic topics and their political ramifications, writing for the *Morning Chronicle* and the *Manchester Examiner*, with a particular sympathy for the work of the Anti-Corn Law League. *The Whistler at the Plough*, his *Letters from Ireland during the Famine of 1847*, and his *Free Trade and the League* were written around this time, when his public influence was undoubtedly at its height.

A meeting with Richard Cobden, following letters Somerville had published in the *Morning Chronicle* in 1842 on the Corn Laws, began his career as a rural writer. He was supported by the Anti-Corn Law League to report on rural conditions. Known to the League's organisers as a rather difficult fellow they called 'Reuben' – whose occasional drinking bouts they tolerated because of his excellent and authoritative prose – he published his writings under the authorship of 'One who has Whistled at the Plough'. Somerville's views on English and Irish rural society were widely discussed at the time, for he was a persuasive, intelligent and often moving writer. He tells us that 'I resolved to write ... in a manner ... which eschewed the didactic and the still less welcome array of dry figures, which in newspapers had hitherto made agricultural politics an uninteresting subject, and to take up a style of narrative and description.'[16] After an earlier tour of Ireland in 1843 – and extracts from his letters written during that tour are published here, as he included them – Somerville visited Ireland again for a second and more extended time. His purpose now was to report on conditions in 1847, the worst year of the tragic potato famine. The result was a remarkable and well-informed account of the structure and problems of rural life during that famine, an account that has altogether been missed by historians.

14 See for example, L.H. Lees, *Exiles of Erin* (Manchester, 1979), p. 25.
15 J. Epstein & D. Thompson (eds), *The Chartist Experience: Studies in Working-Class Radicalism and Culture, 1830-60* (1982), p. 302. See also A.R. Schoyen, *The Chartist Challenge; a Portrait of George Julian Harney* (1958), p. 174; Ward, *Chartism*, pp. 192, 199; A. Somerville, *Cobdenic Policy the Internal Enemy of England* (1854), ch. 5; and his *The Land Plan of Feargus O'Connor* (Manchester, 1847).
16 *The Whistler at the Plough*, p. 4.

'Famine, fever, and the worst ills of the worst times of poor Ireland, were then at their crisis', he wrote in his *Autobiography*.[17] Very small subdivided holdings in many regions, and a rural population that had been growing rapidly since the 1770s, had become inextricably reliant upon the potato. Famine was nothing new to Ireland – there had been such catastrophes before, for example in 1740-1, 1745-6, 1755, 1766, 1783, and 1816-19. However, the significance and scale of the famine in the 1840s, and its chronic associated illnesses (typhus, dysentery, cholera, scurvy, and what contemporaries called 'relapsing sickness'), were unprecedented, and were to have enormous social, economic and political repercussions. The potato crop had been initially hit by a ruinous fungal infection, *phythophthora infestans*, in 1845, which had spread after previously appearing in America in 1843. Because of the prevailing damp conditions in Ireland the blight persisted and intensified in 1846, 1847 and 1848, in very many areas turning the staple crop into a stinking putrid mess: described by one official as like 'acres blackened as if steeped in tar'.[18] There was no remedy for such blight until the later nineteenth-century use of copper sulphate solution. Munster and Connaught were especially devastated, but almost all regions were affected, with the least impact in the north-east. Until shortly before Somerville's visit, the government's handling of the crisis had been relatively generous. From the summer of 1847 it was notable that a far more neglectful response set in, which Somerville himself was not in a position to predict or assess.[19] Some of his comments on public generosity from across the water perhaps need to be read with this in mind. The government's reaction, the political disputes over economic policy, the inadequacy of the public works laid on to provide employment, the operation of the recently established Irish poor law, the efficacy of the soup kitchens and food supplies – these have all been vigorously debated ever since, as they were by Somerville.[20]

Somerville recalled how he 'was sent from England by the proprietors of the *Manchester Examiner*, to travel through Ireland, to examine into its actual condition, without regard to political or religious parties, and to report to that paper what I saw. This task I fulfilled.'[21] In doing so, he himself succumbed to one of the virulent fevers that accompanied the

17 *Autobiography*, p. 256.   18 Woodham-Smith, *The Great Hunger*, p. 362.
19 See e.g. ibid., pp. 408-9.
20 For further discussion of the famine and its historiography, see the select bibliography provided here.
21 *Autobiography*, p. 256. For discussion of other visitors' accounts of Ireland during the famine, see C. Woods, 'American travellers in Ireland before and during the Great Famine: a case of culture shock', in W. Zach & H. Kosok (eds), *Literary Interrelations: Ireland, England and the World*, Vol. 3. *National Images and Stereotypes* (Tubingen, 1987), pp. 77-84.

famine: 'Upon my first arrival in Dublin from England, I was taken suddenly and seriously ill while visiting some of the deplorable abodes of poverty and disease in that city. When I recovered sufficiently to be able to write, I reflected on the chances of recurring illness and death, while travelling in the fevered, famine-stricken, crime-committing districts of the south and west of Ireland; and that if I did not write this chapter [of my *Autobiography*] then, I might pass from the world without its facts being known.'[22]

Unlike so many others, he survived. But the fear and melancholy of death, at this time in Ireland, were pervasive. They seep insidiously and sadly through his writing, enveloping the reader and entreating the need for further understanding. They are the omnipresent background to his accounts of fever, the food depots and public works, the activities of the military, the life-destroying evictions and 'clearances', or the agitations of the Irish poor. Because of the famine, perhaps a million people died.[23] In all, probably over a third the Irish population either died or were forced (often in horrendous circumstances) to emigrate.[24] The famine initiated a long-lasting decline in population, and major changes in agricultural life. Its political consequences for Ireland were far-reaching. And its memory pulses through modern efforts to alleviate such conditions elsewhere. Somerville wrote of 'all the ghastly faces, hollow and shrunken, which I have seen, with death looking out of the eyes ... the masses of population amongst whom I have travelled through Tipperary and part of this county [Limerick], sinking from health to sickness, from life to death – not yet dead, but more terrible to look upon and think upon than if they were dead ... glaring horribly upon the passer by.'[25] In Roscommon, 'the people are literally crawling to their graves, their eyes starting in their heads with stomach torture.'[26] 'No newspaper account of the distress is exaggerated. The people are famishing. It will be my business to give such details as I meet with as soon as I can.'[27] Somerville, a hardened soldier and a mercenary familiar with the ferocity of the Spanish Civil War, could now write that 'Never, in the known history of mankind, was there a country and its people so dislocated as Ireland is now; so inextricably ravelled, and its people in such imminent hazard of perishing utterly.'[28]

---

22 *Autobiography*, p. 256. For discussion of the famine fevers, see Woodham-Smith, *The Great Hunger*, pp. 188-204.
23 See C. O'Grada, *The Great Irish Famine* (1989), pp. 48-9.
24 See Woodham-Smith, *The Great Hunger*, pp. 206-69.
25 *Letters*, p. 56.
26 *Letters*, p. 77.
27 *Letters*, pp. 28. Other contemporaries condemned the view that the severity of famine was being exaggerated. See Woodham-Smith, *The Great Hunger*, pp. 157-69.
28 *Letters*, p. 31.

Somerville's purpose in England had been to investigate the possibility and results of Corn Law repeal. By 1847 this cause was won. In Ireland his priority was to convince a sceptical British public, and their politicians, that a disaster was occurring of enormous and unrecognised proportions. He wanted also to comprehend how conditions had deteriorated to such a point. He was a man capable of compelling rhetorical effect in his writing, but his discussion here was level-headed, accusatory and indignant, but still analytical, always urgent. If Somerville can be said to lay blame anywhere for what he saw, and for the causes of the famine, it was at the doors of the larger Irish landlords, regardless of their faith or politics. However, he went beyond superficial allocation of blame – outlining the structural problems of the Irish agrarian economy, dealing with the problems of entailed estates, tenant right, inadequate leases and the disincentives for tenants to improve land, the Irish poor-law question, dependency upon land, the considerable extent of sub-letting, and the conacre and rundale systems. He made detailed comparisons between the respective circumstances of Irish and English agriculture, and also discussed the reasons for the lack of Irish industrial development compared to England.

It is surprising that historians have hitherto missed his work. In Britain at any rate, this may owe something to the fact that Somerville's views were so sympathetic to the Irish peasant farmers, and highly critical of what he recognised as the incompetence, greed or wastefulness of an all too often parasitic landlord class. Certainly, Somerville had a political stance and his own economic views to communicate, like all other commentators. The passages in this book where he outlines his own version of political economy are not always compelling, though they bear witness to the extent to which even his assertive and independent mind was constrained by certain intellectual axioms of his time. However, it is worth noting his dismissal of the population theory of Malthus, even in Ireland during the famine, and indeed some more recent historians have cast doubt on whether the famine was predominantly a case of Malthusian over-population.[29] Among many contemporaries, Malthusian argument coupled with free-market dogma and anti-Irish prejudice were used to justify limited intervention during the famine. This was not a stance Somerville shared, although he was worried that traders might avoid supplying the worst hit areas of Ireland if they suspected that government intervention and supply would lower prices. Somerville took pains to declare his politics and economic views throughout. It is clear that he saw the causes of the famine as lying in avoidable

29 See in particular J. Mokyr, *Why Ireland Starved: A Quantitative and Analytical History of the Irish Economy, 1800-1850* (1983, 1985 ed.).

institutional, legal and structural flaws rather than in the 'natural' (i.e. inevitable) causes which were emphasised by many in 'responsible' positions as an excuse for inaction. Somerville's journalistic skill, his literary and descriptive imagination, and his sympathy for the Irish people produced a deeply humane account of the hardships suffered, their structural causes, and the inadequate attempts to relieve them.

Somerville's own background was Scottish Calvinist. He spoke 'broad Scotch'. However, that did not stand in the way of his defence of Irish Catholicism. Nor did it stop him condemning some Protestant landlord abuses in the strongest terms.[30] He wrote that 'The reverence with which these poor flesh-worn peasants speak of sacred things is very remarkable';[31] but one finds in him no condescension or anti-Irish sentiment. He criticised the view that 'the Catholic religion ... disqualified the Irish for industrial enterprise', stressing the obvious exceptions to this in Europe.[32] He strongly condemned penal laws prejudicial to Catholics, and the eviction of Catholic tenants in favour of Protestants. With regard to large Protestant landlords, Somerville was particularly outspoken. The small tenantry, he wrote, 'have no security of tenure, and sad experience tells them that to enrich the soil is to invite an ejectment. Many of them ... have leases, but even a lease in Ireland is no security. A landlord has only to make a profession of a wish to exchange a Catholic tenantry for Protestants, and, under cover of such a pretence, he may commit ... the most damnable and detestable robberies.'[33] Further, he commented in scathing terms on that kind of Protestant landlord who 'looks to improved agriculture as a means of church proselytism. He mingles the produce of the farm-yard and the Thirty-nine Articles together, the stall feeding of cattle and attendance at the Protestant church, the instructions on thorough drainage and the instructions in the church catechism. A new dwelling-house, or barn, or stable, or road is equivalent on his estate to a new religion. The use of a bull of improved breed is associated with a renunciation of the bulls of Rome. No man on earth save an Irish landlord could be found to mingle such things together.'[34]

A large number of the worst Irish landlords, Somerville believed, had 'brought Ireland to a condition unparalleled in the history of nations.'[35] As a class, he thought that they stood 'at the very bottom of the scale of honest and honourable men.'[36] Indeed, 'the Irish landlord is only a rent-eater, and his agent a rent-extractor, neither of them adding to the resources of the farm – not even by making roads or erecting buildings.'[37]

30 E.g., *Letters*, p. 103.   31 *Letters*, p. 149.   32 *Letters*, p. 177.
33 *The Whistler at the Plough*, p. 187. Reprinted as an appendix in *Letters*.
34 *Letters*, p. 77.   35 *Letters*, p. 206.   36 *Letters*, p. 118.
37 *Letters*, p. 78.

There was almost a complete lack of trust between landlord and tenant, which explained an absence of agricultural improvement, and much of the unrest and behaviour of the Irish rural poor.[38] The Irish themselves, he insisted, were not 'a naturally turbulent and assassin race'; they should be treated with fairness and trusted, in a way that was certainly not prevailing landlord practice. The tenants were very suspicious of agricultural innovation, because 'they have invariably seen, that such doctrines, and specimens, and injunctions to improve, were only preparatory to their being sacrificed and their land seized. And in a country almost devoid of trade and manufactures, to be turned out of a holding of land is a calamity on a family like a death stroke.'[39] Land – the control over it, and the desire for it – was the key to almost everything in rural Ireland.

He was even harsher on Irish landlords than he had been on their counterparts in England in *The Whistler at the Plough*, a book which itself mounts a considerable attack on English landed power. He appreciated the difficulties faced by some landlords, and the scale of their indebtedness, but his sympathy did not extend far. Land, he insisted, must be made saleable; the law of entail had to be reformed. This was essential if new owners, with capital to invest, were to be attracted. Furthermore, tenants were being politically regulated and intimidated in a wholly unjustifiable manner, and leases were manipulated to such ends, with tenants removed for political reasons.[40] Agricultural improvement was constantly hindered by landlords' policies of exacting exorbitant rents. 'Idle, dissolute, and improvident proprietary classes exact, and compulsorily exact, from the cultivators all their capital, the improving cultivator only being a mark for the landlord's cupidity.'[41] The Repealer gentry were little better than their English and Protestant counterparts in such regards.[42]

38 For further analysis of the classes of rural Ireland at this time, see e.g. S. Clark, 'The importance of agrarian classes: agrarian class structure and collective action in nineteenth-century Ireland', in P.J. Drudy (ed), *Ireland: Land, Politics and People* (Cambridge, 1982), pp. 11–36.

39 *The Whistler at the Plough*, pp. 187–8. For one of many similar assessments, see A. Bisset, *Notes on the Anti-Corn Law Struggle* (1884), pp. 194–6, who complains of 'the disgrace of the frightful robbery committed on those poor Irish labourer-tenants', who after often considerably improving their properties 'had the alternative given them of either having their rents at once raised to the full value of the improvements or of being turned adrift to wander about as vagabonds on the face of the earth, and carry with them to America an exile's sorrows and an outlaw's hate – for though it may be shown to be in accordance with the *form of law*, it was a robbery of the most cruel nature – a robbery that took advantage of the best qualities of the victims to make those very qualities the instruments of their destruction ... The inhabitants of Ireland have taken up a deep and murderous hatred towards the inhabitants of Great Britain'.

40 *Letters*, pp. 89 ff, 116, 121–2.   41 *Letters*, p. 98.   42 *Letters*, p. 97.

Neither were larger landlords helping much towards the relief of the starving poor. 'In no place can I see, or ascertain by inquiry, that the nobility or landowning gentry are contributing [to relief committees], save in the most paltry sums; most of them give nothing at all. A landlord who has nominally an income of £20,000 per annum ... puts his name down, in the county of Cork, for £5. Another in Tipperary county, who either is rich or lives as if he were rich, puts his name down for £4.'[43] Nor did they accept attempts to make them personally responsible for maintaining the poor of their parishes or unions, as was being advocated by some reformers of the poor law. Somerville believed that this would be equitable – 'so that owners of property may be taxed for the poor according to their merits in giving employment to the poor', an interesting view on the obligations of property.[44] However, he added, this would be resisted 'to the uttermost.'[45] Very many landlords, like Lord Lucan, were refusing to pay poor rates, and by so doing were 'dooming their ... people to desolation and death.'[46]

In addition, some were arranging for large sums to be spent on building workhouses on their estates, gaining by selling land to the poor-law commissioners for the buildings (even though these were often remotely sited away from the population). Such landlords planned to have the property on their estates. They would then refuse to pay poor rates, thus guaranteeing the failure of the poor law, and so forcing poor-law authorities to leave the buildings unused. In due course they would adopt these buildings for their own use. Somerville also complained of the way in which many landlords were manipulating the cess (a local rate for the constabulary, roads, compensation against 'outrages' and so on), and extracting tolls and customs. The proceeds of these were being used to adorn their houses, build private extensions, bridges and the like for their own private advantage, rather than for the good of the community and the alleviation of suffering.[47] Similar corruption prevailed in connection with railway construction.[48]

The evictions and settlement clearances at this time have been much discussed. Somerville provides further documentation. Not only did landlords 'prevent, whenever they can, the erection of new houses';[49] but they were clearing their land of inhabitants to take advantage of the current public 'provision' for those people.[50] The poor law, the soup kitchens and the armed police all facilitated such activities. While in England, rural depopulation was said to be due to the attraction of urban industrial employment, in Ireland such employment was unavailable, and

43 *Letters*, pp. 56-7.   44 *Letters*, p. 82.   45 *Letters*, p. 67.
46 *Letters*, p. 87.   47 *Letters*, pp. 115-19.   48 *Letters*, pp. 58 ff.
49 *Letters*, p. 136.   50 *Letters*, p. 82.

'clearances' were forced, coercive and intolerable. Somerville complained of how the present time was an opportunistic one for evictions: 'We have England paying out of English taxes all those armed men, and providing them with bullets, bayonets, swords, guns, and gunpowder, to unhouse and turn to the frosts of February those tenants and their families.'[51] He told of how over all the south and west of Ireland the wrecks of dwellings were visible, the roofs torn off, and the walls demolished, testimony to evictions and to measures taken to prevent tenants returning to the homes they had built. In Ballinamuck, the scene of the 1798 French-English conflict, the entire village had been depopulated and destroyed by Lord Lorton, a 'mischievous bigot'. 'Ballinamuck was destroyed because a jury would not decide that one of its inhabitants was guilty'[52] – guilty, that is, of the murder of a northerner whom Lord Lorton had brought in to replace an ejected Catholic tenant. Somerville complains bitterly that English tax payers were having to pay for such repression, with starvation and death as its result.

Catholic tenants had almost no legal recourse. This was too expensive, and landlords' exorbitant fees had to be paid by the tenant. Where damages were awarded against landlords, they were absurdly low, unlike their incidence on tenants. The law overtly favoured landlords. Tenants were impoverished by legal actions; even when they were in the right, they could be ruined because of legal delays. Measures were taken to force tenants into arrears, causing their eviction.[53] One landlord had even purchased from the creditor a debt incurred by one of his tenants, so that he could then evict the tenant. Where leases existed, they were often held by landlords, rather than legally surrendered to tenants. In such cases, political subjugation was the aim.[54] Lord Devon's Commission of 1844 had complained that tenants often had difficulty in enforcing the production of leases.[55] Somerville endorsed this, and felt that the leases themselves sometimes 'read like a sarcastic chapter from *Punch* ... The law-jargon of [the leases of Lord Clancarty or Lord Palmerston, in Galway, Sligo or Roscommon] is hopelessly unintelligible.'[56] A fault of Irish agriculture thus reproduced one often found in England, and constraining and absurd clauses in leases further obstructed agricultural improvement.

Somerville repeatedly dwelt on Ireland's potential for economic and industrial growth. Its lead, copper and iron-ore resources were extensive; its natural harbours, navigable rivers and geographical situation were enviable; its potential agricultural wealth self-evident, even if currently extorted in poverty-inducing rent. There were no insurmountable cul-

51 *Letters*, p. 76. 52 *Letters*, pp. 93-4. 53 *Letters*, p. 188.
54 *Letters*, pp. 121-2. 55 *Letters*, p. 122. 56 *Letters*, p. 155.

tural barriers to industrial wealth, although some to whom Somerville talked felt it a 'crime' to have capital to carry on a business. He comments at one point on attitudes antagonistic to profit, and a reluctance to trade unless under compulsion.[57] He also felt that the Irish were badly served by traditional leaders, 'territorial legislators' like Smith O'Brien, by the pro-repeal gentry, by 'the ancient race of landlords', who all too often knew little of their country, and shared the faults of outside Protestant and non-resident landlords.[58] Beyond all the necessary agricultural reforms, Somerville urged the need for industrial developments, for without them population would be surplus to land, agriculture would lack markets, and a more complex monied economy would not evolve. Many of the stumbling blocks in Irish rural society existed also in England, but England was safeguarded from their ill-consequences by its industrial and urban home markets. 'It is in the natural order of things for agriculture to be profitless without a manufacturing and trading population to purchase and consume the agricultural produce', he wrote, without analysing further the effects on Ireland of the industrial revolution in England, or discussing the constraints on Irish industrial growth imposed by England in the past.[59] For as long as Ireland remained a purely agricultural nation, controlled by near-feudal landlords, it would be liable to famine.

One of the most telling features of Somerville's literary style is his eye for detail – for rents, wages, rates, regional types of farming, the way people armed and conducted themselves, or how the famine had affected particular individuals. Much of his prose comprises close description of the agriculture of different parts of Ireland, and his assessment of its unrealised potential. His versatility also impresses the reader, for example the way in which poetic description of landscape is juxtaposed against harsh realism to considerable effect. He uses a variety of literary devices to persuade his readers, all of which convey his empathy.[60] He had an excellent eye for symbolic example. Throughout, he was imaginative and open-minded about the possibilities of alternative agricultural systems, as found elsewhere. For the historian his use of verbatim oral evidence is especially valuable, a technique not found among many other writers on the famine. Somerville is careful to allow farmers and the poor to speak for themselves. One will not find in his writing the tendency to impose certain stereotyped views onto the people discussed – unlike many

57 *Letters*, pp. 67-8.   58 *Letters*, pp. 145-7.   59 *Letters*, p. 98.
60 Richard Cobden wrote in another context of Somerville's style that 'The difficulty with Somerville [is] to condense sufficiently his narrative – this would not be easy even with one who had a style less flowing and imaginative than he.' See J. Morley, *The Life of Richard Carlile* (1881), vol. 2, pp. 54-5.

others, he was certainly no prejudiced armchair commentator, reluctant to move into the crowd or across muddy fields. He took considerable pains to report circumstances as he saw them on the ground.

In short, it is time now to rediscover his work on Ireland and to absorb it into modern analysis of the tragic event it documents. Had Somerville written to support the political establishment, ignored conditions he witnessed, or pretended (like many others) that they were 'natural', inescapable or just another case of 'Irish exaggeration', his future in England would have been more secure. However, as proved when he was in the army, such a course was never his inclination. As the only (and very brief) biographical account of his life put it: 'Sympathetic and sensitive to a degree, he might have fared better in this world had he been less so.'[61] He was outspoken to an extent that many found embarrassing, and this had already cost him a British military flogging. His concern for the Irish rural poor and their plight overrode any temptation to political ingratiation. He was often criticized for the social views he stated, and he gained little economic security because of them.

After his work on Ireland he continued to write for many years, but largely in another country. He emigrated to Canada in 1859. Sadly, his wife died just eleven months after his arrival there, although they left a number of children who settled in America and Canada. Despite many literary initiatives,[62] his own fortunes did not improve. Late in life he listed his writings, including his account of Ireland, and remarked that 'it will be seen that many of the subjects are, unfortunately, such as an author may become poor upon, rather than popular and well remunerated.'[63] His earlier sympathetic attitude towards the Irish in the 1840s seems to have taken some knocks following the Fenian attack on Upper Canada in May, 1866, under General John O'Neill, with the seizure of Fort Erie, and the attacks on St. Armand and Frelighsburg.[64] On these occasions he defended the Upper Canadians, on the grounds that their livelihoods and new homes were being threatened, and that they were not themselves involved in the controversy in Britain over Ireland.[65]

61 W.M. Sandison, 'Alexander Somerville', *Border Magazine*, XVIII, no. 207 (March, 1913), separately printed as a supplement, to which reference is made here, p. 6.
62 See the Bibliography of his writings in my edition of his *The Whistler at the Plough* (1989 edn), for further information on his considerable literary output. He also founded and for a while edited the *Canadian Illustrated News*, was editor of the *Church Herald*, and wrote on behalf of the Immigration Department of the Ontario Government, again much concerned with Irish affairs.
63 W.M. Sandison, *Alexander Somerville, "The Whistler at the Plough"* (1913, reprinted from the *Border Magazine*, March, 1913), p. 8.
64 The Fenian Brotherhood had been organised in Dublin in 1858, and in New York in 1859 – they planned to establish a republic in Canada.
65 He wrote a *Narrative of the Fenian Invasion of Canada* (Hamilton, Canada, 1866).

Somerville died in 1885, aged seventy-four, in poverty in a squalid boarding house in Toronto. For some years he had been sleeping throughout the year in a woodshed outside, with the snow in winter seeping through the window – much as it had done, no doubt, around his father's moveable pane of glass, in the cottages of his childhood in the Lothians. And it is certain that, all those years later, he had not forgotten the deplorable scenes he had witnessed during the famine: men like 'the phantom farmer, Thomas Killaheel', who had followed him at one point, while on the hillside two 'spectre children' had stood leaning on their long and narrow spades, 'spades made for spectres to dig with.' Thomas Killaheel 'said nothing, but looked – oh! such looks, and thin jaws! ... The lean man looked as if his spirit, starved in his own thin flesh, would leave him and take up its abode with me. I even felt it going through me as if looking into the innermost pores of my body for food to eat and for seed oats. It moved through the veins with the blood, and finding no seed oats there, nor food, searched through every pocket to the bottom, and returned again and searched the flesh and blood to the very heart; the poor man all the while gazing at me as if to see what the lean spirit might find; and it searched the more keenly that he spoke not a word.'[66] Thomas Killaheel may have spoken not a word, but Alexander Somerville wrote for him. What follows is Somerville's eye-witness account of that worst tragedy of Irish history, 'the great hunger'.

A SELECT BIBLIOGRAPHY OF THE IRISH FAMINE

There has been a great deal written on the famine, its structural and immediate causes, and its effects on Ireland. For further discussion of this and related issues, the reader might find it helpful initially to consult the following:

K.H. Connell, *Irish Peasant Society* (Oxford, 1968).

J.S. Donnelly, *The Land and People of Nineteenth-century Cork: the Rural Economy and the Land Question* (1975); his *Landlord and Tenant in Nineteenth-Century Ireland* (Dublin, 1973); and his 'The Great Famine', in W.E. Vaughan *et al.* (eds), *The New History of Ireland*, vol. 5 (Oxford, 1989).

P.J. Drudy (ed), *Ireland: Land, Politics, and People* (Cambridge, 1982).

R.D. Edwards & T.D. Williams (eds), *The Great Famine* (Dublin, 1956).

66 *Letters*, p. 153.

J. Mokyr, *Why Ireland Starved: A Quantitative and Analytical History of the Irish Economy, 1800-1850* (1983).

C. O'Grada, *The Great Irish Famine* (1989). (And see his detailed bibliography.)

G. Ó Tuathaigh, *Ireland Before the Famine, 1798-1848* (Dublin, 1972).

W.E. Vaughan, *Landlords and Tenants in Mid-Victorian Ireland* (Oxford, 1994).

C. Woodham-Smith, *The Great Hunger: Ireland, 1845-9* (1962).

I

DUBLIN, *20th January 1847*

I devoted my first day in Dublin to inquiries at the relief committees—at that for the city of Dublin and that for the country generally. I was referred to the inspectors of the poor, who in the different parishes take the office upon them, each a week at a time, of visiting the dwellings of the numerous applicants for relief. I visited some of the poorest districts of the city, also the wharves where vessels were unloading cargoes of food, and the offices of some parties extensively connected with the railway works in the interior of Ireland.

I have also read several of the pamphlets relating to the present crisis of Ireland, of which the booksellers' shops in Dublin possess many.

One, entitled 'The Case of Ireland Stated, by Robert Holmes, Esq.' was advertised by bills in every street. It was selling at the price of two shillings, so, thinking two shillings might be worse disposed of than in getting 'The case of Ireland stated,' I parted with them. Robert Holmes, Esq. I was told, is a barrister of long-standing and an able man. He was the brother-in-law of the celebrated Robert Emmett. No man knew Ireland or loved Ireland better than he did. This made me the more desirous to have the case of Ireland stated by him. If I say that Nero, playing the fiddle while Rome burned, was similarly employed to Mr Holmes, my meaning will be understood; but even fiddle-playing might have some excuse if Nero neither cared nor professed to care for Rome. Mr Holmes professes to care for Ireland, and yet fiddles her sentimental tunes in her ears while she is famishing. He contrasts the generous manner in which Rome treated her conquered provinces with that in which England has treated her conquered countries, and particularly Ireland. For one single practical suggestion or symptom of a practical thought in the writer's mind, the pamphlet is read and read in vain. It is long, wordy, eloquent, and useless.

Not so a pamphlet entitled 'Observations on the Evils resulting to Ireland from the Insecurity of Title and the existing Laws of Real Property, with some Suggestions towards a Remedy.' There is no author's name to this; but I believe the author is Mr Pym. Here are a few brief passages, in which he states the case of Ireland:—

'*Landlord*—Title doubtful, or difficult to prove; so much so as to interfere with the sale of the property.

'*Tenant*—Has no lease, or a lease at so high a rent that, being always in arrear, he is always liable to be ejected.

'*Landlord*—Estate heavily mortgaged, or liable in a jointure or pay-ment to the younger members of his family; so that his nominal income is barely sufficient to pay the annual demands, and he has consequently no capital to improve the property.

'*Tenant*—Bound for a rent that takes all he can spare beyond a mere subsistence, and consequently cannot improve his farm.

'*Landlord*—Estate being entailed, or closely bound by settlements, he has only a life interest in it, and is therefore disinclined to spend money on improvements which will not be immediately remunerative.

'*Tenant*—Having no certainty of possession, he will not, of course, give any labour or expend any money for which he does not expect an immediate return.'

On a former visit to Ireland, I found those leading facts, as here stated, to be prevalent everywhere; and everywhere then and now the natural results shew themselves. Thus, says Mr Pym, 'A country natu-rally fertile is left almost unimproved and only half cultivated; the fields are undrained; the rivers, left without care, overflow their banks and turn good land into marsh; straggling hedges and uncultivated spots deform the face of the country; the hay or corn, insufficiently secured, is exposed to the weather; and much land capable of culture is left to its natural wildness, or is so ill tilled that it is but little better than waste.'

It may be as well to proceed to business at once. I am only entering upon Ireland at present; but I have been through the country before, and have studied its agricultural condition, and the causes which make that a bad condition. And the business to be done is to authorize the sale of the land by act of Parliament. A supply of food for the starving peasantry is a temporary necessity, and must be attended to immediately; indeed it is being performed to an extent never known in the history of nations. But this is only a temporary expedient. Remedies, permanent and compre-hensive, must be applied to Ireland, and the first of the permanent remedies must be the simplification of the transfer of land. All land in Ireland must be made saleable. Capital will then flow in to improve it, not before. When the land is bought and sold on commercial principles it will in like manner be leased to tenants. It may be a daring thing to say that the law of entail must be abrogated, but no one step can be taken to save Ireland from the recurrence of those terrible visitations of famine which come so often upon her, or from the continuance of that squalid misery which is always upon her, until this is done. And now is the time to do it.

'This fertile but neglected land,' says the pamphlet before me, 'is occupied by an embarrassed gentry, striving to maintain the position in society to which their nominal income would entitle them, and by a pauper tenantry, multiplying to excess, outbidding one another in the ruinous contest for land, and at length resorting to lawless violence in order to retain its possession as their only means of subsistence. The peaceful and industrious annually retire by thousands from the scene of contest, to exert, in the forests of America, the intelligence and energy which, under more favourable circumstances, would have strengthened their country with a happy and independent peasantry.'

The unembarrassed landlord of an entailed estate stands thus—'He is in reality not the owner; he cannot deal with it as an owner; he is merely a trustee for others; he has no interest in its future, though permanent, improvement, except so far as he may wish to benefit his successors; he can never reap the benefit himself; he cannot sell; he cannot dispose of a part, even though the alienation of a part might greatly enhance the value of the remainder; he holds it during his lifetime, as his predecessor has held it, unaltered, unimproved, to transmit it to his heir, clogged with the same restrictions, alike injurious to him and to his country.'

So much for an unembarrassed landlord. Here is the landlord with an entailed estate and debts upon it:—'As is unfortunately too often the case, he has received the estate, encumbered under a settlement, with a jointure to the widow of the late possessor, and provision for daughters and younger sons. In what difficulties is he at once involved—this owner for life of a large tract of country, with a large rent roll, but, in fact, a small property! He cannot maintain his position in society without spending more than his income; debts accumulate; he mortgages his estate, and ensures his life for the security of the mortgagee. Of course he cannot afford to lay out anything in improvements; on the contrary, though, perhaps, naturally kind-hearted and just, his necessities force him to resort to every means of increasing his present rental. He looks for the utmost amount; he lets to the highest bidder, without regard to character or means of payment. If his tenants are without leases, he raises their rents. If leases fall in, he cannot afford to give the preference to the last occupier. Perhaps, with all his exertions, he is unable to pay the interest, or put off his creditors. Proceedings are commenced against him, and the estate passes, during his lifetime, under the care of the worst possible landlord, a receiver under the Court of Chancery.'

There can be no doubt that if the entailed estates were sold, the portions of the younger sons would more commonly be a business education, with means to start in business, instead of some money to buy a spirited hunter, as now. The very name of a castle, with a brother in it, and a wide tract of country, with that brother's name upon it as landlord, is delusive, through all the lives of the younger members of the family, while the tenant of the castle is himself unfit for any good purpose. If his wide domain were sold to those who could make it perform its natural and national purposes, he would have money wherewith to purchase and cultivate and make profit on a smaller estate, or to enter upon other business, or give his sons a business education. Are he and all his race too proud to be men of business because they are entailed landlords? If they be, let them cease to be the chiefs of entailed beggars in any other way they can devise. They must do something. The fertile soil of Ireland and her millions of people are not to be perpetually blighted and famished, that heirs-entail may masquerade as landowners and play at living in castles.

I shall not pursue this topic farther at present. As to the immediate wants of the peasantry, these are urgent. I do not judge from the hordes of people whom I see begging in the streets and at all public places; these have always abounded in Ireland. But persons whom I have seen, whose vocation is not to write in newspapers—men of business, who have recently been in the west and south of Ireland, declare that no newspaper account of the distress is exaggerated. The people are famishing. It will be my business to give such details as I meet with as soon as I can. But, in the meanwhile, let no hand that can help be held back, under the impression that the distress has been exaggerated.

2

DUBLIN, *23rd January 1847*

One of the first things which attracts the eye of a stranger in Ireland, at least such a stranger as I am, and makes him halt in his steps and turn round and look, is the police whom he meets in every part of the island, on every road, in every village, even on the farm land, and on the seashore, and on the little islands which lie out in the sea. These policemen wear a dark green uniform and are armed; this is what makes them remarkable, armed from the heel to the head. They have belts and pouches, ball cartridges in the pouches, short guns called carbines, and bayonets, and pistols, and swords. The only difference between them and the regular military is, that the military do not always carry guns and pistols primed and loaded, not always bayonets in their belts, not always swords sharpened. The Irish police never go on duty without some of these.

In the Phoenix Park at Dublin, a barrack of large size, with drill ground, is devoted to the training of these armed police, from which barrack they are drafted into the provinces, as soon as they are trained to prime, load, and fire, to fix bayonets and charge; to march, counter-march, and so forth; these to be distributed and shaken out upon the land in half dozens or dozens.

The next thing that has struck me as remarkable in Ireland, previous to the present time, has been this—that rent was usually paid through the sheriff, his officers, the keepers put in possession of the pigs and potatoes, corn and cows, and the armed police who assisted the keepers to keep possession. The property distrained upon was sold by any one whom the landlord or his agent appointed; it being legal for a mere labourer to act as auctioneer, if so ordered. The agent of the landlord was usually himself the buyer, at least virtually so. He got legal possession of the crops by means of this distraint and by the aid of the armed police, and he sent the corn, pigs, potatoes, or whatever the property might be, to a seaport town for shipment to England. Arrived in England, they were sold readily. The landlord got his rent by their sale in England, not by their sale under the hammer in Ireland; and the people of England were pleased to find so much food coming from Ireland, though often wondering why the Irish people should be so poorly fed at home, as report said they were, when they sent so much food to England. That food left Ireland by the process I have described. Some landlords and some districts of country might be exceptions; but in the south and west of Ireland, and in most of the midland counties, that has long been the method of collecting rents, and of exporting provisions to England.

The stranger could not get so far through the country, nor be so long in it as to understand this system of distraint, without seeing that the people were ragged to a degree of wretchedness not seen in any other country; that they were lodged with their pigs, the pigs not having a better lodging than a sty, and that the food of the people was potatoes, and only as many of them as the distraint system of getting rent left them. There being all the staff of sheriffs' officers, keepers, attorneys to sue out warrants, fees for warrants, attorneys to work on the other side to urge the tenant to replevin and resist, and so draw from the wretched man costs; there being all these to pay in addition to the rent, while the rent was paid by selling the crops at prices over which the tenant had no control, it is no wonder that the Irish tenantry were always poor and starving, or only kept from starving by a miserable diet of potatoes, while those who saw the Irish corn, cattle, and pigs coming to England, thought the Irish should be well-fed to have so much to spare.

This was rendered all the worse by the next characteristic of Ireland, namely, that those tenants thus distrained upon were tenants in the third or fourth degree. The head landlord was not the receiver of the rents. Some leaseholder was under him, both of them perhaps being non-resident. A person of some capital, of much energy, and little conscience, took a townland or other such portion of an estate. He let that out again at a rent which none of the peasantry who became his tenants could pay, which he knew they could not pay, but which, in the intense competition for land to keep in bare life, they engaged to pay; they not being able to get out of arrears at any time, could always be seized upon by him, and this has been his system—whenever they had anything. He was thus able at harvest or potato time, by the arrears due, to seize, sell, and send to England, or to certain stores to be ready for the English market, the corn and potatoes, before the producer of them eat too much. But this system of exacting engagements to pay rents which could not be paid, which never were expected to be paid, in order to have always the power of seizing the crops and selling them before the producers had time to eat them up stump and rump, was not confined to middlemen; it has been done by the head landlords, and by many of them. As much was left to the miserable tenantry, but no more, than would keep them in life, with strength enough to put another crop in the ground.

But this system went farther. The enmity of Protestant and Catholic led the first, he being usually the landlord, to allow the latter, the potato-eating tenant, to get in arrear, that he might be at any time evicted by means of the law when a better tenant offered for the land. The Protestant landlord, having all the law on his side—all the officials being Protestants, from the lord-lieutenant to the hangman—he was seldom particular about the moral justice of such cases. There were the armed police ever at hand to help the landlord, if the tenant did not yield possession, and betake himself to a ditch, to lie and die quietly. If he took vengeance into his own hand while in that ditch, or behind the hedge that skirted it and the high-way road, there was the hangman for him; that is, if they could catch him, and get the noose on his neck. But such a man was not easily caught in such a country, among such people. To be sure the pursuing law was not always particular about the right man; so as one or two or three were caught and hung up, the law, and the landlords, and the juries whom they employed were pretty well satisfied; pretty well satisfied, unless a fourth or a fifth should be caught and sworn against; then the law was not satisfied until these were hanged by the neck also. And when the right man, the actual criminal, fell into the law's hands at last, he too must go as the two or three, the four or five innocent men charged with his crime, and found guilty by means which could only be found in a country corrupted by faction as Ireland has been;—he must go at last as they went before him.

Such was Ireland up to the time when the mysterious famine came, and, with a warrant more potent than that of all the sheriffs and sheriffs' officers of Ireland, (and they are no feeble band,) seized the crops and kept possession, from each and from all, Protestant and Catholic.

Heaven's purpose in executing that awful warrant is not for me to scan or scribble at. It is only for me and others to believe that good will come of it, and to do our best to turn it to good account, for Ireland's sake.

Let us see what are its results, so far as yet visible. Not the least of them is this, that men who lived in enmity, who nourished political and religious hatred, and threw it on the wind to grow on every spot of the island where the wind blew, who blighted such commerce as they had, and scared from their shores such men of capital and commercial enterprise as ventured to settle among them to sow the seeds of profitable industry—the first element of national power; they are now meeting in common calamity, driven together by the common danger, and calling each other brethren and countrymen.

But where the end is to be I have no penetration to see. People are dying of want, and of diseases induced by want. Those alive are, day by day, becoming too feeble to work. They have just been able to do enough to break up half the roads in Ireland in the process of giving public work for public relief, and in that state, almost impassable—in many parts utterly so—the roads must be left. The feeble beings are not able to continue at them if it were desirable they should. It is not desirable. It is imperiously necessary that the fields should be prepared, and planted, and sown. The people have no seed. They have no interest in the land themselves; they never had. The most they ever obtained was a meagre subsistence; the rent was taken from them as I have described. The pay they now receive is not enough to get them food, at present prices, to keep up their working strength. Such as it is on the roads it would only be on the land; they see no difference. Those who can pay rent will not do it; those who have nothing to pay rent with cannot. The landlords, most of them only nominally landowners, are not receiving rent; and they are without funds and without credit. The estates are mortgaged to their full value. Never, in the known history of mankind, was there a country and its people so dislocated as Ireland is now; so inextricably ravelled, and its people in such imminent hazard of perishing utterly. Apart altogether from the claims which one human being has upon another for life, if that other can save his life, I urge the imminent distress of Ireland upon the attention of England on another ground, which is, that if the land is not sown and planted, the famine of next year will be immeasur-

ably more disastrous than the famine of this year; and if the people are
not fed to keep them from sinking down upon and under the earth,
which they are now doing, the land cannot be cultivated.

3

KILKENNY, *27th January 1847*

Coming from Dublin to Carlow, I had day-light only for the distance
of thirty-five miles. Over that space, consisting of the county of
Dublin and part of Kildare, I saw no land which seemed to have been
corn and potato fields, but what was ploughed or undergoing the process
of ploughing; while several fields which had been lying in grass were
ploughed up ready for seed-sowing. Two-thirds of that country is lying
in grass. It feeds cattle and sheep, and furnishes hay for Dublin. The
farms are nearly all of an acreage, to be counted by the hundred, and not
by units of acres as in other parts of Ireland. The surface of the country
on both sides of the railway is nearly a dead level all the way. The
meadows, even at this advanced period of winter, have a rough herbage
on them. Some of them are partially flooded. The enclosures, fenced by
ill conditioned thorn hedges, seem to range in measurement between six
and ten acres. Several elegant villas and mansions are seen, and a good
many humble dwelling-places; but not so many of the latter as to give
one the idea of a dense population. Were it not for the Wicklow hills, a
few miles southward, running from east to west as we are running, the
country might be likened to Staffordshire, as seen from the Birmingham
and Manchester line of rails.

This Irish South Western, or Dublin and Cashel line, now opened as
far as Carlow, fifty-six miles, is the smoothest line of rails I ever travelled
on; the carriages are well fitted up, more roomy than on the English
narrow gauge lines—the Irish railways being a medium gauge between
the narrow and the broad, and going so steadily as to make the passenger
think he is sitting in a parlour. The station building at Dublin promises
to be almost regal in magnificence.

A railway contractor, whom I have seen, has contracts for three hundred
miles of railway in Ireland; throughout the whole of which he has hands at
work, at the rate of a hundred men per mile. This gives 30,000 men
employed by him alone on railways. I cannot yet give their wages, but shall

endeavour to reach that important branch of information soon.

Of Carlow I have not much to write. It is a pleasant little town on the banks of the Bourne, which falls into the Barrow a little below the town. The latter river, uniting with the Noire from Kilkenny and the Suir from Tipperary, sweeps through a lovely and fertile country, passing Waterford in all the grandeur of a broad, deep, clear, mighty river, hastening to hide itself in the Atlantic Ocean, as if ashamed of having such a volume of water with so little work to do. Around Carlow the best cultivated farms in Ireland are to be seen—so some people say.

Awful havoc was made among the small tenantry a few years ago, in getting them cleared away to make large farms and to substitute a Protestant population for a Catholic one. Carlow town and county is a stronghold of the Protestants—the political Protestants. The land is a free fertile loam, which grows prodigious crops of onions. London is sometimes supplied with Carlow onions. Turnips are also produced in a considerable quantity, and cattle are fed and manure produced in the farm-yard. Wheat is grown as a leading crop, and the wheat is always of good quality.

After writing the foregoing, and staying a night in Carlow, I walked through and around the town. From Mr Spong, seed-merchant, I obtained a good deal of information, of which the following is the substance:—From 700 to 800 tons of bere are sown, or will be sown, within a circuit of twenty miles more than usual; more oats will be sown than usual. The farmers are not generally behind with their work. The small farmers are behind. There are more than a thousand people in and about Carlow town called quarter-acre men. They rented a quarter of an acre of land—some more, some less—for potatoes, and found manure for it. They are not now collecting manure. That article could not, in any former year at this season, be obtained for less than 3s. 6d. per cart load. Now every one of the quarter-acre men are trying to sell what manure they have, and it is offered at 1s. 3d. and 1s. per cart load. This is a sign that they do not think of planting potatoes again. They may be doing this because they have no seed potatoes, nor money to purchase them. There are more potatoes in the country around Carlow than is generally known. The mass of common people have none; they have either consumed all which the disease spared, or had them taken from them for rent, or sold them, (they rented the land from the large farmers, not from the landlords.) But the large farmers have all potatoes stored away. They keep them very quietly. Some have 100 barrels, some 200 barrels, and others 300 barrels. They are beginning to let them be known now, lest they should not be able to sell them at all.

Yesterday, 25th, there was quite a panic in Carlow with wheat and oats; wheat fell five shillings per quarter, and oats about the same; flour and meal did not fall, because the millers and dealers know the prospects of the markets better than the farmers. There are many mills about Carlow, all in full work, grinding meal and flour. It is supposed that the millers and dealers united to spread an alarm among the farmers, to induce them to bring their grain to market, which they were always holding back in hopes of higher prices. It poured in last week, and seldom has such a day of bustle been seen in Carlow as Saturday. Yesterday (Monday) the panic increased. Every farmer offered to sell, but the millers would not buy, in hopes of forcing them still further into the panic.

A great many men have been employed, and are now on public works. A soup-kitchen is open in the town, which supplies 500 persons with soup daily. When the spring advances, work will be plentiful on the land. The small farmers who are not able to cultivate their holdings and get seed will sublet them. Subletting is now going on to a great extent. The country around this town is called the garden of Ireland; it well deserves the name. There are about 500 acres of onions and parsnips grown annually; the parsnips are sown with the onions. The disease did not affect the onions last year; but many of the growers got bad seed from Dublin, because they got it cheap there, and it did not grow. The parsnips were a splendid crop. They are now selling at £6:10s. per ton; and are bought up for the Dublin market to supply the place of potatoes. They did not formerly sell for more than £2 per ton. The farmers generally in Carlow county have seldom been so prosperous as they are this year: that is, the farmers holding above ten acres, say from twenty acres upwards. They have only lost on their potatoes; they have gained enormously on everything else. Turnips are a good crop, and selling at a great price. Swedes at from 35s. to 40s. per ton, and other sorts at 30s. per ton. The owners of the land in this district are Colonel Bruen, Earl Fitzwilliam, Earl of Besborough, (the Lord-Lieutenant,) Lady Cavanagh, (for her son, a minor,) and Mr Horace Rochford. Colonel Bruen is a resident landlord, and has been very attentive to the poor. All the others have taken their share of the burthen liberally. Upon the whole, it is questionable if any other part of Ireland is so well-conditioned. The railway terminus has centred in this place the whole traffic of the south and west of Ireland with Dublin. The hotels were never so full before; shopkeepers were never more busy; mills are grinding night and day, and farmers never had better prices, with more corn to sell. The sufferers are the labouring population—the quarter-acre men, the small householders, *and the small farmers, whose holdings are under ten acres.*

I should like the prize-holders of the Chartist land-scheme to note those words printed in *italics*—they who never handled a spade, and who are supposed to be able to do such great things on two, three, and four acres of poorer land than this is around Carlow; who are to live on the best of English fare and pay so large a per-centage on the money advanced to them to purchase their land and stock it. Miserable delusion! A better soil, a more industrious people, and better managed farm-gardens are not to be found anywhere than around Carlow, and yet every family holding only a few acres is reduced to Indian meal and the soup-kitchen by the failure of their potatoes.

I must proceed to sketch my journey from Carlow to Kilkenny. It is half-past ten; the coach starts at eleven from Carpenter's hotel, where I now am, after it comes down from the railway station where it has just gone to meet the train from Dublin. Other coaches and cars are to start from here to Kilkenny, Clonmel, Waterford, Cork, and other places. Already the professional mendicants are assembling outside the door to besiege the coaches as they come. They arrive muffled up in tattered cloaks, greatcoats, and all manner of garments slung, hung, wrapped, twisted, and tied upon them. Fifteen or sixteen have arrived, and more are coming. Already they begin to unfold to the public eye their sores, which form their stock in trade, to do a little preliminary business with such as me. One woman begins to beg for Christ's sake. 'Oh, it will be the lucky day to your honour if you give me a handsel.' (Another)—'Give something to the poor, for God's sake.' (Another)—'Long life to your honour; God bless your honour; you are a gentleman, any one may see.' (All, but the last)—'Divide it amongst us, your honour, do, for the love of God, divide it; the devil a bit will that old man you gave it to divide with any of us: remember the poor women.'

The coaches begin to arrive from the railway. The mob of beggars now rush to the windows and doors of the coaches and around the cars. When they see a lady and a gentleman together, they assume that she is his wife and may be in the family way. Before her eyes they open their hideous sores, and beg of the gentleman, for the love of God, to give them something. I get upon the box-seat of the Clonmel coach, which is to take me to Kilkenny. 'Oh! now your honour has got the box-seat, you'll give us a handsel: do, for the love of God, give something to the poor. Give the poor creatures of women a handsel, and it will be the lucky day to you.' (A sergeant of the 64th regiment gets upon the front seat.) 'Sergeant, give a trifle to the poor, and the blessing of God be upon you. Do, sergeant, and you'll never want a copper to bless yourself.' (Many voices)—'Do, sir, give something to the poor creatures.' (Sergeant)—'I really have no coppers. I would give you something with pleasure if I had it.' (Several women)—'Well, it's yourself that gives a civil answer any way.' (A Waterford coach comes up and halts alongside of us.) 'Oh, blessings on you, doctor, but we are glad to see you down again. Oh, doctor, good luck to you this blessed day.' (To a lady inside.) 'Give something for the poor baby; please your ladyship, look at its head how sore it is. God be with your ladyship.' A gentleman, mounted on a fine hunter, with scarlet coat, and booted and spurred, living close to Carlow, returns from the hunt and rides through the crowd. A passenger asks some of the mendicants why they don't beg from him. ' From him is it?' they reply, 'sure we know him better; it would not be a ha'penny he would give the like of us.'

The quantity of luggage to go with the coach I am on is unusually great. Men who have shouted to one another, 'Paddy!' 'Larry!' 'Hardy!' 'Billy!' 'Barney!' and 'Dan!' for the last ten minutes by the hotel clock, are lifting it up, laying it down, moving it back, moving it forward, building it up, pulling it down, building it up again, and they are not one whit nearer an end than when they began, for down it all tumbles, Paddy running one way, and Larry another way, and Dan and Billy a third way, to save themselves from being knocked on the head with rolling hat boxes and portmanteaus.

At last, after adding pieces of rope to straps that were not long enough, and knotting rope to rope, the new to the old, the old breaking and other knots being made of new to new, the tarpauling was got over the luggage, the driver got on the box, and off we rattled, overtaking and passing all the other coaches in succession. Hardy was guard and Larry was driver, and never did a better driver handle whip or reins than Larry. He had shewn himself but a poor hand at loading the coach; that was not his business; his business was on the box. Once on the box, Larry was a prince of coachmen.

We came down upon the river Barrow, and rattled along its left bank. Some of the land bore evidence of having been well cultivated; some of it looked the reverse. Ploughs were at work on every hand, and as much seemed to be doing as could be done for the ensuing crops of corn. Some fields of young wheat looked green and healthy. Larry still smacked his whip, and made the horses canter, and admonished us to mind our hats as we passed beneath the hanging branches of the roadside trees. Behind those trees, close on our right hand, a little below the level of the road, the Barrow, rolling broad, deep, and strong, still kept us company. The high frontiers of the Queen's county rose up a mile or two beyond the river, with their cultivated steeps subdivided into innumerable fields; the whole forming a picture which seemed to be set on its edge in the plain, and leaning back upon the walls of the horizon.

Now we ascended through a cutting which hid the plain from view, and again we descended, with the Barrow once more beside us, as broad, beautiful, and idle as before. At one of those points where we came suddenly upon it after being hid from it for a short time, between four and five miles from Carlow, the sight of the noble river sweeping for several miles before us through meadows and trees inspirited and inspired me to enthusiasm. But the way-side houses were beginning to look more miserable, the farms were smaller, much more numerous, and the people poorer. Close on the road-side, on our left hand, when ascending a gentle eminence, we passed a number of mean huts, all standing in pools of filth, the thatched roofs broken, the walls leaning in and bending out, and one or more faces looking over each of the low half-doors; the faces looking squalid, dirty, shrivelled, and famine-stricken. One face was an exception; it was that of a girl approaching womanhood. The under half of her door was open, and she stood in the doorway at full length, her unshod feet in the puddle of a filthy sink and dunghill, which was making itself level with the road outside and the floor of the house inside. She was not dirty in clothing. She had washed her face, for she could not be insensible to its beauty. Poet or painter never saw a face which would more readily strike a light in the onlooker's eyes at one glance than that one.

I shall not in this letter proceed to describe Kilkenny, its country, and its people: there is more distress here than at Carlow. The distress deepens as we go west. At Carlow the potatoes were English reds—they did not all fail. In the south and the west the potatoes were the lumpers; planted always because large and prolific. The disease is peculiarly a lumper disease—they have all failed.

4

CLONMEL, COUNTY TIPPERARY, *29th January 1847*

This is a large busy town of about 16,000 inhabitants; the most fertile land in Ireland lying around it, save on one side, the south, where rises a high hill less fertile, and the river Suir rolling at the bottom of the hill, and partly through the town, driving many flour mills of great extent, and able, from its vast volume of water and velocity of current, to drive as many mills as would grind meal for all Saxon and Celtic mankind.

Clonmel being thus furnished with mills of great power, and the consumption of meal in Ireland being now great, far beyond its consumption at any former time, the Indian corn is conveyed here from Waterford and other seaports, to be reduced to meal. The redistribution of the meal to other districts causes a great traffic with carts upon the roads in every direction. The 34th regiment of infantry is located here with some artillery and the head quarters of the Scots Greys. The latter regiment is broken into detachments lying all over the county of Tipperary and in part of Waterford county, engaged in the harassing duty of guarding the transit of meal. The infantry are similarly engaged, and all of them are worn and wearied with heavy duty. The duty is all the worse that they are continually on their feet if infantry, on horseback if cavalry; and because they are not marching in the ordinary sense of the term—to shift quarters—they do not get marching money, nothing but their bare pay, which with dear prices is not much.

Ascertaining, on my arrival here from Kilkenny, on Wednesday, that military escorts would go out with carts loaded with meal on the following morning, one of them towards Dungarvan, I resolved to accompany them, and made arrangements accordingly.

In the morning, at half-past five o'clock, the low rumble of carts was heard on the streets. At six the sound continued, and so on occasionally until seven. Not knowing at what hour the carts would be loaded and ready to start, nor at what hour the military escort would turn out, I was ready long before daylight to start on the journey with them if they went so soon. The morning was dark and stormy, and the rain poured from the dark sky upon the darker earth.

As soon as daylight served, I went out, and going up the spacious and handsome main street of Clonmel reached the narrower streets which lead down to the river banks, to the bridges over the various divisions of the river, and to the islands which divide the river, and to the great, the gigantic flour, meal, and malt mills which stand upon the islands. That noble stream, the Suir, rolled and roared through the bridges and among the mills; while drivers of carts, millers, meal-dealers, and police, amid hundreds of carts that choked up the narrow thoroughfares, shouted, pulled, and swore at one another. The buyers of meal from Cahir, Tipperary town, and other remote places were there, to purchase for the expedition which will go out to their towns to-day and on Saturday morning, as the expeditions to Clogheen and Dungarvan were going this morning.

Small progress was made in loading, as the loaded carts could not get out from among the empty ones, until after disputes and struggles amounting to a kind of civil war. A party of sixteen men, and an officer

of the 34th regiment of infantry, marched from the barracks on the east
through the town westward, to a point where the loaded carts were to
assemble. Then came two of the Scots Greys, as the advanced guard of
the party of dragoons; then four of the greys; and, fifty yards behind, two
of the same as rear guard. The sergeant who commanded this party rode
on in front, and in himself made the ninth man. There were also some of
the armed constabulary. In all, the escort for Dungarvan consisted of one
officer, two sergeants, and twenty-five men; that for Clogheen was of a
similar strength. I hired a car and attached myself to this expedition for
Dungarvan; it was only going, however, to the Half-way House, about
fourteen miles distant, on the top of the mountains.

When an hour beyond the appointed time for the whole party to start
had elapsed, and the soldiers had been standing in the rain, and in the
deep mud half-a-mile beyond the town on the Dungarvan road, until
they were soaked, the infantry through their greatcoats, the cavalry
through their cloaks, or nearly so, twenty-six carts out of the hundred, or
thereabouts, which were to go to Dungarvan, had reached the place of
rendezvous. The carts were each drawn by one horse; and each driver
had been at liberty to take any number of hundred weights of meal,
according as he judged of the strength of his horse, up to sixteen; none
were allowed to take more. Most of them had 12 cwt. or 14 cwt. The
payment for carriage to Dungarvan from Clonmel, the distance being
about twenty-five English miles, and road bad, was 1s. per cwt. Most of
the carts had come from places far distant from Clonmel. Any owner of a
good horse can get employment for himself and horse in carrying meal.
The poor horses, and the poor men who own them, have no chance, as
none are sent out under the military escort but those supposed to be able
to perform the work. When I saw the loaded carts assembled on the road,
and was told how bad the road was, so bad that Mr Bianconi, the
celebrated car proprietor, has ceased to run his public conveyances
between Clonmel and Dungarvan, it seemed to me impossible that such
small horses could go over the mountains with such loads. But I judged
wrong of them; they went well, and went through places where larger
horses that I have known would have stuck fast.

Five cars were obtained to carry the foot soldiers, the officer commanding, and the two armed constables. I had provided a conveyance for
myself on the previous evening. It was, like the rest, an outside jaunting
car. The seats hold each two persons when required; in which case the
driver gets up in front. The drivers of the cars carrying the foot soldiers
were all sitting aloft in front.

Few travellers stir out here at present without being armed. The pay-
clerks of the public works are attacked and robbed frequently. Land-

stewards and agents are never at any time particularly safe: commercial travellers and merchants, formerly safe, are now liable to be mistaken for officers and clerks of public works. Nor are they in their own character of men travelling through the country with property in their possession quite free from danger, now that highway robberies have begun. Were it not a very serious matter, it would be amusing to see the arming of travellers. And, as it is, the commercial travellers occasionally make merry with one another when they come into the commercial hotels from a journey on the road, pulling off their gloves as they enter, throwing the gloves into their hats; pulling off wrappers from their necks and throwing them down; taking a horse pistol with a spring dagger attached to it from the right side pocket of the top coat; another horse pistol with a dagger to it from the left side pocket; a pistol of lesser size with revolving barrels from the breast pocket of the top coat; then taking the top coat off and hanging it up, cautioning the waiters, and boots, and other persons present, not to touch one of those pistols, for all are loaded and have percussion caps on ready to go off. Then proceeding, the top coat being hung up, to pull a small pistol out of the right hand trousers' pocket; another small pistol from the left hand trousers' pocket; a third from the breast pocket of the coat, with ball cartridges from the same place, and percussion caps from the pockets of the waistcoat; all which being done, they may lock them up in bag or box until the morning, and proceed to sit down to tea and tell the news. Such is commercial travelling, at present, in Tipperary and the counties adjoining.

As I had no pistols, powder, bullets, nor percussion caps, I was seriously warned on the Wednesday evening not to go out on the morning with the expedition to Dungarvan without them, particularly as it was not my intention to return with the military escort to Clonmel. Accordingly, as arming seemed the order of the day, I armed myself, and did it as follows:—I took one of my carpet bags and emptied everything of luggage kind out; took it to a baker's shop and purchased several shillings' worth of loaves of bread, and to a general dealer's shop, and purchased a piece of cheese. I put them in the bag, put the bag on the car by my side, ready, if any hungry Tipperarian or dweller on the Waterford mountains should present a blunderbuss at me, to put my hand into the bag, pull out, present, and throw to him a bullet of bread; not fearing but this style of defence would be more effective than a defence by powder and lead. Besides, it had this other advantage, that if bad roads, or bad weather, or other mischance detained me in the mountains, or if no inns or provision shops could be met with on the road; I could begin and eat my ammunition; which, if that ammunition had been gunpowder and leaden bullets, I could not have done.

Thus prepared for the journey, I joined the procession, which, as already said, at starting consisted only of twenty-six loaded carts; but which increased to the number of sixty-one before we proceeded five or six miles. An advanced guard of two of the Scots Greys rode on fifty yards in front. I followed them in my car. Then came three cars, with the officer commanding, eight of the infantry, and one of the constabulary. Next were four of the Scots Greys. Then came the long line of single horsed carts loaded with bags of meal. Then followed the cars, with eight of the infantry and a constable; and, last of all, two of the Scots Greys, a corporal and a private, came up as rear-guard. The sergeant of the Greys in command of his party trotted and galloped from front to rear and from rear to front, urging the straggling carters forward, and halting those in front until the rear closed up to a manageable distance; for the line was often extended to a great length by some horse, which was too heavily loaded for its strength, stopping and keeping the rest back.

The line of horsemen, cars, and carts winded up the narrow valleys and on the hill sides, gaining a higher and higher altitude at every step, the hills rising still higher above the road as the road ascended, until we had the mountains on each side at the distance of only a few miles capped in snow, with sunshine on the snow and blue clouds girt upon them at their middle height. As we passed along, groups of squalid beings were seen at road corners, or running from the multitudinous houses, hovels, huts, or cabins dotted on the slopes and in the bottoms by the streamlet sides, to see the meal go past them under the protection of bullets, bayonets, and cavalry swords, on its way to feed people beyond the mountains hunger-stricken like themselves, but to whom they would not let it go if bullets, bayonets, and cavalry swords were not present. To look on all this from some prominent place it was extremely picturesque and striking on the perceptive senses. The beautiful grey horses of the dragoons—the men with their large scarlet cloaks flowing from their shoulders to their knees, and covering the backs of the horses, and the horses with their long white tails waving beneath the scarlet cloaks—the long swords dangling from the waistbelt to the men's feet— the feet booted and formidably armed with spurs, one touch of which would have made the gallant greys leap from the ground to the roofs of the ordinary wayside houses—gave a liveliness to the picture which it would not have possessed had it been merely a military line of march. The liveliness of the scene was increased by the cart-drivers, who holloed and whooped to their horses to get them up the steep roads, and ran, half a dozen of them at a time, to push behind the cart of some horse that stopped.

But how miserable was the scene when looked upon otherwise than as a picture; when dwelt upon in thought. Because the land was mountainous and poor, the best of it of indifferent quality, it was thickly peopled. The landowners of Ireland have generally succeeded in clearing their good land of its dense population. In Tipperary there are exceptions; the soil is of the richest quality, and the population is dense; but even in Tipperary some large rich tracts of land are seen lying in grass, as pasture farms, from which the cultivating people have been driven away. Driven from the good land they find refuge upon the bad, such as I saw yesterday amid the Waterford mountains. I found none of it rented even in that wild region for less than 20s. per acre; it was generally 30s. 35s. and 40s. per acre. The owners were various, the Earl of Donoughmore, Colonel Green, the Marquis of Ormonde, and some others whose names I did not take note of. But all of them have middlemen, who become security to them for a moderate rent, and then exact and extract whatever beyond a moderate rent they can obtain from the cultivators of the land. The constabulary stations, with armed men in them, all along the road, to aid in the exaction of the rack-rents, and the meagre efforts made by the peasant farmers on the undrained land—all of it easily drained, but sour with rushes and pools of water, the best of the deep soil buried in foul bogs, the worst of the shallow soil being the portions scratched at under the name of cultivation by the rent-eaten tenantry—those things shew what the natural result is of the disorderly customs of Irish landlords. It was to save the cart-loads of meal from being plundered by those starving tenant farmers of those and other Irish landlords with high sounding titles and long family traditions that the military were employed. And that meal, thus guarded, was going over the mountains to save from death the equally wretched peasantry of the princely English Duke of Devonshire around Dungarvan.

We reached the half-way house, which stands in a gullet on the top of the mountains, about three o'clock. A military escort was to have been there from Dungarvan to take the charge from the Clonmel party, but it did not come. One division of the carts was to leave Dungarvan road at the half-way house, and go by a cross sectional road to Cappoquin, a poor densely populated place in the mountains of Waterford. An escort of armed constabulary was waiting for this division, and took it in charge. The orders of the officer commanding from Clonmel were, to conduct the carts to the half-way house, and no further; so he left them there, and returned with his party. I came back with them. We had our road all down hill now, the Scots Greys trotted out at a slapping pace, the Irish car drivers whipped and holloed to their horses, and came home in lively style. A wheel came off one of the cars, and the soldiers on it were rolled out upon the road, which afforded all the other drivers, and all the

dwellers by the wayside, who saw them, much merriment. Another failed
to come on from the feebleness of the horse, and was likely to detain the
whole, as the rear-guard of the Greys could not pass and leave any of the
party behind. I was asked if I had any objection to take the soldiers on
my car, and, having none, we soon scoured down the hills to the valley of
the Suir, and so into Clonmel.

While I write this at a window looking into the street, another party of
the Grey's has passed with drawn swords at the 'Carry,' going to escort
carts to Tipperary. To-morrow a party sets out for Cahir, which is a
town situated ten Irish miles (eleven Irish are fourteen English miles) up
the banks of this beautiful river Suir.

5

KILKENNY AND CLONMEL, 1st *February 1847*

Kilkenny is situated on the river Noire, seventy-two miles south-west
of Dublin. To the stranger, its most remarkable features are—first,
the rolling river overhung by rocky eminences, with walks below the
rocks and above, and narrow meadows fertile and green, and gardens and
garden-fields mingling with the river, the rocks, and the suburban
buildings. Second, the magnificent castle, family residence of the Marquis of Ormonde, rising above the steep rock, the rock standing on the
river's brink, in all the grandeur of turrets, postern gateways, and feudal
strength. Third, the hordes of professional beggars, who rush upon the
stranger coming into or going out of the town, begging for God's sake,
and promising to divide the money the stranger may give, quarrelling
with, and swearing foully at, one another when the money is given.

Kilkenny, with its suburbs, contains 23,625 inhabitants. It is a city of
history, a city of many legends, a city of poetry, and a city of trade, the
poetry and trade being much the same, of small value. It has 'water
without mud, fire without smoke, and its streets are paved with marble';
so says fame, and fame in this case says truly. The black marble spotted
with white which we see forming brilliant chimney pieces, polished and
shining, is quarried near this town, and the paving stones of the streets
come out of the same quarries. The marble pavement, however, is more
muddy than poetical.

Looking across some garden-fields from the east upon this little city, with its shining slated roofs, upon which are no smoking chimneys, one might suppose it to be dead; or, that it has been smitten by the angel whose mysterious steps are now upon all Ireland, and that it is holding its breath, awaiting, suspensive and motionless, the next movement of the finger of God.

In calling for leave to govern themselves by their own parliament in Dublin, the inhabitants of Kilkenny are more nearly unanimous than are the inhabitants of any other city. The chief difference is now on the questions of physical or moral force. Headed by an alderman of the corporation, the men who have been most conspicuous at local repeal meetings are siding with the physical forcists of the *Nation* party in Dublin, against Mr O'Connell and his son John, the member for Kilkenny. I call them physical forcists because they are so called in Ireland; the more appropriate term is sentimentalists. They are men who, alike void of practical ideas in their writings and of practical doings in the daily business of life, think nationality consists in the mad metre of verses and in flowery and declamatory writing and speaking. What the Irish parliament would do for Ireland is an unsolved problem. But the sentimental corporation of Kilkenny need not wait for a parliament to assemble in College Green, Dublin, for leave to carry out such local improvements as are required in the town. They do not need, for example, to ask the 'Saxon' for liberty to put numbers to the houses and shops of Kilkenny, to render possible the delivery of letters to the persons to whom they should be delivered; to render less common the perusal, detention, and loss of letters, by their falling into the hands successively of a number of persons of the same name, who have no business to have them in their hands. All they require for effecting this, and many other necessary improvements, is merely a little common sense. Self government does not consist entirely in having the power of enacting statutes or of making parliamentary speeches.

The trade of Kilkenny chiefly consists in providing for the wants of a great garrison of soldiers, who, in their turn, are chiefly engaged, conjointly with the armed constabulary, in keeping the inhabitants of Kilkenny in a state of subjection, and in collecting rents and levying distresses for rents in the neighbourhood. Some manufactories of woollen cloth exist; tanneries, breweries, and foundries, have also an existence. Corn-dealers and millers buy corn and make flour, and send corn and flour down to Waterford for shipment. Traders and dealers of other varieties may be found, but the operations of all are feeble. Religious houses, colleges, chapels, churches, Catholic priests, clergy in general, lawyers, constabulary, soldiery, and street beggary, comprise the leading interests, and give the city its distinctive features. A canal to connect

Kilkenny with Waterford was begun many years ago, but was abandoned, after the money raised for it in the first moment of national enthusiasm was spent. It has remained a long, unsightly, stagnant trench ever since. Its banks were planted with rows of trees, which are now large and ornamental, with walks underneath, where the inhabitants of Kilkenny wander and loiter, the poets to make verses, the lovers to make love, the politicians to make prophecies of what Kilkenny would be if there was a parliament in Dublin. Yet with all this making, the canal has remained half made for more than fifty years. The Noire, with a water-power for machinery equal to one hundred thousand horses, has run poetically past all the while, broad, beautiful, and useless.

Most readers of newspapers have heard of Lord Devon's commission, a commission, by royal warrant, to take evidence and report on the laws and customs of landlord and tenant in Ireland. It is not known publicly how that commission of inquiry originated. Circumstances have heretofore prevented me from speaking publicly or writing of the matter. I do not conceive that those circumstances any longer exist, while there is a reason why the origin of the inquiry should be referred to, as I am writing of the locality, and may again write of the landlords, tenant-farmers, land-agents, land-lawyers, sheriffs' officers, sheriffs' men, constabulary, murderers, and hangmen, whose disorderly conduct towards one another, gave rise to that commission of inquiry.

It originated at Bennet's Bridge, five miles from Kilkenny. I was there in the summer of 1843, and saw such atrocious outrages committed by a landlord on his tenantry—a lease-holding tenantry—a landlord who, being a political Protestant, had the law, the law officials, the constabulary, with their bullets and bayonets, and the hangman with his rope, on his side. I saw such atrocities committed by this landlord, that I was constrained to write of him. I wrote an account of his atrocities to a morning paper in London, the conductors of which, with a prudence which was quite excusable, deemed the publication of them highly dangerous, in respect of the libel law which then existed; but my report was privately printed. The proprietor of the newspaper, willing to do what service he could for the persecuted tenantry whose sufferings I had reported, laid a copy of the report before Sir James Graham, who, in his turn, was shocked with the horrible persecution carried on in the name of the law at Bennet's Bridge, and took my report at once to Sir Robert Peel. Sir Robert Peel, with his characteristic promptitude in all such cases, caused a government agent to proceed at once to Bennet's Bridge and ascertain if my report was true. I was still in Kilkenny when the agent came. He confirmed the truth of what I had written. Upon which Sir Robert Peel immediately caused the commission, with Lord Devon at its head, to issue and inquire into the whole question of landlord and tenant in Ireland.

I subsequently printed, at an expense of £50 to myself, (part of which, by the way, was to have been repaid to me by certain parties who have never done so,) the Bennet's Bridge cases of law-breaking by the landlord, called it 'A Cry from Ireland,' and sent a copy to every member and peer of parliament. Lord John Russell on one occasion referred to it as too frightful for quotation in the house, as he could hardly believe the circumstances there related to be true. Sir Robert Peel, in the same debate, said that he had read that pamphlet, that its statements were horrible, but he feared too true. The *Dublin Review* commented on it, and the reviewer said that the facts were within his own knowledge. All the copies of the pamphlet have been distributed; but some, probably many, of the readers of this paper have access to read, or will remember to have read, the substance of the matter now referred to in the first volume of the *League* newspaper, under the head of 'Ireland as she is in 1843.' Those matters are remarkable, not so much for the atrocities of a bad landlord as for the fact that the atrocities were done with the assistance of lawyers, armed constabulary, and the forms of law, in defiance of the law itself and the decisions of the judges at the Kilkenny assizes and quarter sessions, chiefly because the landlord was an adherent of the dominant Irish faction.

It is worthy of remark that he was an Irish landlord, with a family lineage reaching back into the traditions of the Irish kings, and that he was a resident landlord. He is not resident now. The estate is in Chancery, and a receiver of the Court of Chancery collects the rents.

That receiver is Mr Mannix, a barrister, a landowner of considerable extent in the county of Cork, and largely connected with land as a receiver under Chancery. I saw him the other day, and derived much pleasure and instruction from his practical conversation. He is a thoroughly practical man. In the first place, he expressed his belief that the Bennet's Bridge tenantry were a worthy and industrious set of men (those men who had been harassed until they were known by the disorder and crimes of their neighbourhood as devils in human form, and as black sheep. Does any reader remember the *black sheep* celebrated in 1843?) To illustrate the working of the Court of Chancery with property under its control, he stated that the house of one of the tenants at Bennet's Bridge requires, at the present time, to have repairs done which will cost £3. To obtain leave to expend this sum of £3 on repairs, application must be made to the Court of Chancery through an attorney and Chancery barrister in Dublin, which will cost £5. A pamphlet which I recently quoted, 'Observations on the Tenures of Land in Ireland,' speaks of estates going through gradations of indebtedness until they fall into the hands of 'the worst possible landlord, a receiver under the Court of Chancery.' This must not be understood as applicable to the receiver as an individual. He is bound by the court, and can do nothing but receive the money and pay it into court.

Mr Mannix is not politically associated with the whigs or liberals; but he gave his unqualified approbation to Lord John Russell's measures, as proposed on the 25th of January, particularly his proposed simplification of the sale and titles of land. We happened to meet at Kilkenny, and again at Clonmel, and were in the same hotel reading the newspapers together when the report of Lord John Russell's speech reached Clonmel. To sell an estate of land at present, if encumbered with debt, in which case only estates require to be sold, Mr Mannix told me that one-half of the purchase money would be swallowed up in proving and conveying the title to it, unless it should happen to be an estate of very great extent. But estates of great extent are usually entailed and not saleable. The only way to avoid giving the half of the purchase money to the lawyers is to purchase from the different parties, often fifty or sixty in number, their opposition to the sale, though that opposition may be only the exercise of a fictitious right. To do this is often more expensive than going to the Court of Chancery to obtain an order for the sale in defiance of those fictitious rights.

Let me illustrate the operation of these absurd customs and laws of landed property in Ireland, by a supposed case clearly intelligible to Lancashire.

Cotton is the raw material from which we manufacture clothing, as land is the raw material out of which we manufacture food. If a bale of cotton were subjected to the same laws as a parcel of land in Ireland, lawyers would go to work to make out for the manufacturer, who intended to purchase it, a title; that title must set forth its whole history; the history of its transit from the plantation to Mobile; of the person to whom it was sold there, and the custody in which it was kept; of its shipment, and the custody of the persons in whom it was vested at sea; of the interests of all the owners, if more than one, of the ship; the same of the insurance office; of the entrance of the ship into the docks; of the interests of all the persons to whom the docks containing this bale of cotton belong; of the landing of the bale, and of the proprietorship of the lurry which carried it to the warehouse; of the proprietorship of the warehouse which contained it; of the merchant and his family lineage and history who imported it or to whom it is consigned; of the family lineage of the merchant who has bought it from that importer, and who now proposes to sell it to the manufacturer; of the family lineage of the manufacturer who proposes to buy it; and of every other incident of its history for at least sixty years, supposing it to have been more than sixty years in existence. All this must be set forth on parchment in dreary redundance of phraseology by lawyers, and the consent of all persons who have had, or have been supposed to have, any interest in it for sixty years must be obtained and set forth separately in legal deeds before the bale can be sold once, and at each time that it is to be sold, or any part of it. And if any one of those parties who formerly possessed it, or had an interest in it, at the plantation, on the canal to Mobile, at Mobile, in the ship, in the docks at Liverpool, or in the warehouses, refuses to give consent to the sale of this bale of cotton after it is in Lancashire, their opposition must either be purchased up, or a bill must be filed in Chancery, setting forth all the history of the cotton, with affidavits to every particular, with fees to lawyers of prodigious amount, and subject to delay not less than six months, probably much longer. After all that expense and delay, the cotton bale might be sold and transferred to the new purchaser, who might then, not sooner, proceed with his own head and his people's hands to make it into cotton for human comfort or adornment.

We know that none of those things require to be done. The bale of cotton is the property of a merchant at mid-day. Before night it is not only conveyed to a manufacturer as his property, but is conveyed, if need be, thirty miles to his mill, and may be all made into cloth to-morrow.

Why should not land be as easily sold and purchased as a bale of cotton? There is more danger of fraud or wrongdoing in transferring cotton briefly and cheaply than land. Cotton soon changes its shape and location. Land always remains in the same place, to prove its own identity and to be witness to any fraud that may arise in selling and transferring it to a new purchaser. No other commodity under heaven might be so safely sold, the money paid for it, and a receipt given in twenty minutes of time, as a piece of land.

Since I wrote these remarks, I have seen the speeches of the liberal candidates for the representation of Manchester, delivered in the Free-Trade Hall on the 28th ult. I rejoice that my humble pen is writing in harmony with the sentiments, on the sale and transfer of land, so eloquently uttered by them.

Leaving Kilkenny, and taking the route to Tipperary, I found many people working on the roads for the public pay of tenpence per day. The roads are sadly cut up and disordered by the expenditure of that public money.

The soil continues to derive its character from the lime-stone on which it rests for many miles. The farms are chiefly from twenty to sixty acres for the first eight miles out of Kilkenny. The worst of the land is under cultivation, the best lies wet, rushy, and boggy, and neglected because it is wet. Though drainage is easy in most places, it is rarely attempted. At the distance of twelve or fourteen miles from Kilkenny, the land presented such a shocking aspect of foulness and disorder, the top water and springs of one field running into and over the field of another farmer below; and all the surface and spring water of that field, natural to itself, and acquired from above, running upon another still lower, until many hundreds of acres of the best land, that which lies lowest, were abandoned, the miserable tenantry preferring to give the high rent of thirty and forty shillings per acre for the thin, high, and dry soils, verging on the moorland, rather than have the rich soils below at any price; such, I say, was the shocking aspect of the foulness and disorder of that property, that I halted to inquire its landlord's name and its history, feeling assured that it must belong to some absentee, or be under the keepership of Chancery. It was neither; it was part of the estate of the Marquis of Ormonde.

I came next upon ground belonging to Sir Whelan Cuffe. Much of it was in a similar condition, though in one part I saw an attempt making at drainage. Any landlord expending his own money has a right to follow his own plans; but as public money is to be advanced for the improvement of Irish land, I protest against that money being sunk in such drains as those of Sir Whelan Cuffe. They are cut out on the pasture land less than eighteen inches deep, about half that width, the sods laid up to dry, and again put into the place from which they came. And this is done though there are stones close at hand—a mountain of stones more than sufficient to pave the whole surface of Ireland. The public money must be spent on works of substantial improvement, from which there will be some probability of it being paid back.

Gradually ascending the side of a rocky mountain, I passed a huge stone lying on the road-side, and was told that it marked the boundary of the counties of Kilkenny and Tipperary. Going down the south side of the mountain, the road was steep for several miles, with an impetuous stream rushing out of the mountain and keeping it company. The houses were numerous, the land attached to them small in measure, and seemingly poor in quality; but I was told it was kindly land, and yielded well to a moderate amount of labour. Farther down, in approaching the great plain watered by the river Suir, the land had all the appearance of the most generous fertility. It was divided into small enclosures, by earthen dykes, occupying much space. The owner was the Earl of Clonmel.

Reaching the vicinity of the river, and proceeding westward, on a road not surpassed for breadth and hardness in the kingdom, and amid scenery and fertile land hardly equalled in the kingdom, I passed, at two and a half miles from Clonmel, the handsome lodge-gate of Captain Bernal Osborne, M.P. Many alterations have been effected by that gentleman in that estate (its name is Newtown Abbey) within the last three years, since he married the amiable young lady whose inheritance it was. Much work has been created for labourers, and a superior class of dwelling-houses built; also a national school, near the lodge-gate, ample and elegant.

But, going forward, I found everything changed from what I had yet seen in Ireland. Large flour-mills, worked by the powerful river and its tributaries; ample farm-fields with young wheat upon them rich in promise for next harvest; green clover, as if the month had been May; and villas beautiful and numerous facing Tipperary on the Waterford side of the river, and shewing that Clonmel had wealthy inhabitants. Its evidences of trade when I arrived in it proved that the villas were not merely outside show. The flour-mills and stores were of a magnitude to amaze me, and all the more so, perhaps, that I had never heard of them before. They belong, I believe, every one of them, to members of the Society of Friends. Indeed, with the exception of Mr Bianconi, once an Italian boy, now and for a long time an extensive car proprietor, working about 1600 horses, the Friends have made the trade of Clonmel, and that within the lifetime of the present generation. And it is but bare justice to them to say, that while their great establishments are giving work and wages to many people who would have been otherwise unemployed, and are grinding and sending out the meal of the Indian corn upon the markets of Ireland, which but for such mills as theirs could not have been supplied fast enough to the people in this emergency, their broad benevolence is the chief support of many thousands of people bereft of food, and who are flocking to Clonmel, or, who being there, are flocking to them for subsistence.

A glorious mission of peaceful industry, moral example, and general benevolence, has their settlement in Tipperary fulfilled! Even the native inhabitants, inspired to enterprise and perseverance in business by the example of these industrious Friends, once strangers, are more enterprising and flourishing in Clonmel than in other towns of Ireland.

6

Dungarvan, County Waterford

Coming over the hills, the other day, to this place, I was accosted by a man who carried a gun in his hand, and asked if I was Captain Somebody, whom he named, of the constabulary. What he would have said if I had been the captain I do not know. He proceeded to tell me that he was a farmer and a tailor; that he had twelve boys (men) at work for him; that he contracted to make greatcoats for the constabulary, and paid the boys 7s. 6d. per week; that he had as many potatoes as would plant three acres of ground; that he had three hundred barrels of oats, sixty barrels being thrashed and lying in the barn; that the barn had been twice attacked in the night; and that he had been to Clonmel to buy a gun and a pistol, and percussion caps, for himself and the boys to defend the oats and the seed potatoes.

On mentioning what this man told me to some gentlemen who are neither to be despised for their want of sagacity nor suspected of the want of liberality, they said that the man might be telling the truth, but it was just possible that he had been buying arms, like many others, and contrived an excuse for being seen with them in his possession on the highway. For myself, I saw no reason to doubt the man's story; most of the farmers have corn in their possession, and all who have it feel uneasy about it. They are purchasing arms and amunition to defend it, and are doing this the more anxiously and generally that they see the common people, the very poorest, procuring arms everywhere.

This is a most unhappy state of affairs. My attention was called to it as soon as I landed in Dublin, and frequently since. The first tradesman's shop I entered in Dublin was that of an inspector of a relief committee of St Michael's parish. He told me of the deplorable poverty of the people. But while I stood in his shop, a countryman in a frieze coat was looking at some samples of gunpowder, and selected the sample at 2s.6d. per lb. of which he took and paid for a pound weight. I thought nothing of this at the time, and ever since have believed the accounts in newspapers and public rumour to be much exaggerated. I am exceedingly sorry to say, and feel constrained to write it, that as regards the county of Tipperary, Waterford, and Kilkenny, report has not exaggerated the amount of business doing in arms and gunpowder, nor has report come up to anything like the truth. Nor is it the farmers and provision dealers who have property to defend who are arming themselves; the people who are working on the public works for five shillings a week are pinching their bellies of food, clubbing money together, and buying arms.

In Clonmel, with the exception of the flour and meal mills, no other shops are doing business at present with spirit, except the dealers in guns and pistols. I was staying there eight days in the Commercial Hotel. The commercial travellers came in day after day complaining that nothing was doing; no money could be got and no orders, all except those travelling for Birmingham gunmakers. One of these came to Clonmel on Tuesday last after mid-day, and he told the other commercial men and me, in the public room in the evening, that he obtained the offer of more orders that afternoon than he had obtained at other times in a month. He said his terms were always six months' credit; but the Clonmel tradesmen had been offering him ready cash if he would book and execute their orders at once; such is the excessive demand for arms. I find it the same in Dungarvan and throughout the county of Waterford; and the same at the poorer town of Carrick-on-Suir. I write on this subject with pain; but I feel that I would not do my duty if I did not call attention to these astounding facts.

The following auctioneer's bill, bearing the royal arms on the top, and printed so as to have an official appearance, belongs to a person who holds sales by auction and sells large quantities of arms of all kinds, to purchasers of all degrees, but chiefly to the very poorest looking of the road-working people:—'Whereas, many evil-disposed persons avail themselves of the present scarcity of food, as a pretext to commit acts of violence against property, and otherwise disturbing the peace of the country, his Excellency the Lord Lieutenant is pleased to grant to all her Majesty's subjects, without distinction, the power to have and to keep any description of firearms for the protection of the public peace and likewise their own homes and property; without any restriction, except an invoice or certificate of the person from whom the arms are purchased. T. M. is privileged by his Excellency, and fully empowered by the honourable Board of Excise, to offer for sale by auction to the peaceable inhabitants of this town, five hundred double and single barrelled guns of various sorts, and one thousand pairs of pistols, warranted all double power proof; five hundred thousand best percussion caps, a large quantity of powder flasks, shot bags, and belts, wash rods, turnscrews, nipple wrenchers, &c. &c. Sale to commence on Saturday, 30th January; for a short time only. T. M. licensed auctioneer, Castle-street, Dublin. N.B.—The auctioneer's invoice is all the license required by the purchaser for keeping arms. Auction each day at twelve o'clock.'

The words *Castle* and *Dublin* are printed conspicuously, with the *street* between very small; and thus the bill has attracted much attention. But that, and the royal arms on it, and the *whereas* are only the trick of a smart auctioneer. I notice the thing as illustrative of this disordered country.

Since writing the foregoing, the commercial traveller, Mr T——, has informed me that the statement which recently appeared in the newspapers, as to a government agent being sent to Birmingham to ascertain how many guns had been sent to Ireland since the expiry of the Arms Act, last year, was not correct as regarded the number of 2000, which he was said to have reported as the whole number sent to Ireland. Mr T—— represents only one house, and there are many Birmingham houses represented in Ireland. His house alone had, up to that time, sent more than 2000 guns to Ireland, from the time of the Arms Act expiring. He estimates 800 guns and pistols as having been supplied to Clonmel alone previous to his visit on Tuesday last. He was kind enough to shew me his order-book, and he has taken orders for half as many more. Besides which, there was another Birmingham traveller in Clonmel only a fortnight ago, who took very large orders; but the firm for which that traveller took the orders has intimated to the tradesmen who gave them that they cannot fulfil the orders but for cash payments, the truth being, that the excessive demand for fire-arms, and the disordered state of the country, have alarmed the firm in question and made them hesitate to give credit. And this alarm on their part arises from the fact that they do little in the fowling-piece trade; they are in the musket, fusil, and carbine trade.

In reply to the question, if Clonmel was to be looked upon as a wholesale depot supplying other towns, Mr T—— stated that he and other travellers visited all the other towns near it, and received orders for arms there in the same proportion to the general trade done in those towns. I asked him if fowling-pieces were the kind of guns in most request. He said the trade opened after the expiry of the Arms Act last year with fowling-pieces chiefly and pocket pistols, but now the trade was in military pistols, soldiers' muskets, and bayonets, fusils with bayonets, house guns with bayonets, and fowling-pieces. The fusil is a shorter musket than that of common infantry regiments; the sergeants of the infantry carry fusils, and some entire regiments carry them, from which they are called fusileers. The fusil (pronounced fusee) is a size between the carbine of the heavy dragoons and the full-sized musket. The house gun, Mr T—— informed me, is a short fowling-piece, with a bayonet to fix on it; it is sold cheap, and is in great request.

The retail prices in Ireland are various. A countryman came into a shop one day when I was present, and asked to see the fowling-pieces exposed in the window. The shop keeper handed one of them to him, and said the price was twenty-one shillings. The man said the price was too much, and wanted it cheaper. The shopkeeper put the gun in the window again, saying he could not take less for it, and could not waste time, as he was busy. The man then asked to have the gun handed back, upon which he laid down twenty-one shillings and walked away with it. Mr T—— told me that his firm had supplied that piece, and all of its kind in that shop, at ten shillings and sixpence each. It is said that those pieces are resold singly in the inland villages at thirty and forty shillings each.

I shall not speculate on the purposes which the buyers of these arms have in view. My deliberate opinion is, that the people, as a body, have no fixed purpose in view. A kind of mania has sprung up among them to furnish themselves with arms without their knowing why or wherefore. Distressing as the potato failure and the consequent high prices of food are, that very distress has caused more money to circulate in Ireland, and to circulate among the poorest of the people, than they were ever accustomed to before. When they had potatoes to eat, they handled very little money.

This town of Dungarvon belongs chiefly to the Duke of Devonshire. It is represented in Parliament by Mr Shiel, who sits by favour of the Duke. Some new streets and a square have been built by his Grace, and the town, as a town, has been beautified and improved at his instance. As to his farm-land, I see little in its management to commend; and I probably know too little of it to be justified in condemning it, farther than this, that it partakes of all the evils peculiar to Irish landed estates.

The Marquis of Waterford has an estate in this neighbourhood, which he proposes, so says report, to sell. The rental is about £2000 per annum. The lawyers will get about £5000, and his Lordship, probably, £35,000, if he sells it. The purchaser, if a business man, with an additional £20,000, may make a good property of it. If Lord Waterford devotes his £35,000 to the improvement of some portion of his other property, he, too, will be a great gainer.

To shew what can be done with land in Ireland, I may refer to a tenant of Lady Osborne, about three miles from Clonmel. I was in the coach-building establishment of Mr Jones, a thorough practical man, when this tenant came in to receive cash for oats which he had sold to that gentleman. He willingly gave me, at the request of Mr Jones, an account of his agricultural operations. The following are the chief points of interest:—He occupies thirty acres and pays £60 of rent annually. He paid £100 within the last twelve months for manure, in addition to all the manure made by his own cows, pigs, and horses. He lost his potatoes as others did, but he thanks God that he has had enough of produce left to pay his rent, to get a fair return for his manure, pay all his debts, and have something over!

He was advised by Mr Jones and another gentleman present, as his land was in such good condition this year, to prepare some of it for Swedish turnips. He said he would sow turnips if he saw his neighbours doing so; not that he needed an example from them, but that, if he sowed turnips and they did not, all his would be stolen from him by the hungry people.

The refusal to pay rents by many of the tenantry who can afford to do so; the entire dependence of the mass of the people on the English treasury—in other words, on English industry, for food; the exertions which all parties possessed of landed property are making to oppose Lord John Russell's measure for throwing the burthen of Irish pauperism partly on them as well as on England; the embarrassed condition of the Irish landlords; the impossibility of reaching them unless by sale of their estates; the impossibility of effecting such sales but by a measure far more comprehensive than that of Lord John Russell; all those things, and others related in this letter, conspire to make the present condition of Ireland matchless in its necessities, matchless in its perils.

P.S.—Since posting the foregoing statement as to the trade in fire-arms, and the quantity sold by one Birmingham firm in Ireland, I find that the sales of that firm are a mere fraction compared with the sales by others— one other is alone receiving orders, through *one* of its travellers, at the rate of £2000 per week for guns and pistols, chiefly guns. This is equivalent to 4000 guns per week. The orders are only executed in part to each customer from the impossibility of getting the articles supplied. The articles are fowling-pieces, and muskets with bayonets. The muskets with bayonets amount to about one-fourth of the number of fowling-pieces. The prices, wholesale, are from eight shillings and sixpence to seventeen shillings for musket and bayonet. These are sold, retail, at prices varying from £1 to £1:10s. The shopkeepers easily obtain those profits, as the demand upon them is greater than can be supplied. The gentleman engaged in this gigantic gun trade gives me his opinion as follows:—That the operation of the law previous to the expiry of the Arms Act last year drained the country of fire-arms even of the most innocent kind. There was thus a vacuum, as it were, for the supply to rush into as soon as the law permitted; that the Irish people do everything in masses, being peculiarly disposed to operate together, as under a mania; that the farmers feel themselves and their little stores of corn insecure in this season of dearth, and some of them arm themselves for defence, seeing which, all rush to do the same thing. The difficulty in judging of the matter aright is, however, that the farmers are liable to be visited by bands of men, who take the arms from them, and who have no stores of corn to defend with them.

7

LIMERICK, *9th February 1847*

I had intended to write a letter, instead of this, from the county of Clare or Galway; but the snow-storm which enwraps the country and fills the atmosphere with smothering drift prevents me from getting further west for the present. And the state of the roads is already such as to render it doubtful if even this letter will reach Manchester in time for next Saturday's paper.

But there is no want of matter to write about here. Long before I reached this city I had matter enough, of the deepest interest, for a volume, instead of a column or two in a newspaper. The difficulty with me is to select the topics of most pressing interest, and postpone or leave untold what cannot be now published. To begin and continue to tell of all the ghastly faces, hollow and shrunken, which I have seen, with death looking out of the eyes, might horrify and appal the reader, but would not, I fear, instruct him; the masses of population amongst whom I have travelled through Tipperary and part of this county, sinking from health to sickness, from life to death—not yet dead, but more terrible to look upon and think upon than if they were dead; living, but with death and his attendants in possession of the human tenement, and keeping possession until the indwelling spirit of the clay is ejected, thrown out, out at the windows where it is already seen struggling to stay within, and glaring horribly upon the passer by; those masses of population would afford, in description, scope enough to fill all this paper, from title to printer's name. But the means of relieving them from present suffering and impending death are the topics which I shall rather choose.

On the subject of subscriptions to relief committees, a very few sentences shall at present suffice. Government doubles the subscriptions of private individuals, so that by a subscriber giving £50, the relief committee gets £100. The munificent contributions from England, and the government duplication of them, (the government being in that case only the dispensers of taxes paid chiefly by Englishmen who work, who take off their coats to work, and sweat with their coats off,) these contributions are in many places the only dependence of the people for subsistence. In no place can I see, or ascertain by inquiry, that the nobility or landowning gentry are contributing, save in the most paltry sums; most of them giving nothing at all. A landlord who has nominally an income of £20,000 per annum, but who, it is believed, has positively £10,000, puts his name down, in the county of Cork, for £5. Another in Tipperary county, who either is rich or lives as if he were rich, puts his name down for £4. The town of Bridgewater in England alone has contributed for Irish relief above £1100 in the course of a few weeks. Its population is about 10,000. The population of Clonmel in Ireland is about 16,000. Its contributions to the relief fund are about £1000, being by far the most liberal of any town in Ireland according to the population. But with the single exception of Mr Bianconi, the rich car proprietor, who gives £25, the 'Saxons' resident there, or the 'Celts' favourable to Saxon alliance, are the liberal contributors. The only titled or landed subscriber is the Earl of Clonmel, who gives £20. The millers, most of them, give £100 or £50 each, their daughters and sisters giving sums of £20 and £50, in addition to an endless stream of private beneficence. From a few shillings up to £5, but seldom more than 10s. is the range of the subscriptions of the shopkeepers, gentry, and anti-Saxon aldermen and town-councillors (Mr Bianconi excepted) of Clonmel. And they have been making speeches, writing, and printing, and publishing all manner of anti-Saxonism, at least twice a-week, up to last Saturday.

But, to pass to more comprehensive and permanent measures of Irish relief, let me glance at the proposition to give sixteen millions sterling out of the imperial exchequer to make Irish railways. In the report of the debate on Lord George Bentinck's motion there is the following:—

'Captain Osborne thanked the noble member for Lynn, Lord George Bentinck, for the able and energetic manner in which he had taken up the cause of Ireland. He looked upon the noble Lord as the only party leader of that house who had brought forward a really great plan for the redemption of Ireland, (the proposal to advance sixteen millions sterling to make railways). He could assure the government that the people of Ireland looked for some comprehensive plan for the amelioration of their condition.'

The people of Ireland and the landlords of Ireland must not be mistaken the one class for the other. Both may be poor, and need relief; but the means by which they became poor are very different. Mr Roebuck might speak more softly in the hearing of the Irish landlords in parliament; but, in whatever tone he might speak of their disposition to job for their own exclusive benefit with public money, he could only offend them. So must any one else who speaks or writes of their jobbing dispositions and practices. Yet, is truth to be withheld, and sixteen millions sterling laid hold of, in addition to the ten or eleven millions spent, and to be spent by the government in Ireland for Irish relief, merely because a class of men, far more remarkable for their corruption than for their impeccability, splutter and explode in the face of every one who estimates them according to their past doings? I protest against the inference that the Irish people are insulted, or should feel insulted, because those very men who have beggared the Irish people and the Irish land cannot suffer to hear themselves spoken of. I would rather refrain from speaking of them; but how can the ills of Ireland be explained and redressed if the owners of her land are not to be named! How are they to be named without blame, and trusted with vast sums of public money without suspicion, when we see some of the most practical and least poverty stricken of them in this very season of famine, distress, and disorder, opposing the public benefit, and deferring the employment and payment of labourers to promote their own private ends—those very men standing up in parliament, demanding in the name of the people sixteen millions to help to make railways, while their own greediness mars the making of railways for which the money is already provided?

The line from Limerick to Waterford would have been employing several thousands of men at this moment, if the capital had been all subscribed. The government, seeing this, came forward to make up the deficiency of capital for the earth works, three weeks or a month ago. No man in England or Ireland knows that fact more clearly than Mr Osborne. No man with the breath of life in him knows better than Mr Osborne why this railway is not now going on, and why time and money are now being wasted in new surveys, while thousands of unemployed men, along the course of the line, are dependent on charity, and on government advances to relief committees, for subsistence. The public do not know the causes of that delay; I shall tell them one, at least, of the causes.

The line, as formerly surveyed and adopted, passed near the park walls of an important landowner in Tipperary; but it did not go through more than a few acres of his estate. The line by that course went in a straight direction, and through level meadows. The important land-owner, either to get it to go through some miles of his property for the sake of the money to be paid for leave to do so, or because he thinks that a railway and the trains upon it shooting along the valley, (miserably bad taste if he thinks so!) in sight of his fine new park, would deteriorate the beauty of the scenery of the Suir river and the Waterford hills beyond— to please himself, in one or the other of these respects, or to effect some purpose equally unworthy, is endeavouring to turn the railway out of the straight line in the plain by the river side, to go round some miles of country, chiefly on his estate, in form of a crescent, part of that course being in deep cuttings. The additional expenses, by taking that erratic course instead of the even one, will be £10,000 for construction, besides the great expense now incurred for new surveys, and the great loss to the public from delay.

But his deviation of the line has a more serious disadvantage. The largest flour mills in Ireland, save perhaps one establishment, were to be served by the straight line. A station was to be made close to the mills. The owner of the mills, having beautiful private grounds sloping towards the river, was willing to have them encroached upon by the railway for the advantage of the station for business. That miller is rich enough to live without business; affluent enough to live, if he chose, in higher style than any landowner in the country; liberal enough to live, as he does, genteelly and beneficently; yet he looks to the advantage of his business, which is the public advantage, and would allow the railway to cut up his pleasure grounds rather than it should not bring wheat to the mill and carry away its flour. Moreover, the station at that point would be a passenger station, and would induce many people to leave Clonmel and return again for pleasure, while by the deviation there will be no point of attraction whatever.

The important landlord, to serve his private purposes, takes, or tries to take, the railway accommodation from the public, and the large mills of the greatest employer of men and money in the neighbourhood, offering no public advantage in return. His influence with the government, conjointly with other landowners of influence, has procured for the railway an advance of public money. Which advance being so obtained gives him great power over the directors of the company. That power seems destined to change the course of the railway. That change in the course of the railway is augmenting the expense and causing delay. That delay is disappointing thousands of men ready to work, and who are starving for want of work. That important landlord is Mr Bernal Osborne!

In the present emergency, one would not be greatly surprised if the Irish landlords, to facilitate railway construction, enlarge employment, distribute wages, and relieve in some degree the charitable from the burthen of supporting the unemployed—one would not be greatly surprised if they offered the land required for the new railways at a moderate and reasonable price. Not a foot of it will they yield at a reasonable price. Take the following case; it is only a sample case:—

A landlord whose estate lies in the way of the Kilkenny and Waterford Junction Railway, whose father granted leases to the tenantry, disputed the validity of those leases a few years ago, and succeeded in abrogating them. By doing so, he caused much litigation, much ill-feeling, some crimes, and great notoriety to himself, his estate, and his tenantry. He broke the leases granted by his father, that he might re-let the farms at higher rents, and refused to grant new leases, that he might be able at any time to augment the rent or eject the tenants. He did not understand that his estate *might* be improved in value by a leaseholding tenantry; that it could not possibly be improved by tenants-at-will, and those tenants holding at *his* will. Neither did he know that leases might at some time, not then far distant, give such of his property as might be required for public purposes a higher value than if the property was held by tenants-at-will. He did not know that railway engineers would lay their surveying eyes on his land; but they did. They could not go round about his land, they had to go through it. He then knew that he would get payment from the railway company for the land required by them, but he wanted more than payment. He tried to get more than payment; and after tasking his ingenuity—some people have said cupidity—to the uttermost, he fell upon the following plan:—He granted leases to those tenants whose farms were to be touched by the railroad, that they might thereby claim and receive compensation from the company. He granted the leases on condition that the compensation paid to the tenants was to be handed over to him. The railway company refused to pay compensation to tenants holding under such newly-made and evil-designed leases. Having failed in this attempt to exact money, he has given notice to the tenants that the leases are not valid, and must be withdrawn. He has caused the tenants to go to law at their own expense—at least he has entered into litigation in their name, leaving them liable for expense, and litigation is still going on, while the works of the railway are at a stand in that locality, because the company cannot get possession of the land until the litigation is ended. The people of the locality, who would be employed on the railway works, are unemployed—are on the point of starvation, and saved only from starvation by the charitable subscriptions from England and the money from government. The subscriptions of the local gentry in that neighbourhood amount to—simply nothing, not one penny.

If this landlord is not named, let no one think that he has not a name. He has one that is known in his county and beyond it. If need be, it shall be told. In the meantime, here he is, an Irish owner of Irish land; ready, not a doubt of it, to cry aloud to the imperial government to give Ireland sixteen millions 'to make railways to feed the poor, starving, unemployed people.'

But railways will do so much good to Ireland that it would be well to facilitate their construction in every practicable way. At present the land requires all the manual labour, to prepare its crops for next harvest, which Ireland can give, if those crops are to sustain the Irish people; and it requires more horse labour than all the work-horses in Ireland can give. Every farmer who has horses able to draw a load of corn or of meal is now in receipt of such pay for his horse labour as draws him and his

carts and horses from the farm. The food of Ireland is coming to her
shores as hard corn. That corn has to be carted great distances to mills to
be ground to meal. The meal has to be carted to greater distances for
distribution. In order to have the escort of military guards, the carts, and
horses, and men, a man to each, are restricted in their locomotion. At the
distance of twenty, or thirty, or forty miles from home they are obliged
to remain inactive a day, or two days at a time, awaiting the meal, for
which there is such competition that they would not be loaded if they did
not wait. While, once more, with the harassed, wearied, worn-out
soldiery, not numerous enough, great as their numerical strength is in
Ireland, to furnish guards so frequently as the carts are loaded and ready
to move; with this disadvantage they must again delay.

I cannot form an estimate of the number of men and horses employed
thus throughout Ireland, and to be employed thus until the end of that
time when Ireland is to be publicly fed as now. But an opinion of the
mischief that is to befall the land and its culture and crops may be
formed from the fact that every agricultural work-horse which I have
seen, and which is able to work, each with its master, or master's son, or
master's hired man, is employed in transporting corn and meal at one
halfpenny per cwt. per mile; a payment liberal enough to make Irish
farmers forsake ploughing to get ready cash for carting.

To produce food from oats, and barley, and rye, instead of potatoes,
three acres of land will require to be sown instead of one acre of potatoes.
Neither wheat nor turnips can be sown in any available quantity this
year, from the deplorable misculture of the soil. Its wetness, foulness,
and poverty, though much of it is naturally fertile, unfits it at present for
wheat and turnips.

The land cannot be prepared in time nor at all, save in some limited
and favoured districts, to sow grain. The horses are otherwise employed.
The peasantry have neither numerical strength nor physical strength to
prepare the land with the spade in the requisite time; no, not an eighth
part of it, to produce corn enough to supply the place of the potatoes,
though every man able to handle a spade began to delve tomorrow and
delved until the month of June.

Wherefore, I, after observing closely, thinking anxiously, and making
many calculations, declare my opinion to be, that if the sixteen millions
sterling were now lying loose and without other uses, it would be the
most mischievous thing for Ireland which could be devised, to embark in
extensive railway works with that money, while so vast a proportion of
the land is untilled, with the horse labour employed otherwise than in
tillage, and while the whole manual strength of the country is but
fractional to the strength required to put crops in the ground.

8

ENNIS, COUNTY CLARE, *12th February 1847*

Looking from this western county town, through the medium of note-books and recollections, upon the counties journied over from the east and the south, the soil not lessening in fertility, the face of the country not declining in beauty, but the distress deepening, human life sinking to the west, (may it indicate the dawning of a brighter morrow!) and looking around me here on hungry Clare, a question arises as to the cause of Clare, Galway, Mayo, Roscommon, Sligo, and other grass-growing counties being so generally devoted to pasturage, giving no employment to the people. With that question before us, it may be interesting to take a general review of Irish agriculture; and it is as fit to take that review from this point as from anywhere else. Space need not be now occupied with lengthened descriptions of the people's sufferings. All that can be said of the peasantry of the west is comprised in the words, hovels, hunger, rags, rheumatics, weakness, sickness, death. All that can be said of the gentry of the west is comprised in the words, castles, pride, idleness, improvidence, poverty, debt. There is hardly a middle condition or a middle class.

Until a period of time not yet reaching a hundred years, the surface of Ireland was almost exclusively devoted to pasturage. If the potato plant goes out of cultivation followed by famine, it came into cultivation preceded by famine. It was long after the introduction of the potato by Sir Walter Raleigh—it was not until three generations after his death—that this plant was cultivated for food. From Raleigh's time it had been preserved in the family garden and eaten at the family table of Sir Richard Blackwell, his grandfather having received some tubers from Raleigh. Blackwell, seeing the excessive privations to which the people were exposed by periodical recurrences of famine, urged the cultivation of the potato plant as a relief from famine.

In 1727 an unsuccessful attempt was made to introduce an act of parliament to compel landholders to till five acres out of every hundred, exclusive of mountain and bog, and to release tenants to the same extent from the penal covenants in their leases against tillage. In 1762 an act passed to grant bounties on corn brought by land to Dublin, which was not withdrawn until 1780. In 1764 the sum of £5483 was paid as a bounty for this purpose. The sums increased annually until 1780, when the bounty for that year amounted to £77,800. The counties of Carlow,

Kilkenny, Meath, Queen's, and Tipperary, received the largest share of the bounties.

There are about one and twenty millions of acres in Ireland, of which one third is not touched by spade or plough or the hand of man. Much of that third part is capable of being profitably cultivated. But a far larger proportion of the other two thirds is capable of being doubled, trebled, or quadrupled in productiveness by the presence of money, labour, wages, and skilful direction, and the absence of entails, leases on lives, tenancies-at-will, and all the other evils which the Irish landlord is heir to. It is almost a universal custom throughout Ireland for the landlord to let the bare farm to a tenant to erect dwelling-places for himself and his beasts, at his own expense, according to his ability and taste. The ability being low, the taste is kept at the same level. It is also common, though not universal, for the landlords to get rid of a tenant by pulling down the house. There being always a keen competition for land, a farm can be readily relet to another tenant on condition of that other tenant rebuilding the house. The landlord having no expense to incur, is not particular about pulling down a house, or a dozen or a score of them. In all parts of the south and west of Ireland the wrecks of human habitations are seen, the roofs having been taken off to get the tenants out. A low state of morals is a consequence of wretched dwelling-places; wretched dwelling-places are the natural result of the tenant being the builder at his own expense for the landowner to be the sole proprietor of the building. Leases used to be granted for 999 years upon the payment of a sum of money. In such a case the leaseholder is the real owner, but he cannot sell. He can only sub-let. The sub-tenant under him divides the property among a lower class of tenants. The law is such, that if the second tenant fails to pay his rent to the first tenant, though the third one, who is the occupier and cultivator, may have paid the rent to the second, the third can be seized upon for the default of the second, and all his stock swept away.

If there be tenants of the first, second, and third degrees, with a head landlord over all, that head landlord recovers his rent from any one of the three. This system gives the landlords a better chance—at least they think so—of getting rent, than if they had only one tenant for the one farm. Therefore they encourage this pernicious system of sub-letting.

Another kind of lease not now granted, but still existing and to exist, is that of a lease on lives, renewable for ever by payment of a fine on the death of the lives named in the lease.

The more common leases now are for sixty-one, thirty-one, and twenty-one years, with one or more lives added thereto. The lives are commonly those of neutral persons not in any way connected with the property. If the lives expire before the term of years, the lease expires with the years, if no other lives are added to it. If the years expire first, the lease does not end until the persons named in it die. The hazard and uncertainty of this system cannot be otherwise than detrimental to agriculture; at all events, a good capital, enterprise, and industry, must be unsettled, checked, and weakened, by this system of uncertainty. Speaking of it to Mr Mannix, the Chancery receiver, whose experience so well entitles him to give an opinion on this subject, I was told that unless some uncertainty existed as to the termination of the lease, the tenants would ruin the land. When the expiry of a term of years approach, they would cease to fertilize the soil, and lay the buildings, gates, and fences in ruins. It is, therefore, requisite, he said, to name lives, so that, their termination not being foreseen, the occupation of a tenant may end before he can do injury to the farm.

With all respect to the experienced Chancery receiver, I deny the expediency or necessity of this system. Tenants have ill-used their farms, but they were ill-used tenants before they did so. The most distinctive characteristic of an Irish farmer is his want of faith, his ever wakeful suspicion in his landlord and in the agents of his landlord. The most trustful and faithful of human beings is the Irishman when he is himself trusted, and has been convinced that he is trusted. This is no idle sentiment; it is capable of proof. Nor can I pass without denial the assertion that the Irish peasant is from choice the enemy of industry and the security of property and of human life. Look at the Quakers of Clonmel and of other towns in Tipperary who have large capitals invested in business, who employ Irishmen and pay them without reference to their religion or politics; who avoid all strife and contention, and do justice to all with whom they have intercourse; which of those Quakers is afraid of the peasantry of Tipperary who know him? Not one of them. And more orderly and industrious working men do not exist than those whom the Friends employ.

I cannot permit the Tipperarians and the Irish peasantry generally to be libelled as a naturally turbulent and assassin race, not even by men of the *Nation*, whose pens are dipped in ink from week to week to excite the peasantry to dip their hands in blood. I purchased a volume of songs and poems at Limerick, reprinted from the *Nation* newspaper, and called the 'Spirit of the Nation.' If it had been called the 'Spirit of the Butchers' Shop' or the 'Spirit of the Shambles' it would have been more appropriately named. From beginning to end it presents the mind with no other idea than that of butchers whetting their knives to cut throats. There is no other sentiment in it. Even as to poetry, for which, according to the preface, the book has been praised by political opponents, I see but very little. The rhymes are harmonious and flow smoothly, but any versifier of talent might disembowel the dictionary and string its words together in such lines, just as easily as a butcher separates, lays together, and dresses raw tripe.

Ireland, rich in natural treasures under the earth and above the earth, richer in rivers to move machinery and to float ships than any other portion of the globe of the same length and breadth, and with an abundant population needing to work, seeking to work, and willing to work, only requires peace, and men of peace, with money and skill in their hands and in their heads. With these Ireland may have, *will have*, manufactures, commerce, wealth, wages, inward order, outward power, and landed estates productive and valuable. Since I wrote my last letter, dated at Limerick, I have stood upon the shores of the Shannon, have sailed upon, steamed upon, mused upon, and wondered at, this river's mighty breadth and length and strength. Two hundred and thirty-five miles long, with a volume of running water equal to the three largest rivers of England, the Thames, Trent, and Severn united; swelling into lakes, four, five, and six miles wide, and from twenty to thirty miles long, as if the Shannon spread himself out to invite the world to launch its ships upon him; again gathering himself together to shew his strength, as if bidding the world build mills upon his shores—mills, if the world likes, to grind all the corn and spin all the yarn of the earth. Standing upon, musing upon, and wondering at, the waters of this river, the awe inspired by its measureless power, and the contemplation of what the Almighty Maker made it for, is only surpassed by the deeper awe arising from the havoc, disorder, famine, and crime, made by men who waste the fertile land upon its shores, as well as its godlike gift of motive power—waste, in the face of frowning Heaven, one of the noblest treasures of nature which God ever gave to man.

See a nobleman, owner of a vast territory on one side of it, an amiable man he is, getting his rents collected, extracted, and remitted to him once a month to London, because he cannot live two months without them! His income nominally £20,000 a-year; his acres three times twenty thousand; his wretched tenantry in misery at all times, dying of famine now; he not able to contribute a sack of meal to their relief; government sending meal to their relief. This nobleman, naturally, I believe, one of the best meaning of men, but born to entailed land and entailed beggary, with the misfortune of being a Lord with dignity and debt upon his head heavier than mill-stones, is no doubt anxious to serve his native country if he can. He has only one way of doing so, and only one way of serving himself; the same measure will serve both. Let him promote the abolition of the entail upon his heritage; let him sell a third part or a half of his acres to purchasers who have money to buy and knowledge and a will to make the money so invested profitable; and let him apply the money he receives to the emancipation of himself, the fertilizing of his estate, the well-being of his tenants, and the profitable employment of some of the people unemployed now. When this is done, that accumulation of poor houses called a town—his own town, with his gaunt castle, both famishing on the Shannon, with the Shannon going idly by—may become a great town, though not exclusively his Lordship's own, and fulfil its share of that world which the mighty Shannon is destined to perform.

9

LOUGH DERG, COUNTY GALWAY, 16th *February 1847*

The county of Galway is one of the most western shires of Ireland, with the Atlantic Ocean running into its deep bays; its high headlands stretching far into the ocean, and its many islands amphibiously existing beyond the headlands and within the bays, as marks which tell of ocean and of time, their unresting progress, their transforming agencies. The county contains 422,923 inhabitants, and 1,566,354 acres of surface, of which 90,030 are covered with lakes and rivers, 1801 with towns, 23,718 with plantations, 742,805 bear crops of grass or corn by the aid of man's hand, and 708,000 are left wild. Such is the information derived from statistical documents: but to my eye it is doubtful in many places whether large portions of the 742,805 acres called 'arable' in statistics are not wilder than parts of the 708,000 acres called 'uncultivated.'

Galway county contains every variety of soil, scene, and industrial resource. The only thing on its surface without variety is the human being. All its people are alike, from peer to peasant, helpless and crying for help.

Cultivation has been discouraged by the landowners, save where the land is so numerously peopled that the population could not be driven away. It is seldom that the thickly populated soil is the most fertile; the most fertile soils have been discultured for cattle-breeding and hunting. The Galway gentlemen and noblemen are noted for their hunting and duelling, from which we may infer that they possess *physical* courage. It would be well if they had *moral* courage enough to make them look their present calamities in the face like men. On grass farms about one man and a boy are employed to 200 acres, their wages being eightpence per day for the men, or fourpence per day with diet: the diet was potatoes and salt, when the potatoes existed. Any attempt to make such landowners support the poor of their parishes or baronies will be resisted to the uttermost.

I am writing in a town which, for the present, I do not name for various reasons, chief of which is that I would hardly get at the truth from one party or another if it were known here that I am seeking information for public purposes. Near this place government has expended a large sum of money in the improvement of the Shannon and in building a bridge within the last six years. It is a real improvement. But, unfortunately, all such works done by government seem to make the people think that government should do everything. I speak here of the upper people, not alone of the poor. There has been frosty and snowy weather for ten days. Turf fuel is cut on the bogs, dried and piled up. It is brought into this large village by the people of the bogs, in donkey carts, and sold, a small cart load for a sixpence. The money is expended on meal, which is taken out to the bogs, the men and asses famishing, and the men telling the stranger how they starve; but as soon as they get out and have filled their bellies, they will not stir to bring another load of turf into the town until their stomachs can bear the hunger no longer; then, not sooner, they bring in a load of turf to get more meal. I asked some persons of consequence here why they or some one did not purchase a large store of turf in good weather, and retail it to the poor in bad weather, when, as is the case now, it cannot be procured from the bogs, and people must go without fires, entirely, or almost. They heard me with a kind of surprise approaching to horror, to think that I should recommend the fuel of the 'poor creatures to be purchased up and sold at a profit!'

The higher classes of people have such a contempt for trade, that they would eat the family estates to the bare rocks rather than earn a living, unless it be in the army or as a priest, parson, or doctor. The poor people imitate them, and will not trade unless compelled. When compelled to try mercantile life in a small way, they have no capital to begin with, and consequently have no profits, or very small ones. If they get a good return on some adventure, they enjoy themselves, and do not think of enlarging their trade.

The expenditure of £30,000 of government money in this vicinity during three or four years created much stir, and put profit in the way of all of them. They obtained a bridge, a harbour, wharves, and navigable water. But the gentry think it degrading to them to make an attempt to trade on the river. The poor people cannot. Common report has always said that the peasantry of Connaught are without capacity to conduct business. I do not believe it. They have nobody to lead them in the right way to get means; such means as they do procure are taken from them and eaten up by the idle gentry. The contractor for the Shannon improvements found the peasantry of Galway not only become good workmen, but good overseers, when taught and trusted. It is not so much the nature of the gentry to be greedy and unjust as it is their necessity. If government be expending money, all the cormorant-sloths of younger sons and younger brothers of the entailed landlords stretch out their hands to get it, and do get it; the peasantry doing the work. If a peasant saves some money in those cases, the squire and the young cormorants eat that peasant up. The Shannon Steam Navigation Company are beginning to create trade, and it will increase.

Capitalists have the ill fortune to be misconceived and misrepresented in more countries than Ireland; but here there is a peculiar inclination to misunderstand the man who possesses money and accumulates a stock in trade with it. I passed a mill the other day, and it was standing. I asked why. The answer was, that the miller was too poor to go to market to buy corn to grind, 'and sure none of them as have corn will trust the poor man.' This was only one of many country mills which I have found at a stand for want of corn, though meal is in such demand that it cannot be ground fast enough. At those places I saw what kind of business was done while the miller was innocent of the crime of having capital to carry on his business. In other places where there is capital, and journeymen millers are *not* obliged to go to beg at a soup kitchen, but where wages are paid, many men employed, and the country supplied with meal, the ignorant-genteel are denouncing the owners of such mills as forestallers, regraters, and so forth, because they have stores of corn laid up to keep their mills going and the country eating.

I cannot let this letter go to England without an account of the Shannon river and its great lakes, on the shores of one of which I now write. The trade of the Shannon is small, the capacity of the river for trade is boundless.

At the city of Limerick, seventy-seven miles from the Atlantic Ocean, ships of 300 and 400 tons load and unload. At five miles below Limerick, seventy-two miles from the ocean, ships of 800 tons load and unload. The running water is, above Limerick, about 600 feet wide, and at the shallowest and most impetuous currents of that width between three and four feet deep; when not running impetuously, the usual depth is from 30 to 40 feet. Close to Limerick, it falls 9 ft. 6 in. Between that place and

Castle Connell, five miles above Limerick, it falls 66 ft. 11 in.; and between Castle Connell and Killaloe it falls 20 ft. 8 in. Altogether, in fifteen miles above Limerick and adjoining the navigation from the Atlantic Ocean, this great river falls 97 ft. 1 in. The water-power, for mechanical purposes, which could be used in that space of fifteen miles, can only be expressed and comprehended by the term illimitable. The space for manufactories, public-edifices, water-courses, streets, and thoroughfares, is far beyond what could be occupied by any conceivable extension of trade; while on gentle eminences and hills, rising above the river and the plain, there are sites for an extent of city, which might arise out of manufactures and commerce, though that city exceeded twice in size the greatest metropolis of the world—London.

The navigation from Limerick to Killaloe, owing to the rapids and falls of the river, is partly by canal and locks. Including stoppages in the locks, the swift passage-boats, drawn by three horses each, the horses being changed every four miles, do the distance in about two hours.

At Killaloe, which is ninety-two miles from the sea, the steam navigation of the upper Shannon begins and proceeds upwards. Iron steam vessels were brought in sections from Liverpool and put together and launched here for the navigation of the upper Shannon. That which I took a passage with, the *Lady Lansdowne*, was 90 horse power. Her fuel was turf, and her engines required for six hours' work 65 boxes of turf, each box containing 20 cubic feet, each 20 feet of the value of sixpence. The fuel for 90 horse power for six hours thus costs £1:12:6. It would be an inconvenient kind of fuel for long voyages or for vessels of heavy loading. The steamers on the upper Shannon convey loads commonly by acting as tugs to heavy barges. The conveyance of passengers between the canal at Killaloe and the canal at Shannon harbour, a distance of thirty-seven miles, is also a chief branch of their trade. The vessels are commodious, well fitted up, and the best cabin fares are only 5s. 10d. for the whole distance of fifty-two miles from Limerick.

Between Killaloe and Portumna, a distance of twenty-three miles, the Shannon is a lake, known as Lough Derg. Deep and broad, with islands, headlands, creeks, and tributary rivers, the lake extending back into the rivers, farther than can be seen from the ship's deck, Lough Derg is delightful to look upon and to be upon. Its beauty and serenity, with the shores of Munster on one side and of Connaught on the other, make one feel as if heaven had descended in the olden time to separate men who loved strife and made their country poor by their strife, and held out to them the beneficence of nature to make themselves rich, and still stood, still holding out the gift which they, in the strife of creeds and factiousness of politics, still neglected. The existence of steam packets on the lake may seem to disprove the inference here drawn, that the dwellers on the shore neglect the resources of the Shannon river. Those steamers do not derive much of their trade from the shores of Lough Derg. Tourists in search of health and pleasure from distant places; passengers travelling between Dublin and Limerick by the Grand Canal, which joins the Shannon, seventy-nine miles from Dublin; military stores and troops; corn and provisions between market towns; and, at present, food to relieve the famine; these constitute the chief business of the steamers on the Shannon. But they will, in time, create trade for themselves. It is not yet two years since the large boats were launched on the upper Shannon. As yet they cannot ascend higher than Shannon harbour, thirty-seven miles from Killaloe, fifty-two miles from Limerick, one hundred and twenty-nine miles from the sea. When the improvements of the river now in progress, and soon to be completed, permit, they will go up to Athlone, which is twenty miles farther. Ultimately steam vessels will go to Lough Allen, two hundred and thirty-four miles from the sea, one hundred and fifty-seven miles above Limerick, and one hundred and forty-two miles of direct steaming from Killaloe. At present a smaller class of steamers go twice a-week over the twenty miles between Shannon harbour and Athlone.

Proceeding up the river from Athlone to Lanesborough, the distance is twenty-one miles, most of it a lake called Lough Ree, wider, more diversified, and said to be finer in scenery than Lough Derg. At Lanesborough the water is 15 feet 10 inches above Killaloe. From Lanesborough to the junction of the Arigna river, fifty-two miles, the difference of water level is 34 feet. From the Arigna river to the head of Lough Allen the distance is ten miles more. The Shannon, above Lough Allen, has no distinct character. Several small rivers flow into that lake from Leitrim county, and one from the mountains of Cavan, smaller than the rest: this last is called the Shannon. It wells up in a deep basin 50 feet wide.

From the head of Lough Allen to the sea, the course of the Shannon is 234½ miles; the fall of the water is 146 feet 11 inches, 97 feet of those falls being within fifteen miles of Limerick; 76 feet 5 inches within five miles of Limerick and of the ocean ships, as if nature had been specially regardful to make this the most generally useful of rivers. It waters the boundaries or parts of them, or collects the water tribute of twelve counties—Cavan, Leitrim, Sligo, Roscommon, Longford, Westmeath, King's, Tipperary, Galway, Clare, Limerick, and Kerry. If all the sinuosities and creeks be reckoned on both sides, and such of its islands as are situated in powerful currents, or which possess natural harbours, the entire water frontage of the Shannon, available for business, exceeds

2500 miles. If the tributaries, many of them navigable, be reckoned in the same way, those of them traceable on common maps give an additional water frontage of 6100 miles. If every streamlet of any size, such as are anxiously sought for and made use of by the manufacturers of Lancashire, be reckoned, there will be probably not less than 6100 miles more; in all 14,700 miles of inland water-side extent, communicating with the Shannon, and through it with the Atlantic Ocean, at the most western and most favourable point of the United Kingdom.

The Arigna, falling into the Shannon at Lough Allen, runs through a region of iron ore, *said to be* of boundless extent. Coals are *said to be* found there also. Turf fuel is found abundantly everywhere. I cannot hazard an opinion as to its applicability to steam machinery on a large scale. If water power were used it might serve for heating purposes well enough. I can only speak of the vastness of its quantity. It is hardly possible to conceive a time when the turf of Ireland would be all burned, or any amount of consumption which would burn it. Calculations of its extent and duration, and its reproduction (for turf bogs grow,) have been made by Professor Kane and others.

Since the remark was written in the foregoing on the beauty of Lough Derg, twenty-five miles long and from four to twelve miles broad, lying in heavenly peacefulness, as if it had come upon earth in the olden time to keep King O'Brien of Munster and King O'Connor of Connaught from fighting, and still lay there to separate Munster and Connaught when inclined for war, and to unite them when inclined to hold commerce; since those remarks were written, Lough Derg has been up, as if all the unrested spirits of all the O'Briens and O'Connors of Munster and Connaught had come upon him; the large steamers have been tossed as if they had been in the Irish Channel or on the Atlantic, and tossed, perhaps, more dangerously that they had less sea-room. Yesterday the gale from the west was so severe, and the waves of Lough Derg so mad, that the steamers did not face the fresh water billows, though manned and piloted by salt water sailors.

It may be a question if this lake has more heavenliness in its serene face when lying at peace with its feathery birds and green islands on its breast, or when, to vindicate the benevolence of nature, it rises to receive the whirlwind, charging it to take and disappear with the impurities of stagnation, that man and plant may each have a healthier life.

10

BANAGHER, 19*th February 1847*

In this letter I shall introduce some statistics of the potato culture and failure, as derived from official sources not hitherto available to general readers.

Estimating the loss of the potatoes by money, it is officially set down at 2$\frac{1}{2}$d. per stone of 14lb. The gross value of the crop at that price is £13,618,392: 4s. Admitting the failure to extend to five-sixths of the whole produce, the money loss at 2$\frac{1}{2}$d. per stone is £13,289,932:18:4. But this is not a fair estimate of the loss. It is only a fictitious money value. The price of potatoes is now 1s. 2d. and 1s. 4d. per stone; this is six times the assumed price. But even this is not the price to make the calculation on. I think a truer *guess* at the amount of potato loss will be that which estimates the value of the food required to supply the place of the potatoes. Let us try.

1. 884,989 children above one year old and under five require $\frac{1}{2}$lb. of meal per day each for ten months; this is 60,052 tons.

2. 2,057,156 persons aged from five to fifteen, 1lb. of meal per day each for ten months, 279,185 tons.

3. 4,517,760 persons aged from fifteen to sixty, 1 5-7lb. of meal per day each for ten months, 1,051,070 tons.

4. 353,795 persons aged above sixty, 1lb. of meal each per day for ten months, 48,015 tons. No allowance is made for 361,424 babies under one year. Total of persons above one year 7,813,700. Total population 8,175,124. Total tonnage of meal for ten months 1,438,324. At 1d. per lb. in the official calculations, the expense of this is shewn to be £13,424,357. But the real price of meal is from 2$\frac{1}{4}$d. to 2$\frac{1}{2}$d. per lb. retailed in country districts. Allowing for the quantities bought at wholesale prices and issued without profit by relief committees, work-houses, and similar dealers in meal, the price has been for a considerable time, is now, and seems likely to continue to be, not less than 2d. per lb. This gives £26,848,714 as the money value of the potato loss.

My only doubt as to the correctness of this estimate is whether the people consume those quantities of meal here reckoned upon, taking them in the aggregate. That they do not all consume so much when we take them in detail is too true; they cannot get it. A family of five persons subsisting on the meal purchased by the wages of 10d. per day paid to one of them can only obtain about 26lb. for seven days. There is a large number of people who are not receiving relief, who do not seek it, and yet go short of a sufficiency of food. Many are not getting relief who seek it, and are starving, some dying. I shall relate in a subsequent part of this letter a case of death which occurred here.

The reason for calculating the duration of the potatoes as food for ten months in a year, is to strike off the sixth part of the year as a balance to the sixth of the food of Ireland which is supposed not to be potatoes. Everybody has used them less or more; and five-sixths of the food of Ireland is supposed to have been potatoes. The allowance for each person, in making the calculation and comparison with the Indian meal, is 2lb. of potatoes per day for children under five years of age, 6lb. per day for young persons between five and fifteen; 10lb. per day for adults between the ages of fifteen and sixty and 2lb. per day for aged persons above sixty.

In the province of Ulster, consisting of the counties of Antrim, Armagh, Cavan, Donegal, Down, Fermanagh, Londonderry, Monaghan, and Tyrone, and containing the following acreage of soil:—3,407,539 acres arable; 1,764,370 acres uncultivated; 79,783 acres of plantation; 8790 of towns; and 214,956 acres of water; there were planted in 1846, with potatoes, 352,665 acres. The population of Ulster is 2,386,373; of whom 1,763,325 are reckoned dependent on potatoes. This gives six persons to each acre of potatoes planted.

In the province of Munster, consisting of the counties of Clare, Cork, Kerry, Limerick, Tipperary, and Waterford, containing 3,874,613 acres arable; 1,893,477 acres uncultivated; 130,415 acres of plantation; 14,693 acres of towns; and 151,381 acres of water, there were planted 460,630 acres with potatoes in 1846. The population of Munster is 2,303,150, of whom only 93,011 are equivalent to the proportion of food which was not potatoes. This gives 2,210,139 as dependent on potatoes, and an acre planted for each five persons.

In Connaught, consisting of the counties of Galway, Leitrim, Mayo, Roscommon and Sligo, containing 2,220,960 acres arable; 1,906,002 acres uncultivated; 48,340 acres of plantations; 3877 acres of towns; and 212,864 acres of water. There were in 1846 planted with potatoes 206,292 acres. The population of Connaught is 1,418,859, of whom 1,031,460 is the number entirely dependent on potatoes, or answering for that equivalent. This is six persons to each acre of potatoes.

In the province of Leinster, consisting of the counties of Carlow, Dublin, Kildare, Kilkenny, King's, Longford, Louth, Meath, Queen's, Westmeath, Wexford, and Wicklow, containing 3,961,188 acres arable; 731,886 uncultivated; 115,944 of plantations; 15,569 acres of towns; 51,624 acres of water. There were planted 217,854 acres of potatoes in

1846. The population is 1,973,731, amongst whom the consumption of potatoes is equivalent to 1,089,270 depending on them entirely. This gives nine persons to each acre of potatoes planted.

I have related those details rather to shew the general characteristics of the surface of Ireland than for any value in them as relates to the potato question. The word *arable* is a misnomer. That word, as usually under-stood in England and Scotland, means land which is under tillage, or only laid down in grass in the tillage rotation. In the statistics of Ireland, it is applied, seemingly, to all land which is not lying waste. Thus the grazing regions of Roscommon, Galway, Meath, &c. though lying con-tinually in grass, and not employing over one man to two hundred acres, are called *arable*.

A much greater breadth of land must come into cultivation now to supply the same amount of human subsistence as the total of 1,237,441 acres of potatoes did. The cultivation is so generally defective, and soils so variable, that no attempt can be safely made to say how much land will require to be sown with oats to produce food in the place of potatoes. Some have said three acres of oats instead of one of potatoes. If the manure be applied to the oat crop or to some grain crop which would 'have been applied to the potatoes this will turn out an error of calculation. Three acres of grain should be more than equal to one acre of potatoes, unless the grain culture be very bad. Yet six acres of oats may be of less value than one acre of good potatoes.

The Irish agriculturists must grow root crops to feed cattle and produce manure. To effect this no plan will equal that of compelling them, by loans of money secured on the land, to employ a given number of men per hundred acres.

At the place where I write, a father, mother, and two children came, a short while ago, into the street at night, and lay down on the pavement; they came from a neighbouring town, they said, because they could get no food there. About eight o'clock the woman went to the door of a house adjoining, and begged a piece of turf to make a fire in the street, for her husband was dying. It happened to be the house, the temporary lodgings, of a naval officer of her Majesty's service, and it need hardly be said that the request was at once complied with, and more than turf given. About ten o'clock the poor woman called to the door again, begging for a piece of more turf, for that her husband was dead, and they were lying beside the cold body. The officer went out, and found this to be the case. He proceeded to the constabulary station, but the constables would do nothing with the dead body, nor the survivors who lay beside it, till the morning. He proceeded elsewhere, and procured some straw for them and made a bed, and got stakes and put shelter over their heads with the straw for the night, and made and administered a warm meal for them. In the morning he was astir in time to relieve them, and going out met some of the constables, the principal one of whom talked loud and angrily to the woman for having her husband dead on that side of the street; 'Just,' said the honest English sailor to me in relating the case, 'as if there should be etiquette observed in dying of hunger.' He added, 'The most heartless and unfeeling people towards one another, whom I ever saw or heard of, are—.' I leave it blank, as I am willing to believe that the overwhelming amount of the distress rather than the people's natural feelings, makes them callous and hard-hearted.

II

ROSCOMMON, *24th February 1847*

Yesterday, William Smith, Esq., sub-sheriff, with Captain Granville and detachments of the 55th Infantry and 8th Hussars, and a strong party of police, (the armed constabulary,) under head constable O'Malley, proceeded to Ballinacarriga to take possession of land from James Hanley and six others for non-payment of rent. This property belonged to the Rev. Charles Dawson, who was murdered on those lands in the year 1835. There were great crowds assembled, but no breach of the peace was attempted.'—*Limerick Chronicle, 17th February.*

No breach of the peace attempted! Is the stewardship of seven small farms by a squadron of dragoons, a company of infantry, each man of the company with sixty rounds of ball cartridge in his pouch, and a large detachment of the most completely armed corps in Ireland, the Irish police, no breach of the peace? Perhaps not. Perhaps it is no breach of the peace nor of public decency to eject tenants from Irish land now, and only now, because the munificent charities and liberally-allowed taxes of England are contributed to save such ejected tenantry from starvation. At other times Irish landlords have felt a fear of their land-owning neighbours, and have dreaded to execute ejectments to augment the burthen of the poor-rates; at other times they have had the dread before them of turning the tenantry out to starve. They have no such fear now. Benevolent men from England, with a pilgrim's staff in one hand and cash to relieve the distressed in the other; relief commit-tees to disburse English subscriptions; and, lastly, Sir John Burgoyne, with the English treasury purse in his hand, and all the commissariat stores under his control, to make soup and ladle it out in every village; these come all between the Irish landlords and the death of their evicted tenantry. The present is a favourable time for evictions; the English taxes keep the evicted from falling on the Irish poor-rates and from dying, as such tenants did in other years, in Irish stone quarries and Irish ditches.

In this case we have the great drama of Ireland compressed into one short act—an act so short, that it may be called a piece of bye play, done while the great players occupy public attention with their Irish business in front of the stage in London. We have a 'reverend' and turbulent parson quarrelling, strong in law, strong in political churchism, with his vexed tenantry of another creed. We have him murdered. We have as much public money expended in avenging, or in seeking to avenge his murder, as would have purchased the freehold of all his land; at all events, as much as would have built those tenants decent houses to live in, and as would have put their farms in such workable, though humble order, as would justify the exaction of rent. We have another landlord still quarrelling with them, doing everything to exasperate, nothing to conciliate—everything to oppose, nothing to assist; and calling to his help the military power of cavalry, infantry, and constabulary, and the civil powers of the sheriff's office. We have England paying out of English taxes all those armed men, and providing them with bullets, bayonets, swords, guns, and gunpowder, to unhouse and turn to the frosts of February those tenants and their families. We have English private charity and the English public treasury providing food for those unhoused families. And while this is being done, we have the 'patriotic' knaves of Limerick, Clare, and Galway—this landlord of Ballinacarriga and the rest—calling for more money from England, and calling the English ill names because they do not give sixteen millions at once.

Roscommon is an inland county of the province of Connaught in the west, exceedingly fertile, but little of it cultivated. The population is numerous. Mr James Clapperton, steward of the Ballinasloe Agricultural Society, a farmer's son, from Tweedside, in Scotland, thus spoke of Roscommon, when examined before Lord Devon's commission. 'The produce is capable of being improved very much.'

'Do you think the produce could be increased one-half by improved cultivation?'

'Yes; the want of manure is certainly general.'

'What is the comparison between the land here and the land you are acquainted with in Scotland; is it better or worse than the land in Berwickshire?'

'There is a wider range of soils here than in Berwickshire, and it is not so even.'

'Is it better or worse upon the whole?

'In its natural state it is as good as we have in Berwickshire.'

'What is the rent here compared to the rent in Berwickshire?'

'It is not one-third of what some are there.'

'What would the lands you have described, as let for 21s. be let for?'

'They would be considered cheap at £4 per acre. The land that lets at £1 here would give £3 an acre in the county of Antrim and the North of Ireland.'

That is in the locality of commerce and of the linen manufactures. Mr Clapperton has already enabled some of the tenants of Lord Clancarty to double, triple, and quadruple their produce, by introducing among them a superior style of cultivation. Unfortunately, however, Lord Clancarty looks to improved agriculture as a means of church proselytism. He mingles the produce of the farm-yard and the Thirty-nine Articles together, the stall feeding of cattle and attendance at the Protestant church, the instructions on thorough drainage and the instructions in the church catechism. A new dwelling-house, or barn, or stable, or road is equivalent on his estate to a new religion. The use of a bull of improved breed is associated with a renunciation of the bulls of Rome. No man on earth save an Irish landlord could be found to mingle such things together. Lord Clancarty does so; and yet with these drawbacks he is, agriculturally speaking, the best landlord in Roscommon.

Mr Clapperton, speaking of the district of Ballinasloe, says, 'The upland is of medium quality; light loams and gravelly soils approximating loam are the most prevalent. Very few siliceous or sandy soils. Soils under the strict character or denomination of clay are seldom to be seen in this part of the country. Rich, deep, heavy loams, high in the scale of fertility, are to be seen in almost every locality.'

I find those deep rich loams prevail more in those districts of the county remote from Ballinasloe. The entire acreage of Roscommon is 607,691, of which no less than 440,522 are returned as arable, and only 130,299 are uncultivated, the remainder being under water, under plantations, and under towns. Nearly all the uncultivated is capable of culture at a profit, the country being gently undulating, with few hills. The larger part of that which is called arable is lying in grass.

Where I now write, the people are literally crawling to their graves, their eyes starting in their heads with stomach torture. But it was only this time two years that these people, in their struggles to produce food for themselves, took spades and dug up grass pastures, pleading to be allowed to pay £7 and £8 per acre for the potato crop, besides furnishing the labour and the seed potatoes; and they were fired upon, some of them wounded, and some shot dead by the military and constabulary, because they insisted on having conacre for potatoes or oats. The land, when obtained in small portions for one season only, is called conacre. Four-fifths of all the inhabitants of this county get their bare subsistence from the land by hiring it in conacre from other tenants. They cannot pay the enormous rentals of £7, £8, £9, and £10 per acre. But they engage to pay them in labour. They work for 6d. and 8d. a-day, and their wages are allowed in rent; what they cannot pay thus they pay by the seizure of the crop and its sale under distraint.

In some districts the landlords have refused to grant conacre. The refusal is equivalent to the sentence of death on the population. The farmers can get more people to work for them than they employ, on condition of being paid in conacre; hence those not holding conacre cannot live. Hence they have taken spades and insisted on being allowed to dig and pay £8 an acre to save their lives. But those very landlords and middleman tenantry who are now calling on the English government and the English taxpayers to save these people's lives, to furnish them with money or rent, called out the military and shot them two years since with the spades in their hands. Those very landlords who now raise so piteous a howl for English help, doomed the peasantry of Roscommon to death by starvation by refusing them labour and wages, or conacre instead of wages. And this they did with the finest soil of the British dominions going out of cultivation. It caused them less trouble to lay it down in grass to breed cattle to send to England than to attend to its culture. Yet Mr Clapperton avers that the land let at £1: 1s. per acre in Roscommon to the head tenants would be cheap in Berwickshire at £4 per acre. I know Berwickshire well, and I can support Mr Clapperton in that opinion.

But we shall now look at the causes of Roscommon poverty as discoverable in the evidence of the persons examined by Lord Devon's commission in 1844. In the first place we shall see that the Irish landlord is only a rent-eater, and his agent a rent-extractor, neither of them adding to the resources of the farm—not even by making roads or erecting buildings.

John Donellan, parish of Carn, county of Roscommon, deposed that he held fifty acres; that the head landlord was never seen on the estate; that there was an agent who was never seen on the estate but to collect rents; that his name is Thomas Berry, a lawyer living in Dublin; that he, Donellan, had spent upwards of £100 in building a house; was now served with notice to quit, and could not get a halfpenny for what he expended, though a former agent, the present agent's father, had promised to allow half the expenses.

Mr Berry has notice sent to him by the commissioners of this statement, and gives the following curious explanation: 'Those farms were taken by the father of this complainant (three in number, 170 acres) at the beginning of 1823, not for any term. The rent of two of them was 22s. and 24s. 8d. per acre. It was not considered that the landlord should be under the obligation to assist a tenant holding so much land, and who merely built a house sufficient for his own accommodation. The house in question is a very ill-built one; the walls are bulged out; there is no foundation in the ground; the roof was never more than thatched, and the interior, whenever I visited it, was dirty and dark, the upper story of the house being a filthy roof for storing the feathers of the fowl.'

This may be a reason for doubting that the house cost £100; it is not a reason for absolving a landlord from the duty of erecting substantial and permanent buildings on his farms. 'Donellan,' says this excellent land-agent, 'merely built a house for his own accommodation.' That is, finding it inconvenient to live with the bare farm below his feet and the bare sky above his head, he made himself a place to live in, and as it was merely for his own accommodation, though it probably was to enable him to occupy the farm and to pay rent for it, the landlord it seems had no interest in the house!

Donellan continued—'The farm was taken under the promise of a lease. The time will expire next May. It was often called for and the lease-money paid; but we cannot get a lease. I always heard my mother say the money was paid to the father of the present agent, and all the tenants did the same.'

Mr Berry says—'I mentioned about this period (1838) the claim to my father, who had been the person who let the ground before I succeeded, and asked him whether any negotiations or agreement had been made between him and any of the tenants for leases. He told me that there had been a treaty in the year 1824, and that some of the tenants were to get leases for seven years, but, in fact, no leases were ever executed or made; *and I also believe that some money was paid*—some small amount of money, not for the entire price of the leases, but merely as an instalment for getting them.'

Donellan continues—'Three years ago I held forty-three acres more, at the time of the poor-law valuation, and I found out by the valuator I had not within three acres and a half of what the landlord was charging me. These forty-three acres were a different take, though a part of the same property. Sixty-five sheep died one season rotten, and I was not able to hold the land, and he would not let me back upon the land.'

Mr Berry says of this—'There was little hope that the accruing year's rent of one of the farms would be paid, and which afterwards turned out to be the case. It was then intimated to me that Donellan would set up this *alleged promise* of a lease as a defence,' (against ejectment). 'He (his father) told me *that there had been a treaty for leases; and I also believe some money was paid,*' (for the leases). 'The complainant states further that three years ago he found out by the poor-law valuation that he had not within three and a half acres of what was charged. I inquired into the matter, and found such to be the case. It would have only been fair in the complainant, when he stated that he had been charged for three and a half acres more than he held, to have mentioned, and not have suppressed, the fact that they were allowed for all the money that they had so paid by mistake.'

Yes; but it would have also been fair for Mr Berry to have acknowledged, and not have suppressed, the fact that this allowance was only deducted from the arrears which were not paid, nor expected to be paid. In point of fact, Donellan had paid for three acres and a half which he did not occupy whenever he paid any rent. He was all the poorer in consequence. When he was too poor to pay rent and was ejected for its non-payment, it was no advantage to him to have a certain number of figures changed from the debtor to the creditor side of the agent's books. This part of Donellan's case illustrates the nature of Irish land agencies. The following carries the illustration farther:—

Commissioners—'Have you had receipts when you have paid the rent?' Donellan—'We used to have receipts; but we have got none for the last three years, or anybody else.' (Meaning anybody else on that estate.)

To which Mr Berry replies in his evidence—'I have not given receipts these three years back, because I have given a great deal of work to do to the tenants. At the time of paying the rent there are so many small accounts to settle, that, not to keep those who were in attendance too late at night, I have endeavoured to dispatch the persons paying rent as quickly as possible, and I have not given receipts on that account.'

Commissioners, to Donellan—'Does Mr Berry hold many agencies in the country?' 'I do not know that; he holds about 600 acres,' (on that estate). 'He only comes once a-year for the last four or five years; he got some of the ground into his own possession, he got some houses built, and he used to come then often.'—Land in his own possession, houses built on it; work done by the tenants; many small accounts to settle; tenants having to go home and not wishing to detain them late, no receipts given!

Mr Edward Byrne, a farmer—'I think the condition of the large farmers is rather improving; the small tenantry are getting worse. There is no labour to be had in the country except what they are given by their masters. Wages run about 8d. a-day during the summer months. In winter the rate of wages is less. The conacre prevails a good deal. The rent varies from £5 to £6, £7, £8, and even to £10; only in a few instances £10 where a man has improved by highly manuring some small spot. The rent of conacre is recovered by civil process, and by sale of crop when unpaid within the period agreed upon.'

Mr Walter Burke has 1000 acres, all in grass save 100 acres. He is a landowner and a farmer. His 100 acres are let out in conacre. He considers the legislature should interfere 'to remove them from the crowded manner they are living on the lands, for two reasons—first, they are in a very abject state themselves, and there is a great injustice done to the landlord. I should recommend that there be some summary mode of expelling those persons from the land without going to the extreme expense incurred by the present law. There is a class of landlords whose only means of subsistence for themselves and their families is the income arising from the possession of bills obtained from the tenants, which is attended with a good deal of expense.'

That is, to the 'poor landlords,' as Mr Burke would feelingly call them. But the expense is infinitely greater and is ruinous to the poor tenantry. The landlords compel them to join together in giving these bills in payment of rent, the tenants becoming thus jointly and severally liable for one another. The landlord gets the bills cashed at the bank, and the tenants are then the creditors of the banks; they pay for the landlords' accommodation eight, ten, twelve, and as high as sixteen per cent. Some of those landlords are in parliament, and, as a matter of course, are loud in their demands for money from England to relieve the poor Irish. I shall quote from the evidence of their tenantry when, in my progress through the country, I reach their estates.

Mr Burke continues—'I should recommend a summary mode of expelling tenants, after letting them run into a certain arrear; it should not be before a year's rent is due.'

Commissioners—'What would you do with those people when expelled?'—'I do not know. The government is well acquainted with the mode of treating them.'

If Mr Burke does not know what to do with 'those people' of Roscommon, the real strength of any country, the human arms, and hands, and feet, and heads, and hearts, I know what I would do with Mr Burke and his 1000 acres of land, 900 of which is pasture, the people upon which and around which are at this moment crying for food and dying for the want of it, while Mr Burke is crying to England for money, and calling England ill names because money does not come to him in millions of greater number. I would compel him to maintain his proportion of the Roscommon people, or consent to sell the 1000 acres, or such portion of them as are his own; and I would make a law to render the sale of Mr Burke's acres as easy as the sale of a bushel of corn. That is what I would do with Mr Burke, and with all the land and all the Burkes of Ireland. It would be for their own good to have this done to them, if they would only think so. But, think so or not, they must consent to it before long. Roscommon must be ploughed.

12

STROKESTOWN, *26th February 1847*

My last letter, though written from Roscommon, began with a notice of the eviction of tenantry in the county of Limerick in the previous week, and complained that landlords should choose the present time to clear their land of people, only to take advantage of the public provision for those people. This letter must also begin with a reference to Limerick county, though it chiefly refers to Roscommon.

Mr William Monsell of Tervoe, a place in the vicinity of Limerick city, has written a letter to the *Times*, which has been reprinted in Ireland, and is attracting much notice. He professes to advocate an effective poor-law for his country; but deprecates the proposed enactment of Lord John Russell, because its scope of taxation is too wide. Mr Monsell says that the landlord who does his duty to the people should be exempted from paying the same amount of poor-rates as those landlords who do not do their duty. Wherefore he pleads that the taxation for the relief of the poor should not be regulated by electoral districts, as the government proposes, but by some smaller and fairer division. Lord Stanley has made the same objection to the bill, and Lord Lansdowne has promised to give attention to Lord Stanley's objection. Nothing at first sight seems to be more equitable than the proposition of having limited districts for poor-law taxation, so that owners of property may be taxed for the poor according to their merits in giving employment to the poor. Mr Monsell's letter is overflowing with sentiments of humanity for the poor, and so it has got a place in the *Times*.

But, practically, his plan would be extremely unfair to ratepayers and to the poor. Practically he is not himself entitled to much consideration on the subject. Whatever the tenants may do to employ the people out of their income, he at least draws his rents and employs none—none at present. I have this fact on the authority of a poor-law commissioner, who is prepared to prove it if it is denied. His plan of taxing estates separately, in 'units,' or in very limited district, to adapt the rates to the pauperism of the estates, would allow him and his land, and the large estates of some of his relatives in the county of Limerick, to escape taxation for the paupers, many of them probably living in Limerick city, who were cleared as cumberers of the ground from his estates.

If the bill has not yet passed, and the alterations are not yet made, let this new move of the Irish landowners be narrowly watched. It has one purpose, and one only, to relieve the owners of estates which have been cleared by the eviction of tenantry from paying rates to support the evicted, now that they are paupers crowded into villages and towns.

Returning to the subject of conacre, I may remark that it has been virtually the currency or substitute for money of the millions of the Irish peasantry. The metal currency and paper currency of commercial countries has been little known in the agricultural provinces of Munster and Connaught. There the people have had an earthen currency—conacre was the standard of value. The employer and employed with their pieces of earth transferred the earth to one another thus:— There being no money to represent the value of the acre of earth, the employer in the month of March called it his labourer's acre, and the labourer accepted it, and at once owned himself to be in debt for it to the amount of £8, though he knew he would receive no value from it for six months. He began at once to pay his debt at the rate of 8d. per day. The £8 per acre and 8d. per day were fictions. There were no such sums of money, nor any money. The labourer had in reality acknowledged himself to owe two hundred and forty days' work in March. He began to work, but he was working down a debt; he felt the debt daily. But it did not become less by the hardness of his work. It only became less by the number of days he 'put in,' the easier he could 'put in' a day the less did his conacre seem to cost. He knew that £8 was an exorbitant rent. It was eight times the rent of the farmer, and twelve times the amount of the valuation of the farm land for taxes and poor rates. Conacre being his pay, and to him the standard of value, he tried to assimilate his labour to the value of conacre. In so doing he acted according to the law of man's nature, to give no more for value received than he could help. In that commerce where money is the standard of value and medium of exchange, the exchangers of commodities put a value on every fraction of the commodity—fraction of money, fraction of work performed, and fraction of time. They become industrious, economical and enriched, by giving as little as they can give for value received. But the Irish peasant, actuated by the same law of nature, becomes indolent, wasteful, and is not enriched by giving as little as he possibly can give for value received. He gives 240 days' work for the conacre. To work well would be no enrichment of himself, to do as little as he can do, only the fourth part of a day's work in a day, leads him to believe that he is getting his conacre at the rate of £2 per acre instead of £8.

And yet there are sensible people who gravely moralize on the indolence of the Irish peasant, and discover that he does not work well because he is a Celt. A Saxon is as ready as any man alive to do as the Celt does if so dealt with. The Celts work otherwise when they are otherwise paid.

This conacre system, which gives the peasant and his family their twelve months meagre food in a piece, renders shopkeeping impossible, for they have no money to go to provision shops with. Hence, in such an emergency as the present, when a new kind of food has to be provided and sold in secluded districts, and there are no shopkeepers or trading classes to buy and sell it, the fault is not that of the peasantry, but the system under which they have been reduced to live which dispensed with shops.

'But it is only the Celtic people, as we see them in Ireland, Wales, and the Highlands of Scotland, that consent to live thus,' it will be urged. In return I point to the eastern division of Somersetshire, in England, where there is a Saxon population, with all the Saxon features of face, and body, and mind, and where, in the grazing districts of that eastern division, the conacre system of Ireland prevails with precisely the same results as in Roscommon. At Castle Carey, in Somerset, the farmers are bound not to plough more than a limited portion of their farms, the remainder to be kept in old grass, as in Roscommon. There is a superabundant population in that part of Somersetshire. The soil is fertile and peculiarly productive of potatoes. The land has been hired for many years at £9 and £10 per acre from the farmers for the six months of the potato season, the hirers finding manure, as in Ireland, selling the potatoes to help to pay the rent, working to the farmers to help to pay the rent, and eating potatoes, before the disease destroyed them, three times a day. The disease destroyed almost every potato in Castle Carey district in 1845, and the poor people who had hired the conacres there were in the same state when I visited them in the winter of that year, and are the same now, as I see the hirers of conacre in Roscommon. The greater liberality of the English poor-law, and the partial existence of employment in manufactures near Castle Carey, made the only difference.

It is the want of manufactures and commerce that reduces the peasantry, whether in Ireland or in England, to the conacre system. An exclusive dependence on agriculture always leaves its dependents to be pursued and overtaken by famine. It induces social disorder; and social disorder leads the owners of land to be always calling for 'more power.' The social disorder of the ill-fed people and the 'more power' of those who ill-feed them scare away commerce and manufactures. In the evidence taken by Lord Devon's commission, I do not find so much as one man who goes beyond a desire for more agricultural employment or for more power. The prevailing desire amongst the upper tenantry and the landlords is to have more power to eject or otherwise dispose of the people. This, together with the complaints of the tenantry that they are not protected from the landlords, is the staple of the great blue books of the commission. Here are a few more specimens of the evidence. The conacre spoken of is that hired by those who are not so fortunate as to be employed to pay the rent by work.

Mr Devenido of Mount Pleasant, between the towns of Strokestown and Roscommon—'Conacre prevails to a great extent. The rent is from five to seven guineas. Payment is enforced by seizing the crop and selling it by auction. There have been many outrages in my district: the cause was the price of conacre. The people thought it too high. It has been reduced £1 in consequence.'

Mr Samuel Brown of Knockcroghery—'The labourers now, (July, 1845,) speaking of the country generally, are not improving. *They are in the same state of destitution they have always been in.*'

Mr Christopher Harrison, farmer, Cloonowrish—'I paid £83 to the out-going tenant. I improved the house and also the land. I laid out about £45 in the course of a fortnight. When my landlord found I had expended that sum, I received notice of ejectment.' (This tenant's case rather illustrates the confusion arising from excessive competition for land in Roscommon than the rapacity of a landlord. Mr Harrison took the farm from another tenant and went into possession without consulting the landlord.')

Mr Godfrey Hogg—'I farm about 900 acres, grazing land and in tillage. It is very hard, if a man has expended his money upon a farm, upon the notion that he was to continue, that he is to walk out and leave his family beggars. We held 100 acres, and went on draining and erecting buildings and improving the farm; we went on upon the faith of getting the land at a fair value, and, instead of that, we were charged an increased rent from fifty to eighty per cent. and, in fact, the tenants on the property who had not improved, got the very same quality of land at 10s. an acre which we were charged £1: 7: 6 an acre for, the increased value having been obtained by our industry, and having drained the farm, the other part of the ground they got for £1: 5s. and we were charged £1: 10s. The neighbourhood in which I reside is very populous.

The people are in the greatest state of misery, (22 July 1844,) and I think it is owing to absenteeism. The population varies from 22,000 to 23,000, and there is not a resident gentleman in the entire neighbourhood if I except the clergymen of different denominations. The state of the people is the most miserable you can conceive. There are a great many proprietors, and none of them ever come near the neighbourhood. They send their agents, and they come at stated periods and go away. They have no resident agents. If they must reside elsewhere there should be a resident agent, or a person who could go and see the state of the tenantry, and the improved state of the tillage that is spreading over the country, (in other parts). *There is not a bit of the green crop system introduced into our country yet.'*

The Right Hon. Lord Crofton—'Tillage farms are very small, under ten acres generally; I might almost say under five. The succession of crops is potatoes and oats, and potatoes and oats; I believe four or five crops of oats and then potatoes. If tenants have confidence in the landlord, they have no objection to hold at will; indeed they generally prefer it. If they have not any confidence in the landlord, they will not lay out money. I have assisted tenants to build houses, but it is not general in the county.'

Mr Kelly preferred to have tenants-at-will, for this reason:— 'The man who has a fixed tenure considers that he cannot be put out. He immediately mismanages his farm; he sublets and subdivides, and so the whole thing is destroyed. A man who has it only at will, knows that, if he conducts himself as he ought to do, his tenancy-at-will is as good as a lease, and he will use his best exertions to have his land in the most profitable and beneficial order.'

There must be an overwhelming amount of disorder in a district of which a gentleman, otherwise so rational and intelligent as Mr Kelly, can say this. He proceeds:—

'There is no property held under the courts in my immediate district; but there is a district a short distance from me held under the courts, (the courts of law). I have occasion to see a good deal of it from the people who occupy it coming before me at the petty sessions, and I can state that it is a very miserable system. That district is not under the courts in consequence of a minority or lunacy; it is in consequence of debt. There are fourteen or fifteen properties altogether; they are under mortgage, and there are receivers.'

'What are the cases which bring the tenantry before you at sessions?'

'The receiver is merely receiver; he has no personal interest in the condition of the tenantry; he merely comes down to get his money, and away he goes. The people have disputes about the mearings, or bogs;

they have nobody to go to settle it for them, and they fight it out with the slane, an instrument they cut turf with, and then they come before the magistrates with their heads broken.'

'Has there been any money laid out in the improvement of that property recently?'

'No; nor do I suppose there has been for centuries.'

Such is a specimen of the best county in Ireland, judged by its richness of soil. It only wants labour, human strength, to make it profitable to everybody. It has people willing and eager to work, so eager to work and cultivate the land which the landlords will not allow to be cultivated, that they were shot dead by the military and police two years ago in the fields with spades in their hands, at the request and by the orders of magisterial landlords. They had no choice but to dig up the fields and plant potatoes or die. They offered most extravagant rents for liberty to dig the ground and plant potatoes, but they were refused. They insisted, and they were stuck with bayonets, and had their blood spilt upon the polluted land of the land-cursers of Roscommon.

That was in the spring of 1845. To be denied conacre was to be denied leave to live, to have it at £8 and £10 per acre, where thousands of such hirers had no labour, and no money by which to pay for it, was but a slow death. To dig for life with a spade, was to ensure military execution. To whatever side the people turned they turned to death. The owners of the land would neither employ them nor allow them to be employed. Land that would profitably employ all its population is discultured and lying in wasteful pasture lands. The people are going about, those who can go about, with hollow cheeks and glazed eyes, as if they had risen out of their coffins to stare upon one another. A woman told me yesterday she was starving, but it was not for herself she begged for food; she prayed to Heaven to let her die and give her rest, 'But, oh !' said she, 'if you would take pity on my poor child, for it is dying, and it does not die.' May Heaven have mercy on such a mother and such a child ! They were literally skin and bone, with very little life in either of them, and no food. And they were but fractions of a population wandering to and from a fertile land which they are not allowed to cultivate.

Nor will the landlords who prevent them from cultivating the land pay poor-rates to provide for them. The poor-law commissioner, already alluded to in this letter, has shewn me an arrear of £800 odds of rates in one union. Among the defaulters are one lord, one member of parliament, three baronets, and some scores of squires and squireens all inhabitants of 'castles'; all crying to England for help; all dooming their land and their people to desolation and death, by their own suicidal greediness, pride, and ignorance.

13

LONGFORD, *2nd March 1847*

The county of Longford is nearly in the centre of Ireland, lying east of the Shannon, and watered by that river on its west side. Its population in 1841 was 108,117 in the rural, and 7374 in the town district; total 115,941. Its surface acres are 364 under towns; 4610 under plantations; 13,675 under water; 58,973 uncultivated; and 191,823 arable. But of the arable, so called in surveys, more than one-half is uncultivated, and, with small exceptions, none of it, though generally rich and fertile, is well cultivated. Mr James Kelly, scientific agriculturist examined before Lord Devon's commission in 1844, said— 'I think the county of Longford would give double the quantity of corn it now does if it was cultivated as it ought to be.' Mr Kelly might have gone much farther than to double the quantity of corn, he might have added to that double the quantity of cattle-food.

The soil rests chiefly on limestone and clay-slate. It has some bogs, some level meadows, and many gentle undulations. It has 10,778 farms of more than one acre each, on which were: in 1841, 5840 horses and mules, 23,278 horned-cattle, 13,465 sheep, 18,711 pigs, 157,719 head of poultry, and 1360 asses, all being of the estimated value of £231,530. The majority of the people live by hiring conacre for the season at £7 and £8. This county contains the large village of Edgeworthstown, the family property of Miss Edgeworth—the 'Maria Edgeworth' of literature and fame. It contains the Dublin College estates, held by the Lefroys, noted middlemen and political partisans. It contains the estates of the Earl of Longford and his residence, and part of the estates of Lord Lorton, and the residence of some connections of his family. It contains the family places of more than one gentleman named White, one of them a member of Parliament. It contains also the vacant ground where once stood the village of Ballinamuck, the place where the French invaders under General Humbert, the last foreign foe that set foot within the united kingdom, surrendered in 1795 to General Lake. But Ballinamuck will be known in history for a more terrible invasion than that of the French. The religious crusade under the intolerant and turbulent Lord Lorton, by which it perished from the face of the earth, will give it and him a melancholy memorial in history. The following extracts from evidence taken on oath by the Devon commissioners in 1844 will inform the reader how Ballinamuck perished, and at the same time how the peace of

Ireland, at least of the county of Longford, has been disturbed; how the security which manufactures and commerce require to nourish their growth is scared away by crimes; how crimes have been engendered; and how the general good of the county has been sacrificed to political churchism, intolerant fanaticism, and personal vengeance.

The Rev. George Crawford, LL.D. Protestant rector of Clongish, in Longford, vicar-general of Ardagh, land-agent to several landowners and formerly agent for nearly all the land in the county, deposed on oath thus:—

'I may fairly say that political and religious considerations would operate in the selection or removal of tenants. I think landlords are disposed to have Protestants if they could. I had the management of Mr M'Conkey's property, and when leases fell out he transferred Protestants to them.'

The same witness states that the clearances at Ballinamuck began thus— 'There were two or three contested elections, and the tenants voted in opposition to their landlord, and with the priest. The landlord, when he had an opportunity, removed them.' (To 'remove' is to eject, to deny the means of life, to doom to starvation.)

Rev. Edward M'Gaven— 'Many clearances have been made all over the country, the purpose is to make the farms large enough to constitute votes. Generally speaking the persons evicted have not been compensated; in some cases: 30s. or £2 was given. Upwards of forty or fifty families have been turned out in the parish of Cashel. That was in 1832 and 1833; there was a change of proprietor. The late Lord Newcomen's estate came into the hands of Lady Ross. Political excitement went very high in this county at that time, and they were turned out, and the farms made so as to make freeholds.' (Freehold is the general term in Ireland for a tenant's franchise.) 'Many of the people went to America, and many of them live in huts as they can.'

'Do you think that religious or political motives have any operation on the removal of tenants?' 'Yes; I think it was both religious and political motives that caused the removal of the generality of them.'

Rev. Martin O'Beirne—'In Ballinamuck and Clunglish there has been an eviction of a great number of tenants on what has been considered political grounds alone. In Ballinamuck the entire houses were levelled. In Drumore, in the parish of Clunglish, there was an ejectment of nearly all the tenants in the year 1834. I was very intimately acquainted with the entire of those tenants. They were persons of uncommonly peaceable good habits, very industrious, and solvent punctual tenants. It was college land. A new proprietor (a middleman) succeeded to the land and to the houses, and the tenants were all removed except Patrick Lynn; he died before they got him out. Baron Lefroy became the lessee of the property in that year. He purchased the lease, and took legal proceedings and removed the families.'

'Under what circumstances did he remove them!' 'On the ground, as it was understood by the people themselves, that they were Roman Catholics, and that, in the event of their becoming lessees under him, they might vote against him. He removed the entire of them, and gave the land entirely to Protestants. Only one of the Protestants was on the land before; he was a poor cottier, living on the edge of the bog. The tenants that were removed applied to Baron Lefroy for compensation. One of them, Patrick Mullinhiff, got me to write a memorial for him, and in the memorial I stated that he could produce receipts for rent paid punctually for sixty years. The families on the townland who were not removed were Protestants. Every Catholic family was removed, save one; and the impression was that they, James and Matthew Lee, were continued, while others were removed, through the influence of some of their relatives, who were Protestants—the grandmother being a Protestant. One of the tenants, Edward Mullinhiff, got £11: 10s. of compensation. He did not consider it at all adequate. A Mrs Hagan got £5. I do not find any other person who got compensation. It is stated that they owed no rent. Some of the tenants have emigrated to America, others died, and others are living in hovels in destitution.

That was in 1844. Mr Lefroy, not the baron, but his relative, the present member for Longford county, is one of those gentlemen who are beseeching the English tax-payers to give money and food to him and those whom his relative the judge has driven to destitution.

The Reverend Bernard Moran—'I am parish priest of Ballinamuck. In 1839, thirty-nine families, one hundred and seventeen souls, were turned out in one day. It was considered it was for their religious principles that they were turned out, and the reason why I say that is, that Protestants were put in their place.'

'Just state what you know of the circumstances of the eviction of these tenants. What took place after the first eviction?'

'The land was first held by Catholics, and Lord Lorton put them out and replaced them with Protestants. Then outrages occurred from time to time, and Lord Lorton gave notice that if any outrages occurred he would turn them all off his property. There were five murders took place; they were all Protestants. They were parties who had been placed in the situations of the previous tenants.'

'What became of the tenants who were removed from the estate of Ballinamuck ?' 'Some died through want. Some went to America. Some are going backwards and forwards in the country. I know the case of one who died in want.'

Rev. James Smith, parish priest of Street, in Longford—'There has been a removal of small tenantry in that parish to a very considerable extent. I could not exactly say what object the proprietor had. The whole of the people have been turned out, and the land given to one. The greater part of the people on a farm of about 400 acres, more than twenty persons, with their families, have been turned clear off it, and all given to one tenant. The tenants owed no arrears. The impression in the country at the time of the people being turned out was, that it was because they were of a different religion to the landlord. It was given to a gentleman who lived near; and he stated that it was for the purpose of grazing the land. The religion of the gentleman who got it is Protestant, and they were Catholics who were turned out. Some of the people went to America, some went to the neighbouring estates, and some went into the town.'

Where they are now if not dead; where they are now on the point of death if alive; where they have now a moral claim, to say the least of it, on the land of Street parish for subsistence; but upon which they will have no legal claim if the confederated Irish landowners and Irish middlemen who assemble in Parliament Street, London, can prevent them and prevent them, those landlords and middlemen will, if the English, in their sense of justice and feelings of mercy for the Irish people, do not compel them to make Irish property responsible for Irish pauperism. That qualification of the proposed poor-law which would limit the area of taxation to small districts will be understood in the case of those Longford estates. The paupers to be relieved are the people removed from the land and housed in towns or on distant bogs. The owners of the estates plead that they should only, if taxed at all for the relief of the poor, be rated for the pauperism existing *on* their estates. But let us return to the Protestant rector of Clongish, the Rev. George Crawford, LL.D. vicar-general of Ardagh, and general land-agent. He says:—

'Almost all the property of the county was under my guidance at one time. I was agent to Lord Granard. That property is now under the courts. I have lived fifty years in Longford.'

'Has there been any extensive clearance of farms in this district?' 'Yes, at Ballinamuck, in my parish.'

'Inform the commissioners under what circumstances the removal of the tenants took place.' 'There were two or three contested elections, and the tenants voted in opposition to their landlord, and with the priest. The landlord did not countenance it, and, when he had an opportunity, removed them. It was on the property of Lord Lorton, in my parish'; it was the small village of Ballinamuck; it was entirely depopulated. But they were chargeable with, or supposed to be guilty of, a great many offences. I cannot exactly say if the first were removed on political grounds. The great clearance of Ballinamuck, which took place afterwards, was not for political reasons but for the bad character of the people entirely. On the first outrage I told them, 'You are doing what is exceedingly wrong; your landlord will visit this on you;' and he echoed my sentiments, and told them so beforehand. Lord Lorton declared publicly his intention. There were four or five families in the rural district; and at Ballinamuck the whole was swept away. Lord Lorton warned the tenants in the court-house at Longford.'

Mr Courtenay, having been informed by the commissioners what the Protestant rector and several Catholic priests had deposed to upon oath, came out upon behalf of Lord Lorton, thus:—

'At this time, 1835, I took in upon some of the land which had become vacant' (the land of persons whom he had turned out of it) 'a very superior man of the name of Brock, with a view to assist and improve the occupiers in the cultivation of their ground, and as an example to the surrounding country. He was a native of the north. He had been recommended to me by several gentlemen of judgment and very great respectability. I put him in possession of a farm near the village of Ballinamuck early in the month of May 1835. My intention was that he should cultivate flax, and that the people in that district should do so, ultimately have looms, and establish the linen trade there, the place being well suited for that purpose. On the 24th of May, in the same year, he was murdered on his own farm about six o'clock in the evening. Every exertion was used to bring the perpetrators to conviction, but without effect. Rewards were offered amounting to £1500. Lord Lorton came over himself to Longford, and every possible exertion was used, but without effect.'

'Was there any conviction afterwards for that murder ?

'No; there was not. Upon this state of things being reported to Lord Lorton, he said—"As soon as the lease of this village (which was then held by a middleman) should fall in he would clear the town, and have every house thrown down."'

The sum of £1500 was a large one to offer *and to be refused* for a man's neck. Suppose the exertions to get some one hanged for murdering Brock had been used to prevent other murders, not by the fear of the gallows, but by the love of Lord Lorton, what might the result have been? Suppose that no tenants had been turned out and doomed to death (for to deny an Irish peasant land, is to deny him leave to live) for voting against the party of Lord Lorton at a contested election. And suppose in bringing a man from the north to teach the people the flax culture and to introduce the linen trade, his Lordship had chosen a Catholic, to avoid the risk of disputes upon topics of faith and church politics, which can be very well spared from the culture of flax and the weaving of linen; and suppose that, further to facilitate the flax culture, he had not given such a stranger a farm from which a number of families had been dispossessed for voting for the Catholic candidate,—might not the result have been favourable to every one; to the landlord, the land, and the people upon the land, to the trade of Longford county, and to its agriculture? Had Lord Lorton even been warned by one murder, might not many lives subsequently lost have been saved—the lives sacrificed by other murderers and by him? But he proceeded. Another Protestant was found and put in Brock's farm, and he was waylaid and beaten until permanently disabled. For this, seven men were tried and transported. How many thousands of pounds has it cost Ireland and England to prosecute, maintain in prison, send over the sea, and provide for at the antipodes, the perpetrators of this one crime?

Then followed the murder of Moorhead, another Protestant tenant, placed where Catholics had been driven out. Next followed the slaughter of Arthur Cathcart; blood enough, one would think, to satisfy even the slaughter-house poets of the *Nation* newspaper. Cathcart was Lord Lorton's bailiff, and had been employed in the mad fanaticism of his master in driving the people mad. They murdered him. But this lord of Ballinamuck, who still deemed it his province to dictate what kind of church the people should believe in, and to impose on them the alternative of his church or death by starvation, would not yet be warned. William Morrison succeeded Cathcart as bailiff to do the same kind of duty, and was also murdered. Cattle were houghed and otherwise injured, and property of every kind was destroyed. At last the climax of all that course of blood and crime and vengeance was arrived at by the destruction of Ballinamuck and the doom of its people to famine and slow death.

Two emperors and a king blot the city of Cracow from the map of Europe, not physically, only politically, and all England and most of the world cry to them shame!

A lord puts his foot on an Irish village, tramples it not only out of the map, but levels it to the level of the bogs, and disperses its people to the four winds of heaven—to live on the wind if they can, to die in the wind if they must; and this Irish lord moves through the streets of London, and sits in the very house of parliament where the extinction of Cracow is reprobated, and does not sink upon the floor of the house with the shame of Ballinamuck: on the contrary, he has the courage to ask the English givers of charity and the English payers of taxes to give money to help those very people to live whom he has made beggars. Even Sodom and Gomorrah would have been saved if there had been ten innocent persons found there. (Genesis, xviii. 32.) Ballinamuck was destroyed because a jury would not decide that one of its inhabitants was guilty. The plain of Gomorrah, travellers say, is now the basin of the Dead Sea, upon whose shores no fruitful or useful thing grows: the place where Ballinamuck once stood, says the traveller whose hand pens this letter, is now the site of a police barrack, filled with armed men, and no other living thing but the armed men, is seen there, and they are kept there at the expense of the English tax-payers.

Mr Courtenay, in the blue books of the Devon commission, is reported to have said—'The town has not been rebuilt. The place was improved and much more peaceable after the throwing down of Ballinamuck.'—*Appendix B. page 73.* Who will doubt that the place is more peaceable?

A few words of application to conclude with. Agriculture can never be well conducted when made subservient to such purposes as have been here related. But agriculture, however well conducted, can never prosper, and make a dense population prosperous, without manufactures and commerce to employ a majority of the people, and enable them to purchase the products of the agriculturists, enabling the latter in their turn to pay wages to their labourers. Manufactures and commerce can never take root and flourish, nor co-exist with lawlessness, bloodshed, and insecurity to life and property. And lawlessness, bloodshed, and insecurity to life and property must continue to result from the bad practices of the landlords who follow and imitate such a mischievous bigot as Lord Lorton, of whom, unfortunately, the county of Longford has too many.

14

LONGFORD, 5*th March 1847*

Mr John O'Connell, M.P. for Kilkenny, has written a letter from London to the Repeal Association, which is reprinted in most of the Irish newspapers. It may possibly attract no attention in England, nor may this notice of it attract attention in Ireland; but the subject is profoundly important; and, as the member for Kilkenny has the temerity to provoke a discussion on such a subject—that of the generosity of the English public to the Irish people in this present season of distress—I shall not shrink from telling him, respectfully yet firmly, that his letter to the Repeal Association now circulated throughout Ireland is a most unfounded and unworthy libel upon the English people. And more, that of all the gentry in Ireland, the repeal members of parliament, so far as I have yet seen their estates and the starving people on their estates, (and I have already visited a considerable number of them,) are the gentry least entitled to accuse the English public of apathy or hardheartedness.

Mr John O'Connell, referring to an address delivered by him on the previous evening in the House of Commons, says in his letter—'I also drew attention to a monstrous sentiment prevailing in some quarters here, that it is in the natural order of things for a population to be suffered to diminish down to the diminished supply of food in a country afflicted with scarcity. I implored of the government and the house not to let this cruel sentiment have influence upon them in dealing with the question of relief to Ireland, and expressed my fears, from what I had seen, that inadequate and insufficient as are the measures proposed by the government, yet, in so far as those measures involve the expenditure of money, the government are absolutely in advance of English opinion.'

I can prove to Mr John O'Connell, and to all whom it may concern, by reference to Irish estates one by one, to farms upon those estates one by one, and by reference to the charity given or *wages paid for actual labour now performed*, giving the names of the proprietors and middlemen one by one, whose reputation is involved in the question, that, whatever the stage of liberality may be now arrived at by the government, public opinion and public generosity in England are far in advance of public opinion and public generosity in Ireland.

Some Irish gentlemen may be too poor to have much to give away in the present emergency; but the poorest of them might give something. The greatness of the necessity seems to be, for them, an excuse for doing nothing at all—literally nothing at all. Moreover, they might pay wages sufficient to keep their work-people out of the public soup-kitchens, and in a condition able to work. I shall here relate a case I witnessed the other day; I might relate twenty such seen within a week.

Seven men were in a field which measured three acres, and which had just been sown with oats. They were employed in breaking the clods of earth, in clearing the furrows for letting off top water, and in otherwise finishing the sowing of the oats. It was about four in the afternoon when I saw them. They appeared to me to work very indifferently; the whole seven were doing less than one man's work. I watched them for some time, while they did not see me, consequently they could not be enacting a part before a stranger. I was soon convinced that the men were, some of them, leaning on their implements of work, and others staggering among the clods, from sheer weakness and hunger. I concluded this to be the case from the frequency of such signs. One of the men, after I had watched them some time, crawled through a gap in the hedge, came out upon the road on his hands and knees, and then tried to rise, and got up bit by bit as a feeble old man might be supposed to do. He succeeded in getting upon his feet at last, and moved slowly away, with tottering steps, towards the village, in a miserable hovel of which was his home.

I thought I would speak to the feeble old man, and followed and came up with him. He was not an old man. He was under forty years of age; was tall and sinewy, and had all the appearances of what would have been a strong man if there had been flesh on his body. But he bowed down, his cheeks were sunken, and his skin sallow-coloured, as if death were already within him. His eyes glared upon me fearfully; and his skinny skeleton hands clutched the handle of the shovel upon which he supported himself while he stood to speak to me, as it were the last grasp of life.

'It is the hunger, your honour; nothing but the hunger,' he said in a feeble voice: 'I stayed at the work till I could stay no longer. I am fainting now with the hunger. I must go home to lie down. There is six children and my wife and myself. We had nothing all yesterday, (which was Sunday,) and this morning we had only a handful of yellow meal among us all, made into stirabout, before I came out to work—nothing more and nothing since. Sure this hunger will be the death of all of us. God have mercy upon me and my poor family.'

I saw the poor man at home and his poor family, and truly might he say, 'God have mercy!' They were skeletons all of them, with skin on the bones and life within the skin. A mother skeleton and baby skeleton; a tall boy skeleton, who had no work to do; who could now do nothing but eat, and had nothing to eat. Four female children skeletons, and the tall father skeleton, not able to work to get food for them, and not able to get enough of food when he did work for them. Their only food was what his wages of 10d. per day would procure of 'yellow meal'—the meal of the Indian corn. The price of that was 3s. per stone of 16lb. This gave for the eight persons 26lb. 10 oz. of meal for seven days; being about seven ounces and a half per day for each person. No self-control could make such persons distribute such a starvation measure of food over seven days equally. Their natural cravings made them eat it up at once, or in one, or three days at most, leaving the other days blank, making the pangs of hunger still worse.

But in this calculation I am supposing all the wages to go for meal. I believe none of it was expended on anything else, not even ⸱alt, save fuel: fuel in this village must all be purchased by such people; they are not allowed to go to the bogs to cut it for themselves. Nor is this the season to go to the bogs, if they were allowed. The fuel required to keep the household fire merely burning, hardly sufficient to give warmth to eight persons sitting around it, to say nothing of half-naked persons, would cost at least sixpence per day. Wherefore, no fuel was used by this family, nor by other working families, but what was required to boil the meal into stirabout.

Now this was one of the best paid men on the estate; all have not such large families as him, but all have as low wages; all have to pay the same price for food and fuel; all have to pay house rent. And this estate is the property, and those are the work-people—not employed for charity, but employed to do the necessary work on the *home farm*—of an Irish squire who keeps several hunting horses, has a number of dogs always about his yard and following the family carriage; in short, has all the show of horses, dogs, carriages, and liveried servants, common to the Irish gentry, which they keep whether they can afford them or not; and he is a repealer, and altogether a mighty fine patriot.

It would seem invidious, and would be very unpleasant, to pick those gentlemen out by name; but if Mr John O'Connell, Mr Smith O'Brien, and the others, of Old and Young Ireland, continue to misrepresent in their letters to Ireland the generous exertions of the English government and the English public in behalf of the Irish people, I shall name them, and name them in connection with conduct which should cover them with shame.

Cattle are dear and corn is dear. The incomes arising from cattle and corn are better this year, in many districts, than usual. In some counties rents have not been well paid; in others rents were never so readily paid, nor the tenants able to pay them, as this year. Yet even there, the apathy of the gentry is the same. This very squire, whose working men are starving as I have related, rails in public against the government; against political economy; and in the hearing of hundreds of people, the other day, of whom I was one, declared that Lord John Russell was answerable for all the deaths that were taking place in Ireland, for that he could make food cheaper if he chose.

As to Mr John O'Connell's assertion of 'A monstrous sentiment prevailing in some quarters here, (in London,) that it is in the natural order of things for a population to be suffered to diminish down to the supply of food in a country afflicted with scarcity,' it is neither more nor less than a monstrous mis-statement on his part of one of the simplest principles of the most philanthropic of mankind—the political economist.

It is *not* said by them to be 'in the natural order of things for a population to be *suffered* to diminish down to the supply of food in the country afflicted with scarcity.' It is said by them to be 'in the natural order of things for a population, to *suffer from* a diminution of food, and to sink in wretchedness and suffering in proportion to the increase in their numbers and the decrease in the supply of their food; ultimately, if the diminution of food becomes excessive and of long duration, to die and diminish with it.' It is in the natural order of things for human beings to die if they do not obtain sustenance for their bodies, just as it is in the natural order of things for agriculture to languish and fail to produce food for a great population when idle, dissolute, and improvi-dent proprietary classes exact, and compulsorily extract, from the cultiva-tors all their capital, the improving cultivator only being a mark for the landlord's cupidity. It is in the natural order of things for the tenant farmers of Ireland to be oppressed and degraded and made bad farmers when their political uses are deemed of higher importance by the landlords than their agricultural uses. It is in the natural order of things for the oppressed tenantry to listen to those who are continually telling them of their oppression, and promising them a blissful change by some one mighty action which cannot be performed, and which would be as worthless if performed as another moon would be in the sky to give them moonshine of their own. It is in the natural order of things, at least Irish things, for the people to be deluded.

It would be in the natural order of things for an Irish parliament of Irish landlords to legislate for themselves and against their tenantry and the great body of the people. Cruel as the political Protestant landlords have been in persecuting the Catholic tenantry for their religion and their adherence to repeal politics, they are exceeded in cruelty by landlords of the repeal party—the very vultures of a heartless, ignorant, haughty, and selfish class of men.

It is in the natural order of things for agriculture to be profitless without a manufacturing and trading population to purchase and con-sume the agricultural produce. It is in the natural order of things for an exclusively agricultural population to be always liable to famine; for it is in the natural order of things for such a population to overstock the land with itself, having no other outlet for the younger branches of families, until they become so numerous and so poor that they cannot afford to cultivate the land: they eat up their seed, their stock, their implements, and consume their own strength.

And so saying, I leave all the rest of Mr John O'Connell's assertion to its own refutation, namely, that 'a monstrous sentiment prevails in

London, that it is the natural order of things for a population to be suffered to diminish down,' &c. It must have required a good deal of courage, to say the least of it, for any Irishman to have written that of the English people in reference to their present treatment of the Irish.

Here is a passage from another gentleman, who is frequently in print on this side of the channel, John S. Dwyer, Esq. of Castleconnell, near Limerick. The letter is one of a series addressed to Lord John Russell. His Lordship is better employed in the service of Ireland than to be reading such letters. Yet this, as an Irish landlord's letter, is a curiosity worth reading. Castleconnell, where it is written, is the locality of the great rapids of the Shannon, powerful for manufactures to an illimitable extent, and upon which there is only one mill, and that for grinding corn.

'Your Lordship is aware that the party of whose name and traditions you are the representative and leader has very slight claims on the confidence of either the agricultural classes of Great Britain or of the Irish as a nation—a party who, when in power, legislated solely for the advantage of capitalists, systematically sacrificing the interests of society to the aggrandisement of money-dealers, merchants, and manufacturers.'

Mr Dwyer, like every other Irish gentleman, tells the government and everybody else that they know nothing about Ireland. 'Oh! sure you know nothing about Ireland.' 'What Englishman knows anything about Ireland !'

Now, I have very serious doubts if the Irish gentry do not know less of Ireland, their mother country—the mother whom they have reduced to beggary and shame—than most Englishmen do who have transacted business in Ireland. At all events they know nothing of England, and I hold that it is essentially necessary that to do their own country good they should know something of England.

For instance Mr Dwyer thinks that the complicated tenures of Irish land are the sole reason for the defective state of Irish agriculture, and he compares those complicated tenures with the 'simple' tenures of England, under which he says she has flourished. Now, in England, the legal harness under which land is held is identically the same as in Ireland. Leases for ever, renewable on fines—copyholds—leases on lives—joint ownerships—tenancies-at-will—and every other obstacle which can mar good agriculture, exist in England. Moreover, the burthens of county-rates and poor-rates are, and have long been, heavier on English land than on Irish land. Hitherto the Irish landlord has laid all the burthens of the soil on the tenant. Even the poor-rate, which he is supposed to pay one-half of, he makes the tenant pay the whole of, deducting his own half afterwards from that half-year's rent which relates to the half-year when the rate was made, the tenant being thus obliged for the landlord's convenience to pay part of his rent before it is due. So far as English agriculture is more prosperous than that of Ireland, it is so in defiance of the complicated tenures.

It is the readier and higher-priced markets in England that makes agriculture more profitable there; and those readier and higher-priced markets are created by the manufacturing and trading classes. Even the rents of the Irish landlords are chiefly obtained from the manufacturing and trading classes of England, who eat and pay for Irish produce. If the Irish landlords would keep that produce at home, and would still have their rents, they must create manufactures, and commence at home; and such gentlemen as Mr John S. Dwyer must cease to think, and write, and act nonsense.

If he knew more of England than he does, he would know that legislation in *favour* of English manufactures is repudiated. It never did good; it always did mischief. Manufactures thrive by being left alone, untouched by legislation.

If he knew anything of England, he would know that she is not jealous, as he asserts she is, of Irish prosperity. The more that Ireland could manufacture, the richer would her population be, and the better customers would England and Ireland be to one another. Lancashire and Yorkshire lie near each other; they are not enemies, yet they are competitors; the prosperity of the one is the life of the other. Ireland and England would be related in a similar manner, if more nearly on an equality of prosperity. It is the interest of England to raise Ireland to her own level; they are the enemies of Ireland who prevent it; those enemies are within herself.

15

ATHLONE, 10*th March 1847*

Athlone is a town containing 6393 inhabitants, standing on both sides of the Shannon, partly in Roscommon, partly in Westmeath. It is in the centre of Ireland, and is the head of a military district. Its military works of defence on the Roscommon side cover fifteen acres of ground. It is garrisoned by 1500 soldiers, horse, foot, and artillery; contains 15,000 stand of arms; two magazines of ammunition and ordnance stores; besides a large number of armed constabulary.

My letters from Roscommon and Longford gave some account of those landlords who find employment for that great military force, the Lord Lortons, the Lefroys, and such like; and the people upon whom the great force is employed, the conacre peasantry, who battle for bare life, and for leave to hire and to delve the ground at £8 per acre.

Mr Richard Winter Reynell gives an account of himself and his land, which also shadows forth the uses of the great military force at Athlone. He says—

'I am a tenant farmer. I occupy between 3000 and 4000 acres of land. About 150 or 170 acres are in tillage; the rest is in grazing. The rent averages about £1:11s. per acre. I give an acre and a half to one bullock for fattening, but in addition to that the same land keeps sheep in winter. Half of my farms are for fattening and half for sheep and grazing, (breeding). Those who cultivate their land in small farms take four or five or six crops of oats from the land successively until it is exhausted; I have known them to do that. In some parts they are now beginning to sow grass seeds since the agricultural society was set up. One of the farms which I hold of 200 acres was in five or six farms before I got it. I do not see a great deal of improvement in the large tenantry. I do not see much improvement in the small tenantry, the labourers are not improving at all. A great number of labourers in my neighbourhood are huddled together in little villages, When there has been an old lease in existence they have got in as sub-tenants in that sort of way. I know a great many in one place, and that is the way they hold. Those under me have a house and an acre of land for 30s.' (Of course the people build their houses, or huts, or hovels themselves.)

'Conacre does not prevail so much now; the landlords generally are setting their faces against it and are advising their tenants to drop it. At particular seasons the poor people are very badly off; there is not constant labour to keep all at work; the usual rate of wages is eightpence and tenpence per day without diet of any kind.'

This is the most extensive farmer in Westmeath; but his system is a specimen of the large farms into which the small ones have been gradually merging. Deducting his 170 acres of tillage, he has full 3500 acres of grass, the latter employing, at an average of 8d. per day, thirty-five persons, men and boys. This is somewhat above the actual numbers, and 8d per day is above the actual average. But to make allowance for something additional paid at present in consequence of high prices, the average wages of men and boys may be called 8d. and they may be rated at thirty-five, or one per hundred acres.

The yearly wages of each, 'without diet of any kind,' (those are Mr Reynell's own words,) are £10:8s.; total wages to the population of 3500 acres, £364; rent of 3500 acres, £5425; total population of Westmeath, 141,300; total acres of Westmeath, 453,468; number of acres arable, or capable of cultivation, 365,218; number of agricultural population, 131,316. The rent of 3500 acres is very nearly fifteen times the amount of wages paid for the labour which produces the rent.

The cattle fed on that land are chiefly sold to the beef-eating English, who pay for their beef and work for the money which they pay. The money which they pay for the beef makes up the rent of £5425. The land was cleared of human beings to make pastures for the cattle. The human beings were starving in 1844 when Mr Reynell gave his evidence; they are better cared for now, in the year of famine, 1847, than in the year of plenty, 1844, because many of them had neither wages nor conacre in that year, there having been no labour for the greater part of them, and the landlords 'setting their faces against conacre' as Mr Reynell states; while this year the English tax-payers are providing the destitute peasantry with yellow meal. The question is, therefore, between the taxpayers, who pay £5425 for beef; and also pay for yellow meal for the surplus population of 3500 acres in Westmeath, while the landlord, who pockets the £5425, does not pay for yellow meal to the people driven from his 3500 acres of pasture.

I think the English tax-payers will understand that question sufficiently well to know what to do. And when they call to mind that they have also to provide guns, gunpowder, bullets, bayonets, swords, lances, cannon, cannon-balls, bombshells, and rockets, and from 1500 to 2000 armed men, and 400 accoutred horses in Athlone, to keep the people in compulsory idleness and the land in comparative barrenness, they will have little difficulty in forming a judgment as to what they should do in respect of making it compulsory on the owners of the 3500 acres of grass lands to employ his proportion of the population, or pay poor rates for their sustenance; the more readily may they come to a decision when they know that it would be for the benefit even of that landlord to have the land cultivated and the people employed.

Another purpose for which the great garrison of Athlone is required, is to protect such destructives of property and human life as the destroyers of Ballinamuck, described in a previous letter, and not yet forgotten by the readers of this letter, I hope. As the interests of agriculture are held to be secondary to the interests of political Protestantism, the profitable employment of the Irish people and the reformation of Irish agriculture become fearfully difficult, though perhaps not wholly hopeless. Not only is all confidence destroyed between the Protestant landlord and Catholic tenant by such persecution as that of Ballinamuck, related in a former letter, and that which will be related in this letter, making the Catholic tenant a poor cultivator and a poor man, but there is more than a natural consequence of that destroyed confidence; there is a positive design to prevent the Catholic tenant from being a skillful, scientific, or improved farmer. Listen to William Fetherston Esq., a landed proprietor and farmer deposing on oath at Mullingar, on the 19th of July 1844:—

'Are there any agricultural schools or superintendents in the district?'—'There is an agriculturist employed by the Farming Society; and there is an agricultural school at Farra, about five miles from here, on the Longford road, under the Incorporated Society.'

'Do you know the regulations under which it is carried on?'—'No, I do not know anything very particularly, except that they have got a very clever person to instruct them in agriculture, and likewise a schoolmaster. I know the Farra school *is exclusively confined to Protestants.*'

'Is that because none but Protestants go there; or is there anything in the regulations on that subject?'—'*It is in the regulations.* There is no agricultural superintendent but the agriculturist. He is a Scotchman, employed by the landlords composing the Agricultural Society.'

So Catholic tenants are turned out of small farms, and small farms are turned into large ones, and given to political Protestants who vote right; and when the public voice proclaims the illiberal act to be persecution, or something very like it, the best excuse that can be offered, that ever has been offered, is, that the Protestants, being men from the north, are the best farmers. Yet here is Catholicism studiously made a disqualification for learning the science of manuring, green-cropping, subsoiling, and draining. The Catholics, forming the great majority of the population, are denied land, denied the information how to make it profitable if they have land; are denied conacre if they have not farm land; are denied work if they have not conacre; are denied poor-law relief if they have not work; and, having no work, have only the choice of facing death by slow degrees with no food in their stomachs, or death by quick degrees with bayonets and bullets, from Athlone, in their stomachs. They were shot dead when digging up land to plant potatoes in 1845.

That the Protestantism sought for and introduced is not mere religion, may be ascertained from the following evidence, taken at Longford, in addition to what was quoted from Longford witnesses in a former letter. Mere bigot Protestantism would have been no good excuse; but this has not even the comparative innocence of religious fanaticism; it is the undisguised use of Protestantism for political purposes, for obtaining promotion in the church, for obtaining a seat on the bench as a judge, and seats in Parliament:—

Mr Keon—'I had, under the Earl of Granard, some leasehold property

on a town-land called Drumlish, near Longford, and a farm belonging to
Lord Belmore, a mile and a half from the town. I have not known one
instance of a tenant on leaving a farm getting compensation for improvements he has made. A poor cottier might get 30s. or 40s. to give
peaceable possession. Under the impression that I would be permitted to
hold Knocknixtin, I expended £300 in the course of six years. I
improved it very materially. There was an objection to my holding it
longer in consequence of my not voting for Mr Lefroy at the election in
this town. At the election of 1835 I refused to vote for him. The agent
applied to me to give up the place. I went to lay a statement before Lord
Belmore, but was taken ill three weeks, and did not reach him. My wife,
finding I was detained ill from home, came, and I sent her. Lord
Belmore received her very courteously at first, and said he would see the
agent. She called again, and the reply to her was, that I could not expect
any favour from those that I would not favour with my vote. She replied
that I also held under Lord Forbes, and that I voted for his interest, and
not for Mr Lefroy.' (He could not vote for the interests of both
landlords, as they were of opposite parties.) 'He said, "He cannot expect
anything from me when he goes against me." '

Mr David Moffat— 'I held a farm under Mr Francis Synge. I was also
sub-agent under Mr Lefroy. I was removed after the election in 1841. I
disobliged Mr Lefroy, the agent,' (relative of the M.P. and of the judge).
'I wished to remain neuter and not vote, in consequence of having
possession of a mill I had built myself. I owed Mr Lefroy money, and he
owed me money; in striking a balance I owed him £40. He served me
with a *latitat*, and brought an execution against me, and sold eighty or
ninety pounds worth of property for £19:10s. The whole of the tenants
will prove that. I do not owe a shilling now. I expended £150 on that
farm; and I built that mill in 1840. It is getting no compensation for that
that I complain.'

Mr Edward Rooney, clerk to the Board of Guardians at Longford,
mentioned, amongst other things, that Lord Lorton's agent, Mr
Courtenay, issued the regular notices for the tenants to meet him on the
26th day of October to pay the half year's rent due in the previous
March; and that when they came, in obedience to that notice, he refused
to receive that half year's rent from some of them unless they also paid
the half year's rent just then due. According to Mr Courtenay's own
statement to the commissioners, he did this with those who did not vote
for Mr Lefroy, because they had 'voted in opposition to the wishes of the
landlord.' Referring to one of those cases, that of Thomas Farrell, a
tenant of Lord Lorton, Mr Courtenay was thus questioned, and thus he
answered, (Devon Blue Books, Part II., Appendix B, page 72):—

'What was the cause of the proceeding in that particular case?'—'My reason for demanding the year's rent from him in October (due on the 29th September) was in consequence of his having voted in opposition to the wish of his landlord, and having volunteered in making statements and affidavits at the election and afterwards.'

Such is the complete impunity with which the Irish political Protestant land-agents have been accustomed to act in such cases, that they do not seem to have any sense of fear or shame. Why should they be afraid? They have had all power and law, and all persons of power and law, from the Lord-primate of all Ireland and the Lord-lieutenant of Ireland, on their side, down to the hangman.

But though Mr Courtenay admits without shame that, after having issued a notice in October for the tenants of Lord Lorton to come and pay the half year's rent due in March, he demanded, in addition to that, without notice, the half year's rent due on the 29th September, and did so because they had voted in opposition to the landlord's wishes: he does not tell all the facts. As they had intimation that they were only to be required to pay as usual half a year's rent, he did not expect them to come prepared with a whole year's rent. They were not so prepared. Whereupon he proceeded, they being leaseholders, to execute a process of ejectment against them because they owed a year's rent. A process of ejectment cannot be taken against a leaseholder until at least one year's rent is due, and has been called for and not been paid. The people offered to pay the half year's rent which he had by a printed notice summoned them together to pay; but he would not take that. He not only sought to punish them for having voted in opposition to the will of their landlord, but he wanted to have on their farms pliable voters for future occasions. So he used the pretence of only calling for half a year's rent, while he demanded suddenly a whole year's rent to get them ejected, and it seems he succeeded.

It may be alleged in behalf of those landlords, that the Catholic tenants are bad agriculturists. It would be wonderful if they were otherwise. But some of them are distinguished even as good agriculturists, and yet they are sacrificed to politics and state churchism like the rest. Here is one of Lord Longford's tenants. The account which he here gives of himself, I have ascertained from other sources to be quite true and within the truth:—

James Kelly—'I held a farm of 29 English acres 22 perches at Ballymacurgan, a mile from Longford town, on the estate of Lord Longford. I was born and reared there, and my forefathers before me. I was dispossessed on the 2d of June 1840.'

'For what reason do you suppose you were ejected?'—'The agent told me it was on account of my voting contrary to my landlord's wishes. That was Mr Kincaid of Dublin. I told him my conscience did not allow me to vote differently after I was sworn. I would wish to stay out of the way and not come forward to vote at all; but the country people threatened any one that would do so.'

'You are quite sure that Mr Kincaid told you that it was in consequence of voting that way?'— 'Yes; he told me he wanted no compliment from me, but to stand to him at the elections. "It is not what you have, but you shall not want anything; we have nothing against you; but we should be sorry your lease should be the first that dropped, (as I was an improving tenant,) that it should come to my turn first."'

'Did you offer to take the same land and pay the rent year by year?'— 'I offered him another year's rent if they would not put me out. I said I should not wish for £500 to be put out of the birth-place of my forefathers; and I had made so many improvements, and squared the land. I offered to take it without a lease. I would rather have it without a lease, because I should not be a freeholder then, and not be in danger of being killed. I made new ditches and squared every field, and planted them so that a bird could not get through them; and there was never a year but I had a bed of quick planted; and was up before daylight. I made buildings; it was not long since I rebuilt some of the offices. I got no compensation. I asked for it; and stopped after the ejectment and did no work. Then the driver told me to go on with my work, and still I expected not to be dispossessed. Everybody told me that they would not turn out such a tenant, who was always making improvements. I hurried and got my crops in, and was just finishing the last ridge when I was dispossessed.'

After reading this, one turns with some eagerness to that remarkable 'Appendix B,' in the Blue Books, to which all aggrieved land-agents and landlords have been admitted to contradict the tenant witnesses, or explain inexplicable things relating to themselves. Mr Kincaid replies to James Kelly thus:—

'Although he states in general terms that he was told by the agent that it was on account of his voting contrary to his landlord's wishes he was turned out, yet on being pressed to say positively whether he was sure the agent said so, he gives a confused statement of conversations at elections and at other times, but no distinct answer to the question.'

So it must not be true, Mr Kincaid, that you dispose of good tenants because they oppose Lord Longford at the elections? It must not be true that you turned out Mr Kelly for that offence, else why have all this fencing with the fact? Let us see how you get out of it:—

'I do not recollect distinctly what I may have said to him or to any of the tenants in the excitement of a contested election. There were a considerable number of voters on Lord Longford's estate, and I used my best exertions to bring them to the poll and to induce them to vote for the candidates that his Lordship wished to be supported, and on all the occasions referred to by Kelly, he not only voted in opposition to his landlord's wishes, but he did so in a tone and spirit of defiance and triumph which was by no means calculated to gain his landlord's countenance. If other causes were wanted for taking the farm from Kelly, they would not have been difficult to find.'

But of course they were not required to be found, his hostile votes being sufficient.

Such is the wretched vassalage of the agriculturists of Longford where people are now gazing with vacant eyes at the bare earth and at the bare sky, with empty stomachs, and nothing in their mouths but prayers to God to relieve them from misery by a speedy death. And some of them are receiving relief in death. Such is the deplorable waste of the agricultural resources of Longford, Westmeath, and Roscommon, counties of great fertility, sufficient to employ all their population. Such are the means by which insecurity to life and property, and crimes against both, are engendered; such are some of the means through which the bad fame of crime deters capital, commerce, and manufactures from taking root in Ireland.

16

MAYO, 10th March 1847

What muse, what inspiration shall I invoke in writing of Mayo? I question if even fable has yet imagined a muse, or patron saint, or pen-and-ink spirit, able to gather into a writer's brain all the matter of Mayo from which ideas may be drawn out at the writer's finger ends. It is at once the most magnificent and most mean of Irish shires. Its mountains and islands rise out of lakes and bays to the sublimation of altitude; the wall-like rocks, founded deeper in the ocean than fathom line can reach, rise a thousand feet in upright majesty, with mountains one thousand and three hundred feet enthroned above them. In caves beneath those mountains, and in passages open from the top, and so deep that the spiritual daylight hardly finds its way down, the tides of the ocean, as if lost and imprisoned, roll and roar in their prisons, and ceaselessly work at, gnaw at, and knock upon the rocks until they waste them away, and again make passages to the open sea.

How narrow seems that blue ocean from hence to the western horizon, where the great ships of America and of England are as small as birds—like small birds on the edges of their nest, their nest the setting sun; it is but a narrow border of blue. But, heavens, what a depth to look down into that sea, a thousand feet below us! And to be able to leap into it! 'You cannot gaze a minute without an awful wish to plunge within it.' Look at this pointed rock, a long narrow stone abutting out and over the gulf, where the tides hold tumult so far down that you can hardly see them; a creature of flesh and blood, body and soul, with hands and feet, creeping out on the narrow rock on penitent knees, to bend his head over the rock, round it, and kiss its farthest point for grace and forgiveness! Well done, sinner of the strong nerve! you have done it; you may return and sin again. Your brother and sister, with less iron in them, or less *ether*, with less sin, mayhap, are giddy—going—gone—down—are down. The ocean has more wreck, eternity has more spirits, and the priest more pence.

There is a mixture of the savage and the sublime in this legend, which gives a fearful interest to more rocks than one on the west coast of Mayo.

But there is a fall which is no legend that we must submit to; a plunge which we must make from the mountains of Mayo, with all their grandeur of ocean, of islands, deep bays, high headlands, lakes, rivers, waterfalls, fertile meadows, and greenness which knows no withering; we must plunge from the grand and the beautiful in the inanimate works of nature—to the most degraded and farthest lost of her works—the men made after God's own image.

There they are; all that remains of them in Mayo, living where the worms live, in holes of the earth; crawling as the worms crawl; but dying of sheer hunger and helplessness in their clay holes, where even a worm would do something to preserve its own life and provide its hole with health. They move not hand nor foot for that purpose.

Mayo is irregular in shape. Its greatest breadth, from south to north, is 58 miles, greatest length from east to west 72 miles. It is bounded on the west and north by the Atlantic Ocean, on part of the west by Galway, and on the east by Sligo and Roscommon. It comprises an area of 2131 square miles, or 1,333,882 acres; of those acres 56,976 are under water, 848 under towns, 8360 under plantations, 800,111 are uncultivated, and 497,587 are arable. Few of the farms are above fifteen acres; a hundred acres are a very large farm; and the greater part of the land is held in rundale or common, and in joint tenancies. The 'rundale' is for all the holders of land in a village or township to have spots allotted to them here and there over several miles; a few perches of good soil in one place, a few acres of poor soil in another place, an acre of meadow in the plain, two acres of pasturage on the hill, half an acre of potatoes separating some neighbour's oats and barley, two miles on the west of the village, and two or three half acres of oats and barley separated by the potatoes, or meadows, or bogs of the neighbour's two miles east of the village. This is rundale; and the general result of rundale is for the several patches of ground to have no fences; for three quarters of a man's time to be consumed in travelling over miles of country, talking as he goes, to dozens of his neighbours, while visiting his farm of six, or eight, or ten acres. Another result is for the pigs and cattle of one farmer to run among the crops of another, and for the whole of the people to have disputes about their marches and rights of way, and to settle their disputes by fighting them out, and renewing the disputes and the same mode of settlement from day to day, from week to week, and occasionally throughout the year; and the next year again, and the next. The disputes never ending, and never to be ended until rundale is ended.

Joint tenancies exist in some parts where there is no rundale. A number of persons join together and take a farm; and all are jointly or severally liable for the rent. One more provident pays his share of the rent, but is distrained upon by the landlord for the default of a co-partner who has not paid his share. A battle ensues, and the neighbours side with the respective combatants and make the battle and the broken heads general. When joint tenancies and rundale exist together, which is often the case, the quarrels are more frequent and the disputes more hopelessly inextricable.

The subsoil in the low districts is limestone and red sandstone, all forming a fertile soil. In other parts the subsoils are granite, quartz, and mica slate. Iron ore is abundant; and excellent slate quarries. Also many other industrial riches above and below the surface earth.

The population in 1841 numbered 388,887, of whom 19,749 lived in towns, all the rest in the rural districts, in hovels of the meanest kind which human beings have ever been known to live in. The employments are entirely agricultural and fishing, grazing predominating greatly over tillage.

There was in 1841 a stock of 23,216 horses and mules in the county, 81,457 horned cattle, 142,193 sheep, 52,286 pigs, 338,268 head of poultry, and 11,007 asses, all being of the estimated value of £956,432.

The principal towns are Castlebar, the head-quarters of the military, the place of the assizes, of the county prison, and the hangman; Westport, a place of some commerce and occupying a situation between the mountains which overlook it and the sea, seldom matched for its scenic beauty even on the beautiful sea-coasts of Ireland: Ballina, Ballinrobe, Bellmullet, and Swineford. The latter place derives its name from a great market for swine held there in the times of old.

The principal nobles and gentles who live there or elsewhere, on rent gathered in Mayo, (and it must be confessed that rent is not easily gathered there); are ten or eleven Blakes, half as many Brownes, as many Bourkes, a few more O'Malleys than Bourkes, some Knoxes, Palmers, Lynches, Kirwans, and a few Lords, of whom are Lords Clanmorris, Lord Oranmore, Lord Arran, Lord Sligo, Lord French, Lord Cloncurry, Lord Lucan, and Lord Dillon, most of them, if not all, making a determined stand against paying poor-rates: one of them, somewhat noted about London for driving a fancy four-horse 'drag,' refusing to pay the tolls, and thrashing a gate-keeper who insisted on having the toll.

It is also somewhat remarkable, the county of Mayo being so poor and always so poorly fed, that, during the summer of 1846, at least one of the gentlemen who scrapes rent enough together in Mayo to live elsewhere, should have been in a condition of cash to purchase a bushel of flour in London, drive with it in a carriage to Hammersmith Bridge, and, watching the moment when one of the Richmond steamers passed under the bridge with a company of London citizens holding holiday, empty the flour over the bridge on top of the holiday Londoners, and drive off at the gallop. If the spirit that prompted the mischief was not remarkable for a Mayo gentleman, the choice of the article for mischief, a bushel of flour, of which London is sending so many sacks to preserve Mayo in life, was at least worthy of note.

The number of officers in the army furnished by those West of Ireland families, and of old majors and colonels retired, and of younger sons waiting for appointments to regiments, is surprising. But those people must do something. As yet they are too proud and ignorant and poor to go into trade. They therefore seek the army, and wait in idleness until the political influence of their families is felt at the Horse Guards, and they get commissions.

The time will come when the landed gentry of Mayo will not be poor and proud of their barbarous lineage, and ignorant of true honour, the honour of industry, of making themselves honourably rich, and the general inhabitants of Mayo industrious and happy. The ironstone shall yet be iron under hammers made in Mayo; the rivers and lakes shall work and help the human hands to work; the bays and harbours shall have ships in them, many in number, weighty in burthen, rich in value. The men and women shall rise out of the earth-holes in which they now huddle together like lean worms in a place of rottenness. They shall rise and build dwellings, and cultivate the ground, and produce food to be sold to a manufacturing and commercial population; and they shall pay good rents then without difficulty.

Is this too much to prophecy? too much to hope for in Mayo? To believe that this is too much to come to pass in a county so stored with untold wealth, so advantageously situated on the front of Western Europe, is to believe that the idle landowners are to breed young military men and succeed each other in generations of worthlessness for ever.

No; the whole human race has a higher destiny than that.

The Rev. Bernard Durcan of Killeaden, at Swineford, on the 24th of July 1844, deposed, before the Devon commission, that—

'The general rate of wages through that district was sixpence per day, without diet. The best proof of that is, that the contractors on the public roads can get any number they choose, and that in the hurried season. The people came two or three miles to work at those wages. That is what makes it necessary for the people to go to England to the harvest. Rents are 50 and 60 per cent. higher than the poor-law valuation of land; in some cases cent. per cent. higher. The county-cess, which falls all on the poor tenants, to be paid in the summer, may be fairly estimated at eight shillings per acre; to meet that demand the people have to sell the potatoes they should be eating. In some districts of this parish, I believe nine-tenths of the adult male population go to England to the harvest every year. There is scarcely a house which there are not some gone from, the young men particularly. Besides the fatigue and hardship they undergo, their own tillage is necessarily neglected. If they could get employment, and even moderate remuneration for their labour at home, they would, of course, prefer it. It is dire necessity that makes them go. There are very few labourers under that name. They generally hold land. Mr Ormsby has some of his land set to labourers, and they are obliged to work when called upon at any period of the year at sixpence a-day without diet. If one refuses to come when called on at the most pressing time for his own business he is fined one shilling and his crop is distrained to make him pay the fine of one shilling. It gives the landlord an opportunity of exercising a good deal of tyranny, if so disposed.'

Mr Ormsby, being informed by the commission what the Reverend Durcan had said about him and his labourers, sought leave, like all other aggrieved landlords, to explain. Here is his explanation, every word:—

'There is no distinction between tenants and labourers on my property. All my tenants are obliged to work, if required, a certain number of days in the year, varying according to the distance they live from me; those in the immediate neighbourhood having to attend oftener than those more remote. I do not give them lower wages than the usual remuneration of the country.

'I had to insist upon a fine in order to ensure regularity in their attendance when called upon, otherwise, I should be altogether dependent on the caprice of labourers.

'In answer to the implied charge of hardship and tyranny, it is enough to state that I frequently have not work for all who are ready and anxious to receive it, and dissatisfaction has often been expressed at not receiving more employment.

'Notwithstanding the reverend gentleman's insinuations, I flatter myself that so far from looking on my work as a grievance, all my tenants are sensible of the benefit they have derived from the employment I have given them.'

I shall not at present proceed farther with this account of the population of Mayo. They are by far the most wretched, and, in the present season of famine, most generally destitute of any people whom I have yet seen in Ireland. At the same time the government provision is everywhere presented to them now. But they are sunk below the power of working, and nothing, or almost nothing, is being done, save on a few select farms, to provide crops for next harvest. In this remark I speak of Mayo only. The central counties from which I have recently been writing are getting well forward with the sowing of oats. They will have more acres under corn than usual in those counties, though nothing like as much as will supply the place of the potatoes. Here there seems to be a dismal blank.

17

CASTLEBAR, MAYO, 15th March 1847

This is the county town of Mayo. It contains 5137 inhabitants; and its parish contains 10,464. The greater part of the former are very poor; the latter are in a state of destitution which defies tongue to tell or pen to write; the greater part of them are occupiers of land, and are allowing the land to lie untilled and unsown, though the weather is favourable for sowing in every respect.

The town contains the assize court-houses; the county prison, the military and constabulary barracks; an infirmary; a workhouse; a parish church, with a lofty tower; a Catholic chapel; a Wesleyan meeting-house;

two schools; and a gallows. It contains two newspapers also, one of them established and managed by the Honourable Frederick Cavendish. This is the *Castlebar Telegraph and Connaught Ranger,* the other is the *Mayo Constitution.*

The town consists chiefly of a street nearly a mile long, with a spacious green; trees around the green; and some houses behind the trees. Hills rise beyond the last of the townhouses; the lake of Castlebar lies at the bottom of the hills; and the river of the same name comes out of the lake, and runs as if it had turned its back upon the ocean—for Westport and the Atlantic are only a few miles from the lake, and this river flows inland. It reaches Lough Conn, a lake twelve miles long, and then finds its way out to Killala Bay, where the French landed in 1798, and from whence they marched thirty miles, and took possession of the town of Castlebar. The hills which overlook the town, the river, and the lake, would appear to be great hills were no greater ones seen behind them. But behind them, on the north-west, towards Lough Conn, there rises the grey head of the giant Nephin, 2646 feet high. To stand on the other hills and look up to Nephin we feel almost as if we stood on the roof of Ireland and looked up at the dome. On the other side of the town is the Reek, bulwark of Joyce's county and Connemara. And Reek again leans back upon that appalling giantess called the Devil's Mother, 2131 feet above the deep waters of Lough Nafooey, near whose solitary waters few wanderers approach without awe. On the shores of Nafooey some outlaws are said to live in ordinary years, but the present season of famine is bringing even them from their solitudes; and that forlorn lake is companionless, save when a vagrant stranger, like me, finds his way to it with a guide; but such stranger going there only to see in it the likeness of that black giantess of mountains, to whom the wanderers, and ultimately the geographers, have given the name already written—for it is her looking-glass—he soon turns away and seeks the haunts of human life and the places of earthly loveliness.

There are many lovely places in Mayo. Close to Castlebar itself, in it indeed, there is the Lawn, the residence and demesne of the Earl of Lucan. The Lawn is pretty. But somehow the question of poor-rates gets into one's head when looking at it and thinking on Lord Lucan. His Lordship has become a defaulter in his poor-rates, and his tenantry follow his example. The other landlords do the same. The most forcible of their reasons for not paying the rates is that £60,000 have been spent in Mayo in building workhouses, and that they are called upon to pay that expense for building. It seems, however, that when the £60,000 were unspent, and seen only in perspective, those same owners of the soil of Mayo used all their political influence to get large sums laid out in building. They seem to have all agreed, then, that the larger the sum which each workhouse would cost, the better would the cost be to Mayo. They only disagreed as to the estates which should be favoured with a workhouse. Those who had the greatest political influence obtained the privilege of having the site of a union house, stones to build it, lime for mortar, and sand to mix with the lime, all purchased from them. Government advanced the money, and they had a scramble for it. The tenants were employed in drawing the stones to the site, which had been paid for in ready cash to the lucky landlord of the political power; other tenants quarried stones, dug out sand, burned lime, served the masons who built, and some of them were masons. All paid their rents to the happy landlords of the political influence at that time, and also all arrears. And why? The money in payment of the work went through the hands of the rent collectors.

We would naturally suppose that the workhouses would have been built in the most central parts of the different unions, or near to the most central towns or villages. But that natural arrangement would not have accorded with the influence of the landowners, who required that the money should be spent on their land. Listen to Mr Cavendish:—

'We have a poor house here, (at Castlebar;) another within eight miles; another within fourteen miles; another within eighteen miles; another within fourteen miles, (those being the five for the whole of Mayo,) all within that small district; when in remote districts there are no poor-houses within forty miles; and the reason of them being built where they have been was at the instigation of the landlords, in order to enable them to sell the poorer part of their land to the commissioners; and next that they may have good substantial buildings on their lands hereafter in case of the poor-law not being carried out.'

To refuse payment of rates; to combine landlords' agents and tenants as boards of guardians, not to collect the rates, and so, not to use the poor-houses for the poor, is certainly the most direct course to take to get hold of the 'good substantial buildings' for some other purpose. Mr Cavendish says:—

'No rates have been collected except by the aid of the police; many sums which have been lately collected have been by the presence of the police; and now there is a charge brought against the union for the two first instalments of £12,000 for building the workhouse, amounting to nearly £800. *It would be a great boon if the government would relinquish that enormous sum.* And if they were to do that it would give to the people an inducement to withdraw their opposition to the poor-rates altogether. In this county there are five poor-houses, and the expense of the mere building of those five poor-houses was upwards of £60,000, not any portion of which has been collected; and as they find it in every union, particularly Westport, Ballinrobe, and here very hard to collect the rates for the maintenance of the poor, they will find it very difficult indeed to collect £60,000.'

The first effort was to get the money advanced by government; the second to get it spent where the strongest landlord could get most of it; the next is to get 'government to relinquish the enormous sum'; failing which they will neither pay nor collect rates. The Earl of Lucan heads the combination.

At first rates were collected in the 'presence of the police,' but a magistrate's warrant was requisite to obtain the presence of the police. The head magistrate at Castlebar and chairman of the board of guardians is the Earl of Lucan; the principal acting magistrate, and treasurer to the board of guardians, is Mr Ormsby, his steward. They do not now issue warrants to the police to go out with their carbines, bayonets, and pouches of ball-cartridges, to give their presence to the rate-collectors, because the house is built; the £12,000 which it cost are spent; and the half of the rates falls ultimately on themselves, though wholly paid by the tenants in the first instance. To ease the landlords in every possible way, the rates were made, by parliament, payable by the tenant. The tenant being thus called upon to pay the landlord's rate, which was to be deducted from his rent, was called upon to pay a part of his rent before it was due as rent. If proceedings were taken to recover the rates, the expenses fell thus upon the tenants. If the tenants did not pay their rents regularly, but paid part on account from time to time, (and that is paid commonly by bills discounted at the banks, the landlord endorsing the bills; the tenants paying the enormous discount; again borrowing money at a loan society, in which the agents are usually the lenders, or from private usurers at 30, 40, and 50 per cent. to meet the bills when due at the bank; the loans being aid by instalments which are in reality doubled in amount;) if the tenants did not pay their rent in full, but allowed arrears to accumulate, they did not get permission to pay in as part of the rent the receipt for the landlord's half of the poor-rate until they were paying the rent of that half year in which the rate was made. Thus, if a tenant was in an arrear of twelve months' rent, and he paid the landlord's rate in presence of the police in April 1844, which was the period of the police being used for that duty, his rent for that half year would be due on the 29th of September following, and he would not pay it until after the harvest of 1845, at which time and not sooner he would be privileged to pay in the receipt received for the landlord's rates in the spring of 1844. It is not common for tenants-at-will to be allowed to run so far into arrear with their rent, as they can be ejected at any time by six months' notice, whether they owe rent or not. But in Mayo a large number of the tenants are leaseholders, who cannot be ejected unless they owe at least twelve months' rent. They are, therefore, allowed on most estates to fall into arrears to that extent, so that a process of ejectment may at any time be brought against them. When a contested election occurs, they get intimation that they must vote for a certain candidate, else a process of ejectment will issue against them. Most of them vote accordingly. To get those tenants on the register is the only inducement to give them leases; to have power over their votes is the purpose of designedly allowing them to fall into twelve months' default of rent. The votes obtained, such things as workhouses, at a cost of £12,000 each, in select localities, to 'enable them to sell the poorer part of their land to the commissioners,' are obtained also. And the tenants are at first called upon for the rates in the 'presence of the police,' and the rates are obtained. But twelve, eighteen, twenty-four, and thirty months go by, and the receipts for rates paid in 1844 by the tenants begin to come into the hands of agents as rent, which suggests to the said agents and landlords that they should join the tenants in an opposition to poor-rates. So the workhouse built at Castlebar, on Lord Lucan's land, at an expense of £12,000, to contain 700 persons, had within it in 1845 134 persons—the largest number it ever contained. It has had fewer since, and has about that number now. The population of the Castlebar union is 61,063 persons.

In the rating of the land, the owners have also taken care of themselves and shifted the weight of the burthen on the occupiers. A demesne, measuring hundreds or thousands of acres, kept as a deer-park, sheep-walk, hunting-field, or forest-chase, for the pleasure of the landlord, though it may be naturally as fertile and valuable land as the farm valued for poor-rate at twenty-five shillings per acre, will be most probably valued for that rate at five shillings per acre.

The only burthens which the Irish landowners have permitted them-selves to bear, with the exception of the half poor-rate on farms, and the low rate on grass lands, is the tithe rent-charge, and this is only nominally their burthen; they have invariably added it to the rent of the tenants. The poor of the peasantry entitled to relief must wait until the rates can be collected from the farmers. The parsons, most of them being of the landlord class, were saved the delay of waiting until a tithe-rate or rent-charge was collected from the farmers. The landlords undertook to pay that and charge it on the tenants.

The county cess was exclusively charged and levied on the tenants or occupiers. Of course when a landlord occupied his own land he had to pay the cess. In many parts of Mayo it amounted, in ordinary years, to a fifth part of the rent. Half of the expenses of the 9000 armed constabulary in Ireland is paid from this cess; the general taxes of the kingdom paying the other half. The grand juries of counties, a body altogether irresponsible to the cess-payers, have had the distribution of this money. In the case of outrages on property they award compensation to the sufferer, usually at the full amount and above it of his loss, and the award is levied on the whole of the occupiers of the barony in which the offence occurred, or in some lesser district determinable by the grand jury. The effect of such awards by the grand jurors, they being frequently in the proportion of six Protestants to one Catholic, and all landlords, has been to make the knaves who have foresworn Catholicism and taken up (I need hardly say in pretence only) Protestantism for the sake of getting a farm, or some official situation and official salary, of which knaves so situated there are many everywhere and a rather large number in Mayo— the result has been that those persons are ever and anon having an old horse pushed into a limekiln, a pig drowned in the river, a haystack set fire to, and sometimes a mud cabin with its roof of rushes set on fire. They go before the grand jury and swear that they believe the outrage to have been malicious, owing to their having been converted to Protestant- ism. The grand jurors believe with them, and award them sums of money, which are levied on the district where the mischief was done, in 'presence of the police.'

That there may have been such offences done by an enemy is likely; but that the greater part are done by persons who destroy their own property to get more for it than it is worth, and who get awards in cases that no insurance office in the kingdom would pay policies in, is just as sure as it is that the five workhouses of Mayo cost £60,000. A grand jury which memorialized the government the other day on the injustice of levying poor-rates on large districts, because in large districts the employer who employed many hands would be rated the same as him who employed few hands, (the real object, however, being to save the landlord who had cleared the population from his estate into the towns from being rated for their pauperism in the towns;) this grand jury at that same assize awarded a landlord £3000 and odds for loss sustained by him through a fire, alleged to have been malicious, the perpetrators not being known; and when it was proposed by one of the jurors to levy that sum on the barony in which the fire occurred, it was successfully objected to, and the levy was ordered to be made on a wider district, because, if made on the barony, the greater part of it would have fallen on the noble lord himself, he being principal owner and occupier in the barony.

Another purpose of the public cess has been to make roads, build bridges, and perform other public works. Under colour of performing such works, private residences have been ornamented, public roads diverted for private convenience, bridges built for private use, and the public wants neglected. No fault was found by the grand jurors with anything designed by the county and district surveyors; and as the surveyors obtain their situations from the jurors, and not from the cess-payers, they always tried to make public works suit the private wants of the gentlemen jurors. These last, paying no cess themselves, laid the cess on the occupiers with a heavy hand, collected it in 'presence of the police,' and always answered to every remonstrance of the cess-payers, that public roads, bridges, angles cut off, hills levelled, and hollows filled up, were the best possible things which could be done in the county with the public money.

But the act of the 10th of Victoria passed at the close of the session of 1846, to facilitate the employment of the peasantry, and it passed in a haste, when half the lords and gentlemen had gone to grouse-shooting. To their astonishment they discovered that this act, which passed in such haste when their backs were turned, contained, not only a clause giving the Lord-Lieutenant of Ireland power to summon grand jurors together in distressed districts and compel them to provide work for the unemployed, but a clause which laid one-half of the cess to be collected for that purpose on themselves. Upon which they at once discovered that roads were useless works, bridges were useless, hollows filled up were useless, and hills cut down were useless. All public money expended in making or improving roads, if it was cess to be collected in the baronies, was declared to be a waste of money. They excepted from this declaration of waste the proposition to send sixteen millions of imperial taxes on railroads. And when Lord John Russell told them that half of the cess would be defrayed by the imperial exchequer, (at the expense of the working men and women of England and Scotland chiefly,) and that the charge of the other half would be divided between them and their tenants, they were still unreconciled to bear that fourth part of the cess; and they still declaim on the utter uselessness of all public works to which they shall in any way be called on to contribute.

When we bring to mind that Ireland does not pay the assessed taxes, nor several of the excise duties, (that on soap, for instance,) nor income and property tax; that the Irish landlords were never until now taxed for public roads, and that they now unite into an 'Irish party' to harass the government and impose upon the English public new burthens for the performance of duties which they neglect, it will be seen that as a class Irish landowners stand at the very bottom of the scale of honest and honourable men.

And yet all that is said of those of them who own the land and the political power of Mayo in this letter, becomes purity itself compared with the deeds done, as shall be related in my next letter, in respect of tolls and customs in Mayo. It is not enough for them to exempt themselves for many years from payment of the public cess, and expend that cess in many cases for private benefit; but £30,000 per annum collected in Mayo in tolls and customs, to do the work which the cess is applied to, has been divided, and is now divided, among a few influential families as private income.

18

CASTLEBAR, MAYO

There is, it appears, not less than £30,000 per annum collected in the county of Mayo for tolls and customs. Those tolls and customs are chiefly collected under patents granted to certain of the landlords; the original purpose of the patents being to secure the landlords from loss in making roads, maintaining streets in repair, and such like public services. In process of time those works were provided for by acts of parliament, and a public cess for their execution was collected from all occupiers of land. In Castlebar district the cess has usually amounted to about one-fifth of the rental. That cess has been expended by the grand jurors in making and repairing the roads, in paving the streets of Castlebar town; in doing all the things, in short, which the patents for tolls and customs intended the money collected under them to do.

Those tolls and customs are farmed out to various grades of collectors. The head landlord receives a rent for himself from some friend to whom he leases the power of exacting the dues. That friend, commonly a relation of the landlord, or political servant who is thus rewarded, sets the privilege of collecting the dues to a third party, at a sum very considerably higher than what he himself pays. This third party may collect the dues; in some cases he does, but not always. Even he is occasionally one of the family who has a deputy farmer of tolls under him. The first under the landlord may be a brother whom primogeniture and entails have made a poor brother. The second may be a cousin, younger brother of some other entailed landlord of lesser degree, in whose family no patent for collecting tolls and market-dues is vested. Next comes the man who contracts to pay a large sum, and who pays men of vigour and energy their daily wages to collect the dues and fight for them, or offer to fight, as necessity may require.

Sometimes a person is found who buys hay and corn and butter and pigs in the town of Castlebar, and who refuses to pay those dues to Lord Lucan's deputies. If he is strong in purse and independent in position, he may go to law and get a decision from the judges of the land, that the lords of the land and the deputies under them have no right to levy those tolls and dues. In such a case they will allow that person to buy and sell in the streets, and pass along the road without toll in future; but they will catch all the rest who are not rich enough to go to law; and especially the tenant farmers, who must not make enemies of landlords and agents, nor of the relatives of landlords, lest they lose their farms. Listen to Mr Cavendish of Castlebar:—

'I took the matter up myself. I purchased articles in the market, oats and potatoes, and refused to pay the toll. They seized my goods. I replevined and made them pay all the costs in an action at law; but the people are not rich enough to do that. They charged 3d. per cwt. for oats, or 9d. per sack of three cwt. I refused to pay that, but offered them 1d. per draught. They seized. I tried the question with them, and beat them.'

'Was the toll so set aside continued afterwards?'—'Yes, it was continued afterwards against those who had no power to resist it. If I buy a load of hay in the country, and direct it to be drawn to my stables, the custom is charged, (though I never pay it,) though it is never weighed, or any account taken of it, but only passing through the street; but the country people pay it. The toll was originally imposed to build a market-house, build bridges, and repair the streets. *The market-house has never been built*, and the bridges are built and the street repaired by present-ment of the grand jury from the public cess; but the public highway is converted into a profit by the landlord. The landlord gets £75 for the toll of the street, and the man under him sets it again, and he gets a profit. Not one shilling is laid out in the way directed by the patent. The toll is an entire profit levied on the public, and put into the pockets of the landlord, his under bailiffs, and tenants.'

The customs, however, would seem to furnish rather a worse case than the tolls. The market is held in the main street of Castlebar. It is paid for by those who bring their goods. All the neighbouring farmers and their wives bring something to be sold; eggs, butter, poultry, and such like. There is no covered place nor place of shelter. If goods are laid on a table in the street, twopence is charged; if an awning or any covering be erected over that table to keep the goods dry in a wet day, or to keep the sun off them in a hot day—(butter may be the article requiring protection—what a word that *protection* is!—to protect the Irish butter interest, free trade has been forbidden to touch butter)—if any article requires the protection of a covering when so exposed for sale, each person is charged double.

In the neighbouring town of Westport, where the Marquis of Sligo is lord of the land, of the town, and of all the power, the tolls and customs exacted under his patent are transferred to a religious society for the conversion of those who do not believe in the creed of that society. The operation to convert begins by exacting money for each horse's load, ass's load, and basketful of farm produce carried into the town and sold in the market-place; and, instead of making and mending roads, and keeping the market-house in repair, the operation converts this money to other uses. This is the beginning of the conversion, and it is the end. The middle portion of the operation consists of quarrels, falsehoods, cursings, revilings, jealousies, heart-burnings, hatreds, broken heads, and sometimes deeper crimes, to obtain the payment of, and to avoid the payment of, those unrighteous imposts.

Speaking of Mayo generally, Mr Cavendish says—

'Almost every year a state of starvation prevails among the poor in this county. It is not for want of provisions, but for the want of money to purchase them, there being little or no employment.'

There being no employment which affords wages, the next result is thus stated:—

'The great ruin of this country is the subdivision of lands in small proportions. Whenever a son or daughter is married, the father gives to each a portion; and as the families here are in general very large, he divides his holding into very small portions. The landlords find that they can collect their rent better by the lands being sub-divided. If they make a setting to one man he may not be able to pay his rent; but if the setting be made to several he may get a little from each. But the grand failure is in the want of confidence between the tenant and landlord; they are jealous of each other. The landlords do not grant leases in consequence of political feelings; if they grant leases the tenants do not always vote according to their landlord's wishes, and the landlords are, therefore, against granting leases.'

This refusal to give leases is not universal however. To control the tenant in his votes, and yet get him on the register to vote, which he cannot do unless he holds his land on lease, the expedient of keeping the lease in the landlord's or agent's possession is resorted to. In the county of Longford several cases were mentioned to me of agents having been paid what was called the 'lease money', years ago, for the leases, and that they still held them in their own possession. Some such cases were also sworn to before Lord Devon's commission, in some of which the agents gave up the leases in their possession to the rightful owners—the tenants—and excused themselves for having retained them for years by the plea of an *oversight*, though the tenants said that they had called for them nearly every time they went to Longford, which was once a week or once a fortnight.

Those agents being lawyers as well as rent collectors, I was at first inclined to think that the leases were retained in their hands because all the fees for drawing them might not be paid, or that they held them as collateral securities for bills discounted at the banks, or held them to have an advantage as to rent over the tenants at some future time. In some of those cases in Longford and the adjoining midland counties of Ireland, I found, however, on further inquiry, that the agents, being lawyers, they offered the tenants leases, and took the 'lease-money' from the tenants, though they knew that the landlords, their superiors, would not execute the documents nor grant leases. They, it seems, took the 'lease-money' for its own sake, and kept it and did no more, the tenants reposing under the security of parchment and stamps as they thought, but awaking at times to be thrust out upon the bare highway as tenants-at-will; calling for the leases at last to protect them from ejectment, and being coolly told that they had never been executed; seeking to recover the money which had been paid as fees or 'lease-money' years before for the execution of the documents, and being told that lawyers never do such preposterous things as return fees; and finding, when they proceeded to law with a man of unreturnable fees, having got some legal hawk to assist in pecking at that legal hawk's eyes, that the statute of limitations intervened, and that they got nothing, while the last penny or potato which they had in their hands when ejected for want of a lease was taken from them, and gobbled up by that second man of law, who knew all along that they could effect no good against the first man of law.

As I found it in Longford and the midland counties, so is it in the western county of Mayo. But here it seems the control of the tenant for political uses suggests the propriety of giving him his land on a lease, and keeping that document out of his own hands. A landlord looking to the improvement of agriculture, the social advancement of the tenantry, and the better employment of the labouring population, sets his farms to his tenants on lease to give them security, to make them feel that they may invest money and manure in the soil and have no fear. The Mayo landlords, it seems, or some of them, give leases to the tenants for the undisguised purpose of making them feel insecure, and in that feeling of insecurity become willing to vote as the landlords desire. To get workhouses built through political influence at £12,000 each, in the most inconvenient places, as my last letter shewed, and then refuse to pay rates or get them collected; to use the political influence to get commissions and promotions in the army—every body in Mayo, not a policeman, a peasant farmer, or priest, or parson, is a colonel, or major, or captain. Leases are granted to make voters; but they are held in landlordly possession and not by the tenants, lest the tenants do not vote for the landlord's candidate.

James Conry, Esq. master extraordinary in Chancery, and commissioner for taking affidavits at Castlebar, gave the following evidence before the Devon commission, on the 31st July 1844, on oath:—

'In cases where leases are executed they are more frequently withheld by the agent or landlord. The landlord executes the lease for electioneering purposes, and it is held in the possession of the landlord, and on the property of Lord Lucan; that is the fact; the leases are all in the office of Lord Lucan. There were a great quantity made in the year 1826; they are all retained in the office.

'What advantages can be derived from that?'—'If the tenant displeases the landlord in any way he can turn him out, and he has no title.'

'Would it not be in his power by a simple process of law to enforce the production of the lease?'—'It would be difficult for a man without means to do that.'

It would be difficult for a man without means to go to law with his landlord, and dangerous, whether to make him produce the lease held for a political use or to make him cease to exact tolls, customs, and market dues in Castlebar for family emolument. Mr Ormsby, the steward of Lord Lucan, denies this, and everything else sworn to by every other witness who says anything unfavourable to his Lordship; but the denials and the temper in which they are made only prove the general accuracy of the other witnesses, and make Lord Lucan look a worse landlord than he was before his intemperate steward rushed to his rescue.

Mr Conry also says that the farms are put up to a kind of auction, and there being *no employment of any kind for the people but on the land*, they bid against one another in the desperate hope of getting the land at any price. But it should rather be said that they *write* against one another.

'Generally, written proposals are sent in to the landlord, and those are held to be equivalent to an agreement, (when there is no lease;) for those documents are preserved by the landlord, and the tenant has nothing.'

Mr Conry also states that on estates where a number of tenants hold a farm in common, each being liable for the rent of the whole, and the whole for the default of one, instead of proceeding against them by distraint when some one of them falls into an arrear of rent extending to twelve months, which distraint would cost from £2 to £3, 'processes of ejectment are brought down from Dublin and served upon the parties, and a vast bill of costs run up.' The costs are as much as £20 in those cases. And those processes of ejectment are brought, though it is not always desired to get the tenants ejected. The agents are lawyers, or associated with lawyers, and they do this to obtain costs for their own emolument.

This explains why the enormous number of ejectment processes in the county of Mayo, recently spoken of in the House of Lords, were issued; and why Lord Lucan and others say in that house that processes of ejectment do not signify that the tenants were ejected.

19

LIMERICK, *22nd March 1847*

Though a previous letter was dated here, I have not yet described Limerick city and county. Even now the city must be omitted, but the county has pressing claims to notice.

Its greatest length from east to west is fifty-four miles; its greatest breadth from north to south is thirty-five miles. It is chiefly a plain lying south-east of the Shannon, gently undulating. The soil is fertile beyond anything that can be expressed in common agricultural language. With good roads in some parts, and the best of hard stone to make good roads everywhere; with intersecting streams that drive mills and make meal and flour; with other rivers navigable from the Shannon inland, with the Shannon, broad and deep, all along the western boundary, rolling to the Atlantic, with water more than sufficient to float all the ships of the world at once; with the city of Limerick situated on that river, containing docks and harbourage, and affording a first-class market for agricultural produce; with all those advantages, Limerick county is still a poor one, if we may judge it by the employment it gives to the population and the wages paid by its agriculturists to their work people, ninepence and tenpence per day in ordinary years; one shilling per day in this extraordinary year of high prices received for their corn and cattle; still a poor county, if judged by the enormous proportion of its people unemployed by its own resources; still poor, if judged by the common evidences of poverty and disorder, an overwhelming military force in the principal town, barracks for soldiers in the smaller towns, stations, seventy in number, for the armed constabulary in the villages; still poor, if judged by the crimes committed in the struggle to sustain human life on the smallest amount of food now, and on the worst quality of food always before now, which human beings ever subsisted on; but a rich country if judged by the amount of rent paid to its landowners, and by their grandeur of castles, parks, mansions, equipages, ancient family lineage, and new dignities outshining family lineage.

There is Sir Lucius O'Brien, and William Smith O'Brien, M.P. for the county, and other O'Briens, all descendants of the kings of Munster. There are several O'Gradys; and there is 'the O'Grady' of Killyballyowen. There is John Fitzgerold Fitzgerold, 'the Knight of Glin' Castle, Glin on the banks of the Shannon, very ancient; and next door to him, at Mount Trenchard, there is Lord Mounteagle, almost bran new. There is the Earl of Devon, owner, but, I regret to say, only as yet nominal owner, of a large tract of the very richest land near Newcastle. There is William Monsell, Esq. of Tervoe, who writes so fervidly in favour of a poor-law which shall authorize rates to be levied on each estate separately, according to the pauperism on that estate. And there is the Earl of Dunraven, his father-in-law, whose great estates are, like his own, so well cleared of population and paupers. There is the Earl of Clare, Lord Guillamore, Lord Clarina, Lord Cloncurry, Earl of Kingston, Lord Muskerry, and about a hundred other proprietors, resident and non-resident, for whose names and titles space is not allowable in these columns. One of them, Squire Westropp, may be named, however, as it was from a part of his estate that the sub-sheriff, constabulary, 55th infantry, and 8th hussars were employed about a month ago in ejecting tenants for the non-payment of rent.

And this fact recalls to my mind that the English Earl of S—— owns an estate in this county from which some years ago, before English newspapers took much note of Irish affairs, and before Irish papers dared to publish and comment on the acts of landlordism, 1500 persons were turned out homeless, landless, penniless, and potatoless, at the point of the bayonet, in one day. Mr Doolan of Fairy Hill, Portumna, county of Galway, formerly commandant of the police in Limerick county, told me a few days ago that he had the command on that occasion, and that he saw many of those people lingering on the roads and dying of want months after. Some of them are still paupers in the towns and villages.

Mr Doolan also stated, and authorized the use of his name in connection with it, that while in that command he was employed in obtaining evidence in cases of murder, and in paying the witnesses to go to America after they had given evidence. One case of murder was as follows:— A farmer was distrained upon for rent, and his potatoes, stored in a pit in the haggard, were under distraint watched by two keepers. The farmer's family had no other food but those potatoes. The keepers would not allow them to have any potatoes, the orders being against it. In desperation the family at last rose upon the two keepers and murdered them. They were tried and hanged, but not all at once. The father was hanged first; next two sons; next their mother was hanged; and at last one of the daughters. The whole expense of the trials and the rewards to witnesses was £10,000, for which Mr Doolan holds vouchers, and to the correctness of which he says he is ready to make oath. He says that his undoubting opinion is, that had the most ordinary feelings of humanity, simple fair play, been observed towards those people, no murder would have been committed. The two lives of the keepers would have been saved, and the five lives of father, mother, daughter and two sons, would not have been given to vengeance and the gallows. And there would have been saved £10,000, expended on a special commission, on different trials, on prosecuting, counsel, witnesses, and hangmen; besides the saving to England in not being called upon to augment the garrisons of Limerick and the other towns with additional cavalry, infantry, and artillery.

But the most extraordinary part of this drama of cruelty, vengeance, and judicial butchery, is probably this, that the owner of the property on which the distraint for rent was made and the murder committed, lived at the time in Yorkshire, lives there still, draws, it is believed, about £60,000 per annum out of his Irish estates, chiefly in the county of Limerick; has not been in Ireland once during the present century, though an Irishman born; and averred to Mr Doolan, on the latter paying him a visit a few years ago, that he had never, before Mr Doolan told him, heard of the distraint, the murders, the trials, and the executions; that he left everything to his agents, and that it was their business, not his, to know those things.

Mr Doolan was concerned, as commandant of the police, in another murder prosecution, for which there was a special commission which cost, with the outfit of the witnesses to Canada, £30,000—*Thirty thousand pounds* of national taxes, besides extra military expenses, for one murder; that murder occasioned by the inhuman conduct of an Irish landlord with the law of landlordism at his command.

Lord Devon's commission of 1844 did not receive evidence on any cases of agrarian outrage beyond a very recent period; nor did it take note of such cases save when they came out incidentally. Mr Doolan states that such cases as the ejectment of 1500 persons by the Earl of S——, which led to awful misery and crime, and enormous military expenses, could not occur now. The Earl of Lucan in the House of Lords, two weeks ago, doubted the truth of a statement made by Lord Brougham, that 400 ejectments had been effected in the barony of Tyrawley, county of Mayo 'because,' said Lord Lucan, 'there is now so much noise made about those things in the newspapers, I do not think so many ejectments could have taken place without us hearing more about them.' The fear of the newspapers is the reason given by Mr Doolan for such things being impossible or unlikely now.

My last letter from Mayo allowed some light to fall upon the ejectment cases in that county. To get rent for the landlords and to get the largest amount of cost for the agents are the causes of ejectments being brought against the small tenantry. They are brought in hundreds, though not intended to be carried into execution.

As to the impossibility of such a case as Lord S——'s ejection of 1500 persons being repeated now, because of the newspapers, I shall here relate a case not yet three years old, which the newspapers have allowed to pass with less notice than enough. It occurred in Suffolk, on Lord S——'s estate there, and exposes the injustice and evil working of the feudal privileges of land and landlords being permitted to exist in this commercial age of England.

Anne Manning, of Wangford, in Suffolk, was tried at Ipswich for setting her cottage on fire, and found guilty, and sentenced only to eighteen months imprisonment because of peculiar circumstances in the case. I was present at the trial, and, from what I heard then, I made inquiries, and ascertained these appalling facts:—

That it was customary for the Suffolk labourers to steal pheasants' eggs from one gamekeeper and sell them to another gamekeeper who was anxious to breed up a large head of game for his master. All of the labourers were habitually low paid in Suffolk, through their superabundance of numbers, as they are in Limerick, and through the waste of the corn crops by game and bad farming. Therefore, with low wages and inadequate employment, it became a trade eagerly pursued by the farm labourers, that of robbing the pheasants' nests and selling the eggs to the gamekeepers, probably to those from whom they had been stolen. One of Lord S——'s gamekeepers had lost so many eggs that he was afraid to face his Lordship. His Lordship was over here seeing his Irish estates, and sent notice to Suffolk what day he would return from Ireland. The gamekeeper dreaded that day the more the nearer that it came, and at last, in desperation, shot himself. The evidence on the coroner's jury found a cause for the suicide in the depression of spirits, arising from the loss of pheasants' eggs, and a consequent diminished number of birds. Another gamekeeper imitated the first, and also shot himself. One of the men who had stolen those eggs, the husband of Anne Manning, was committed to jail for three months, by the magistrates, for the offence. During his imprisonment, his wife, with a family of very young children, was left to her own resources at out-field labour for her own and their support, the wages for women at field labour being only 8d. per day. Her cottage rent, which had been paid weekly before her husband was catched stealing the pheasants' eggs, fell into arrear. The landlord of the cottage distrained upon the furniture for the rent, and upon a certain day the poor furniture was to be sold. The wretched woman became desperate, and said the furniture should not be sold. To prevent it, she set fire to the house. This was in June 1844, when incendiary fires were unhappily so common in Suffolk, when the madman Lancaster, convicted of some of those fires, urged others to kindle them, and excused himself for kindling them, because *it was for the good of the farmers and the landlords to burn the corn and make it scarce and dear!* And it was at the assizes at the end of July that Anne Manning was tried for the burning of her cottage, her husband in prison for the eggs, her little children in the workhouse. The late Mr Justice Williams was the judge; and it was reported through the courts and Ipswich at the time, that he declared himself unable, as a man, to pass sentence on that woman, as a judge. At all events he did not pass sentence on her. She was taken into the adjoining court, and Mr Baron Alderson sitting there, adjudged her to eighteen months imprisonment, a light punishment for arson; and even he was overcome with emotion as he did it.

But to quit Suffolk and its poor farm labourers, and return to Limerick with its poorer, where Lord S——'s estate, depopulated of £1500 persons in one day, is situated. I find in the Devon Blue Book, Part II. page 595, that a Mr Michael Byrne, in complaining of the county-cess being entirely paid by occupiers who have no control over its expenditure, says—

'The landlords will not pay one single shilling of the charges for repairing roads and bridges, and for the police and gaols and dispensaries. In the case of a new road, as in the case of Lord Stradbroke, made by the occupiers in the barony which it passed through, Lord Stradbroke did not pay one shilling, though it improved his estate 50 per cent.; they made roads through the mountains which improved the value tenfold—it fell upon the people totally unconnected with his estate; that I think very unjust. I must pay for all the improvements on Lord Portarlington's estate, though he does not pay one shilling. In the last session there were fourteen of the great people (voting away the money as grand jurors) that did not pay one shilling tax of the kind. They are benefited, but they do not pay the tax.'

'Do you consider that the tenants do not take into consideration the amount of the county-cess at the time they are proposing for land?'

'It is very little calculated. *They are so anxious to get into a farm, they make no calculation. They are anxious to get anywhere, whatever farm they can, and then struggle away.*'

In those *italic* lines is written the agricultural and whole social history of Ireland. They were uttered before the commissioners on the 15th of August 1844. Immediately following which Lord S——, who was in Ireland at the time, (in fact, it was this very visit in 1844, the return from which the gamekeepers in Suffolk so dreaded, the eggs being lost, that they shot themselves;) Lord S——, in a very angry tone, denied that the county-cess was spent in making the road through his mountain property as alleged by Mr Byrne. His Lordship says, Appendix B, page 53 —

'Some ten years since, £50,000 were granted by parliament for improving roads and opening lines in districts requiring them.'

He then proceeds to say that he expected a part of this money, but did not get any of it to make roads through his mountain property, though he went to the expense of having surveys made to plan where those roads should be. His Lordship adds that, for 'such persons as Mr Michael Byrne' to be bringing the names of landlords before the public who went to the expense of private surveys for private roads, expecting to get public money to make them, and who did not get the public money, is a very hard case.

It is clear that Lord S—— did not make the roads on his Limerick estate, he says so himself; and as they are made, I am inclined to believe Mr Michael Byrne's account of the source of the expense. The view from those very roads of the great plain of Limerick is thus described in the 'Hand Book for Travellers in Ireland,' published in 1844, by the Messrs Curry of Dublin:—

'In ascending by the *new* road which winds along the slopes of the hills, the eye ranges over one of the most extensive fertile plains in the kingdom, and in this fertile but wretchedly cultivated district, except the larger towns and demesnes there are few objects on which the eye can with pleasure repose. The numerous low clay-huts, exactly the colour of the soil, afford no relief, and the widely scattered seats appear as mere specks on the surface of the immense space. In the autumnal months, however, when the various corn crops are ripening, this bald, though from its extent, sublime scene is enriched by the golden colours of the waving grain.'

I quote this passage because I have not seen Limerick plain in harvest; and also to shew that other writers than myself call it 'fertile, and wretchedly cultivated.' This great plain of Limerick has had for many a year all the advantages enumerated at the beginning of this letter. It has landlords resident and non-resident, Saxon and Celtic, all of whom, or any one of whom, might have done whatever they chose—some of them have even manured the soil with human blood, all have done what alone landowners can do, thinned out the population; but still the fertile plain is wretchedly cultivated.

20

RATHKEALE

This is a town seventeen miles from Limerick, on the road to Killarney, containing 4201 inhabitants. It is a mile long, beginning on the top of a gentle eminence descending on the slope to the river Deel, which is navigable to the Shannon, and ascending the rising ground on the other side. It has a church, a Catholic chapel, some schools, a prison, a court-house, a barrack for soldiers, a barrack for police, a post-office, an hotel, some flour mills, a number of small shops, a fever hospital, and fever enough to fill the hospital until it runs over and drops out—drops out its dead into the grave-yards and fills them. It is a very ancient town, with old castles about it, and old legends, and has probably had fever from the earliest times until now, as it is only now that its street is getting a drain to carry the filth from places where filth never could escape from before, and where it lies, and runs and oozes out, to lie most odiously and pestilentially even now. This drain is being cut over the brow of the eminence through a hard rock, and formed wholly to the river at an expense of the Board of Works; in other words, at the expense of the general taxes.

The land around this town for several miles is a free fertile loam, easily cultivated, capable of bearing any kind of farm crop, affording rents varying from £2 to £3 per Irish acre, and well cleared of those obstructions called men and women, which are more formidable to the Irish landowner than the forest trees of the American backwoods are to the Irish emigrant. Yet the men and women are still so plentiful that the farmers can obtain the best of the men as ploughmen for £4 per annum and their diet in the farm house. Married men who live in their own houses receive 6d. per day and their diet of two meals per day. The best ploughing, ploughs, horses, and smartest workmen whom I have yet seen

in Ireland are now ploughing in the fields between Limerick and
Rathkeale, and to the distance of two miles beyond Rathkeale on the
opposite side. Going over those two miles we reach a country lying
chiefly in grass, and employing at the rate of four persons (at 8d. per day
for boys and 1s. for men) to each £400 of rent! The estate of
Cahermoyle, belonging to William Smith O'Brien, Esq., M.P. for the
county of Limerick, is one of the first met with in this direction, lying
almost in grass, entirely depopulated, and employing the population,
which are crowded into the villages and towns adjacent, at that rate and
that only. The Earl of Devon's estate is another in grass; but only some
of its farms are discultured. The whole of Mr O'Brien's are uncultivated.
They are chiefly large, well stocked with cattle, which, when fattened,
find their way to Cork and to England. The population of Cahermoyle
and the other estates are on the public works at 1s. 4d. per day; those
employed by Mr O'Brien in the demesne of Cahermoyle are paid only 1s.
per day, without diet, or any part of it. But as I shall devote a letter to a
full description of this and the adjoining estates, giving the rents, taxes,
wages, food, produce, and the prices of the produce sold, I shall not go
farther into those statistics at present, but return to describe that country
of matchless fertility lying between Limerick and Rathkeale. I cannot,
however, return from Cahermoyle, which is about five miles from
Rathkeale, without saying that, on the borders of Mr O'Brien's property
the most deplorable dwellings and the most appalling misery which I
have seen in Ireland is to be seen now; not on the Cahermoyle estate, for
this reason, that no population, not even to cultivate it, is allowed to get a
footing there.

Leaving Limerick by the road which goes south-west, taking us, if we
go far enough, to the lakes of Killarney, in the county of Kerry, and from
thence to Derrynane Abbey, and other remarkable places on the sea
coast, we go out by a street which in amplitude and elegance may be
classed with the best streets of any town or city in the United Kingdom.
And leaving that street behind, and with it Limerick, and losing sight of
the Shannon, and feeling as if there was room for heart-sickness because
the Shannon is out of sight—so beautiful upon the visual senses, so
suggestive with its broad waters, deep and clear, of contemplation deep
though not clear, of what such a river was made for, if not to be made to
do more for mankind than it has yet done, and of what it may and must
do for the mankind on its shores before many years are over; losing sight
of the Shannon and leaving Limerick, we have several miles of road of
such a breadth, hardness, and smoothness, as to be unsurpassed anywhere; though not always so ample in breadth, it continues good
throughout the county. The limestone rock, which abounds everywhere,

affords road metal of the best kind, cheaply and abundantly. That same limestone rock bears upon its surface a fertile soil, laid out in larger farms than we see in other parts of Ireland, and seemingly better cultivated. It also affords good building stones for the cottage dwellings of the county, and these dwellings we see in many parts standing with substantial walls and without roofs, the roofs having been taken off to get the indwellers out, as if they had grown too large within to be got out at the doors. They had, in fact, only held too tenaciously, somewhat as the limpet does on the sea-rock, which suffers its shell to be broken and itself exposed to death rather than quit its hold; the instinct of self-preservation being the same in the shell-fish of the sea-rock and in the tenant-farmer of Ireland, neither knowing how to live if they quit their hold.

Those roofless houses are more numerous as we approach Rathkeale, where the landlords have been making clearances more recently. The landlords who cleared the population from their estates ten, fifteen, and twenty years ago, have now large farms, with Scotch ploughs drawn by two horses each, held by Irish ploughmen who have been taught by Scotch ploughmen, and all signs of human wreck have been cleared away with the people who were wrecked.

That better cultivation prevails, with better rent paid to the landlords, and more produce sent to market on those farms that have been cleared, is undeniable; and the fact is not to be lost sight of, that the more produce that can be raised upon any estate with the least of it consumed on that estate, even if it be for the benefit of the landowner in the first instance, is for the national good ultimately. But this is not so if the consumers beyond the estate, who should eat and pay for that produce, are not profitably employed at work which enables them to pay for it. The Irish landlord sees his English brother Lord, or if he be an Englishman with an Irish estate, he sees his Irish estate encumbered with a dense population which eats the heart out of the soil, and he forthwith sets to work to clear the Irish estate, expecting to make it resemble that of England. He does not seem to know that the English land is 'cleared'—(I use the offensive word in reference to England, because it is the universal term, and appropriately so in Ireland)—by the manufactures and commerce of the country drawing the rural population to a more profitable from a less profitable employment. The English landowner is kept free of a population that would eat the heart out of the soil, and starve when too poor to cultivate it, not by any good act or design of his own, but in despite of all his class prejudices and class legislation. He has despised the trading and manufacturing people of his country, to whom alone he is indebted for not having his land over-run and over-eaten and swallowed up by a dense rural population like his Irish brother, and he has legislated against those people. The Irish landlord, or he himself on his Irish estate, following in the same course of destructive and anti-national ignorance, despises the manufacturers and traders, clears away the rural population by a force applied by himself behind, without regard to there being a place in the world for those people to go to, and not as in England by a force applied by others before them to draw them out and provide profitable employment for them. The Irish landlord also legislates for his class against manufactures and commerce. And yet these people who have been cleared by him from his estate, and who have found an outlet, and food, and life, beyond Ireland, have chiefly found the outlet through the commerce and manufactures of England, while nearly all the rent paid into his pocket, and carried away in his pocket, to be spent in whatever part of the world his own convenience finds a pleasant place, as a predatory bird carries its prey in its talons or its beak and flies aloft, or flies afar, to enjoy it at leisure, has come into his hands through the market provided for his farm produce by the people of England, who work and make wealth, but not upon the English land.

Such are the very different means by which landed estates are cleared in England and in Ireland. Irish agriculture is more profitable where the dense population is thinned out, the cleared soil being at the same time a fertile soil. But where is the right, legal or moral, human or divine, to clear away the inhabitants without making industrial provision for them elsewhere and elsewise than in agriculture? The right is not to be found even in the expediency which political economy would suggest, of providing a larger quantity of national food at a cheaper cost, because the national loss of having so many millions of the population dependent on charity and national taxes, and exposed to famine, and ever on the verge of social disorder, with a vast army of military and police ever required to check the disorder, is nationally a loss far exceeding the benefits derived from the larger quantity of national food produced at a cheaper cost.

But even the augmentation of produce for the markets does not always follow a thinning out of the population. In the first twenty miles of country seen from the public road south-west of Limerick the marketable farm produce has been augmented. The soil is so fertile and so easily worked, that it could not fail to give more corn to the market, the population on the soil being reduced, if ploughed and sown even in the most simple way. But to speak justly of the cultivators in that district, they seem to have advanced in agricultural progress far before the rest of Ireland, except, perhaps, a part of the county of Carlow. They are approaching the present agricultural condition of some parts of Suffolk and Norfolk, or that of the Lothians in Scotland twenty years ago. But this approach is only in the style of culture, crops, and rent; the wages of the ploughmen are not more than half, on some farms little above one-third, of the wages of ploughmen in Norfolk or the Lothians. The Limerick men are not able to work well from sheer emptiness of stomach, consequently their work becomes dear labour. The farmers and landlords who employ them are despisers of political economy, because political economists have denied the liability of the English tax-payers to support Irish paupers. Political economy while it proclaims the wrong of state provision superseding private exertion, and asserts the rightfulness of wages being regulated by the supply of workmen and the demand of labour, never teaches that a private employer of labour should give his workmen barely half enough of food, which results in his getting less than half enough of work. Political economy teaches a doctrine directly opposed to this. It teaches that the labour is cheapest which is best—that an article may be dear though it be low priced. It would teach the Limerick farmers and landlords that, though they can get labour done for 8d. per day, the supply of men being so much over the demand for them, and though they are under no *legal* obligation to pay more, it would be for their own profit to pay more and keep the workmen in a condition to work efficiently.

Political economy is in itself the very essence of humanity, benevolence, and justice. It is its conflict with selfishness, error, ignorance, and injustice that makes it appear otherwise to some eyes at some times.

Having left Limerick city behind us three miles, we pass Patrick's Well, a village named after St Patrick. Near it is Attyflin, seat of Squire Westropp; Greenmount, seat of Squire Green; and other parks or demesnes or pleasure grounds, with landlordly residents in them, named Fort Etna, Richmond, Jockey Hall, Kilpeacon, Maryville, and Faha.

On the seventeen miles from Limerick to Rathkeale we pass close to or near the residence of Sir David Roche, M.P., the ruins of Dunaman Castle and the round tower of Dysart, Carass Court, seat of Squire Browning, and Croom Castle, once a stronghold of the Fitzgeralds, and often besieged by their mortal enemies and near neighbours the O'Donovans. The war-cry of Crom-a-boo (Fitzgerald to Victory) which is still the motto of the Fitzgerald race, though that wild race is now headed by the tame Duke of Leinster, was derived from this castle and its battle-grounds around it. The Rev. Thomas Croker has repaired a part of this warlike ruin, and lives in it. Near it is Croom House, with Squire Lyon within. Not far from that is Islanmore, the nestling place of Squire Maxwell; and two miles from that is Cherry Grove, the seat of Squire Harding. Islanmore and Cherry Grove! there is poetry and prettiness in the very names; though the prettiness is not confined to the names.

But all of them recede to nothing in comparison with Adare Castle, its old Abbeys and Monastery, and village on the river Mague, about ten miles from Limerick, the seat and demesne of the Earl of Dunraven. Here we have broad meadows, and green uplands, and noble forest oaks, miles of them; and open glades and wooded thickets; the wandering river loitering in the woods before taking its course of six miles to the Shannon with the traffic of Adare through lands called the Golden Valley, but richer with yellow butter at all times and yellow corn in its season than if it were paved with gold; three abbeys of ancient times on the green banks of the loitering river, the shadows of their venerable towers upon the water; lofty trees around the towers, with colonies of rooks in the lofty trees, and ivy on the old grey walls, with birds innumerable in the ivy; one abbey restored from ruin and made a parish church; another restored by the same good taste and liberal hand, Lord Dunraven's good taste and liberal hand, and given to the Catholics as a chapel, to whom all the three belonged once; the third standing between the two, being converted into a mausoleum for the reception of Lord Dunraven's body when he dies. May he yet, as a living man, enjoy for many a year the repose of beautiful Adare, to which, as far as the reconcilement of adverse creeds can go, he has done so much—alas! that it should be so seldom done in Ireland! to give tranquillity.

21

ARDAGH, COUNTY LIMERICK.

This is a village of poor houses, forming two long rows, on a gentle slope from west to east, surrounded by a deep calcareous loam on limestone subsoil, some of it in tillage, most of it in pasture. Nearly all the houses are hovels, whose ill-built walls of stone and mortar, though stone and mortar are natural products of the district in measureless abundance, are falling or have fallen, and have been patched up again in every style of wall-building save the styles of elegance and strength. The houses not built of stone and mortar are made of clay, not so high in the walls as the others, and more crooked. The roofs of most of them are thatched, or have been thatched. From the absence of tillage in the district, straw to repair the roofs is not obtainable, and the inhabitants are all too poor to purchase slates. The landowners have no immediate personal interest in repairing those dwellings, or in building new ones, consequently they do not repair or build. On the contrary, they prevent, whenever they can, the erection of new houses. The overgrowing population must erect dwelling-places where the landlords cannot prevent them, which is in some narrow siding or nook of a public road, with no garden, yard, or haggard behind, or on some small patch of ground which belongs to a person who makes more profit by letting it be covered with clay-huts than he could obtain from it if covered with corn crops; or upon land held by lease from some head landlord, who, though he tries, cannot prevent the erection of new places of human abode.

In the last case the new places are usually seen behind the rows of old ones, when you can get through the old ones or round the end of the row to look behind. With low crooked clay walls, those huts of the married children of the parents who live in front, look as if they were stricken with age, and were decrepit and feeble, and not able to stand up; or, which is a fact as well as a similitude, they are crouching down behind for fear of being seen by the landlord or his agent. They are narrow and low for this reason; and as they are at first built to accommodate a youthful pair, newly-wedded, who are content to be in a small space, and who have not the means of adding many more feet of clay to the walls, the inducement to keep to a mere hut operates on every side. In due time, and frequently sooner, children accumulate, and grow in size and number, and they in their turn build huts behind, and have children, while still the old people, or the youngest sons and daughters of the old people, live in front. All have pigs and asses in the huts with them in ordinary times. They have not all pigs now, for the food of the pigs is no more; but all have dunghills and pools of stagnation in the narrow places between and at the end of the huts, and not unfrequently within them. That there should be fever and other diseases originating in filth, dampness, and foul air, is only a natural consequence at the best of times. That there should be an aggravation of those diseases and death with them now, when to filth, dampness, and foul air is added famine, is not to be received as a wonder, but as a natural result. The wonder is, if wonder there be, that gentlemen of wealth, humanity, and patriotism, possessing broad lands, and so much fresh air that they know not what to do with that great share of earth and heaven which has fallen to their lot, should deny their neighbours and fellow-creatures room to live and work.

The nearest and most remarkable landlord to this village of Ardagh is Mr William Smith O'Brien, M.P., Cahermoyle; his residence is about half a mile distant. The Cahermoyle estate is almost wholly laid down in large grazing farms, on none of which are the overgrowing population of

the district allowed to build houses; they have only the choice of going, and they must go, to Ardagh, and obtain leave to erect a hovel, in rear of the other hovels there, at an enormous rent, paid to the inhabitant of the hovel who permits the new comer to come; or they locate themselves in some nook of a field, or siding of a road, without a foot of ground, save what the clay-hut stands on. Mr Smith O'Brien permits none to settle on his estate in that manner, nor in any way else.

Part of his property is in the Newcastle poor-law union, and part of it in Rathkeale union. The portions of it in Newcastle union are rated for the poor at ninepence in the pound, there being two half-yearly rates of fourpence halfpenny each. His farms, which are in the Rathkeale union, are rated at tenpence in the pound per annum, only one rate for the year having been made there; while Rathkeale district, being more densely peopled, is rated at 2s. 6d. in the pound. Thus, the poorer district of Rathkeale pays three times more money for the relief of the poor than the rich grazing farms of Cahermoyle.

The entire population of Ardagh, and of the farms of Cahermoyle, and every other landed property, is employed on the public works, save five men who are draining within the demesne of Cahermoyle, and men and boys at the rate of about one full grown man and two half grown lads to 350 acres of ground. Those men and boys have only been kept on the farms and prevented from going to the public works by being hired for the year. The wages on the public works have been 1s. 4d. per day. They were not paid by piece-work, but at 1s. 4d. per day overhead, married and single, weak and strong, all alike. The farmers have not given higher wages than 10d. per day, that being 2d. more than the wages given previous to this year. The men hired by them are paid, the highest, £1 per quarter, or £4 per annum, with diet in the farm-houses. But a man receiving £1 per quarter is a first-rate ploughman or herdsman; the more common rate for hired men is 15s. per quarter, £3 per annum and diet. The boys receive from 5s. per quarter up to 10s. according to their strength. The ploughman of Mr Barry, a tenant farmer, told me that Mr Barry's service was considered the best in Ardagh parish; it was a most excellent house for diet; they had meat twice a week. None of the other farmers thereabout gave their men meat at all, save perhaps once in six months. Mr Barry, he said, had a brother who had carried on business in England, in Ipswich, had recently died there, but had made a small fortune before his death. In visiting him in Ipswich, the Irish farmer had seen the Suffolk ploughmen getting bacon to eat, and as they performed at least double the work that the Irish farming men did on their potatoes and milk, he very wisely thought his men would work better if they had better diet. So he gave them pork or bacon; and this is the 'meat' which the grateful ploughman who told me of the circumstance eats twice-a-week.

If two lads at 5s. and 10s. per annum respectively, and one married man at 6d. per day and two meals of potatoes and milk on each working day, are constantly employed on a farm of 200 acres statute measure, with a few extra hands at the time of planting potatoes in March; at the time of hay-making, in July; at harvest, say three weeks in September; and at potato-digging, say a fortnight in October, the wages of the extra hands at those times being 1s. and 1s. 4d. per day with diet; that farmer of 200 acres giving such an amount of employment is considered to be, and comparatively is, a liberal employer. But it is rare to find such an employer. The great overplus of population not so provided for hire conacre for potatoes, or shift in some other more miserable way than on conacre.

Mr Smith O'Brien employed some men in the winter of 1845, as a relief for the potato failure of that year, in making a road through the demesne of Cahermoyle; he paid them 10d. per day. The men whom he now employs in draining the demesne are paid 1s. per day, which is 4d. less than the pay on the new roads, which are being made in various directions on and around his property by the Board of Works. As the farming men only remain on the farms who are hired by the year and dieted in the farmers' houses, and they do not all remain, the 1s. 4d. per day of the Board of Works being a temptation too strong for them to resist, and as the expense of providing them with meal at 3s. per stone in the absence of potatoes is an inducement to their masters to let them go to the public works, in some cases to release them from their hiring to allow them to go, so the 1s. per day, the highest wages paid by Mr Smith O'Brien, only procures him men who have houses or conacre from him, and are bound to work for him.

With meal of Indian corn or of oats at 3s. per stone, labourers under the Board of Works on the roads around Cahermoyle are only able to procure 42 lb. 5 oz. of meal per week; which, divided among a family of five, or six, or seven persons, of which families there are many in small unhealthy huts in Ardagh and on the adjoining farms, gives an allowance less than can possibly sustain them in health, even had they wholesome dwelling-places to live in. But Mr Smith O'Brien has men working for him who live in such huts, with such families, and in greater hunger, for they have less food by one-fourth.

I was told that of five men employed in the demesne of Cahermoyle, four of them might be reckoned as employed there in charity. If they be so employed, the charity or relief is one-fourth less than that paid by government in the locality. But I demur to their employment being called charity or relief. They were performing work most necessary to be done—draining; work which, if done to the extent required on the Cahermoyle estate, should employ 200 men six months of the year for five years; an estate which, if cultivated as it should be to yield the greatest amount of produce for the food markets and of profit to the owner, should employ as many men per 100 acres as Mr Morton's Whitefield farm in Gloucestershire. The geology of Cahermoyle and Whitefield is the same. The present state of Cahermoyle is similar to the previous state of Whitefield. Weeds, rushes, inferior grasses, inferior cattle; utter waste of manure from the cattle; corn growing portions of the farms over-cropped and exhausted; potatoes planted for the one or two workmen on each farm to live upon as the chief part of their wages; these are the characteristics of the estate of Cahermoyle. These were the characteristics of Whitefield farm up to 1840, when Mr Morton entered upon it. The likeness of the two places extends farther. Cahermoyle, besides being on the same geological stratum as Whitefield, is seven miles from the Shannon. Whitefield is about seven miles from the Severn. Cahermoyle is twenty miles from the city of Limerick; Whitefield is nearly the same from the city of Bristol.

But here the likeness ends. Whitefield contains 240 acres; Cahermoyle upwards of 1000. The best land of the latter is superior to any of the land of the former, and constitutes more than a half of the whole; the best land, the alluvium, of Whitefield, is but a few acres; of Cahermoyle it is 400.

The expenditure for drainage, buildings, and useful roads on Whitefield was £7827. The expenditure on drainage on the farm land of Cahermoyle is nothing; that on the useful roads for improving the value of the land is nothing by landlord or tenants; the Board of Works, with the public money, is improving the farm roads.

Besides the sum of £7828 expended on permanent improvements on Whitefield farm by the landlord, the Earl of Ducie, Mr Morton, the tenant, has stock and working capital on it to the amount of £4500. The rent, before he took the farm in 1840, and before the capital was expended on it, was £200 per annum; tithe £33; poor rate £28; and road rate £4. The rent is now augmented to the amount of five per cent. upon £7828. The farmer calculates upon ten per cent. on his working capital of £4500; on £200 per annum, as remuneration for his personal services on the farm; on wages for ten men at twelve shillings a-week each, and on all the payments to keep implements and roads in repair. What he obtains over all those returns is profit. And he has had profit after all those returns.

I apprehend that such a man as Mr Morton is the true benefactor of his country, and that if Mr Smith O'Brien would turn his attention to his own property to enrich himself by producing human food from that land so naturally rich, now lying waste, he would be a patriot.

Since writing the foregoing, I have been on another farm of Mr O'Brien's where the natural quality of the soil far exceeds that of Gloucestershire. Mr Sheehy, one of his tenants, holding about 150 acres, at 24s. per acre, has only one lad in his employment, and not another person, not even of his own family, employed in cultivation. The land is just sloping enough to be of easy drainage; a stream of water runs through it fit for irrigation or machinery; the Board of Works has just made a road through the farm; a fine rich loamy soil all in grass and rushes covers the whole surface; the limestone rock is everywhere on the farm within two, three, four, or six feet of the surface; a kind of coal, excellent for burning lime, is found in the mountains within one hour's walk, and roads were made to it by government grants of money several years ago, and more roads are being made to it by government now; but no attempt is made, has been made, or seems likely to be made by Mr O'Brien to manufacture lime or bring lime to his farm land. The farm-buildings are clay huts, the roofs fallen or falling in; the fences are crooked mounds of earth with crooked ditches beside them; all manure from cattle runs waste into the ditches; the cattle lie in continual wetness, and are overtaken by periodical epidemics; but when fattened, (as fattened they are despite all the wreck and waste of the land, the soil is so rich,) they go to the contractors for the navy in Cork and to England to be sold.

Such is Mr Sheehy's farm, with only one lad, at 10s. per quarter of wages and his diet, employed on it; the other man, who has a family, and who used to be on the farm at 5d. per day and his diet, is now on the public works at 1s. 4d. per day.

On Mrs Nolan's farm, near Cahermoyle, rich grazing land, about 100 acres, one lad only is employed. Her second workman has also left and gone on the public works. She has a field unsown, and she has been waiting to see if the government would give her seed to sow. This farm, I believe, belongs to a Mr Studdert. But it is difficult to know who the landlords are. Smith O'Brien and several other gentlemen hold land as middlemen, at a very low rent, in this neighbourhood, under Dublin College.

Mr Patrick Power has a farm of about 240 acres. Some of the fields, I see, have been in tillage, and are laid down to rest to recover from their exhaustion. They lie thus without grass or crop of any kind, but weeds that rise spontaneously for five or six years. Meanwhile, all his cattle manure runs to waste; the cattle lie without straw or bedding to make manure; the roofs are falling in above them; epidemic diseases periodically destroy them; two women only are hired in summer to make the butter; only one lad at 10s per quarter is on the farm at present. The herdsman, Walsh, is on the public roads, at 1s. 4d. per day, with Mr Power's consent, and Walsh's mother, a widow, is doing the herdsman's work in payment of 30s. of house rent. I went with her to her house. It is three paces square inside; was erected by her late husband; the roof is propped up by poles standing in the middle of the floor. I had to crouch nearly two fold to get in at the door; the floor is a puddle hole; the roof is broken in; the daylight is seen through it every day; the rain comes through when there is a shower.

Three similar hovels, and no other houses are on this farm. They had all a few perches of haggard or garden, but since the failure of the potatoes in 1845 and 1846, the rent of 30s. each was not paid, and the haggards have been taken from them. James Muksey and Donovan, two of the cottier tenants of the hovels, are on the public works at 1s. 4d. per day. The highest wages they ever earned before was 8d. per day. Mathew Daly and his wife, another of the cottier tenants, are both sick of fever in their wretched hut, without fire, without food, without air or light, but what comes through the roof, which is nearly touching their fevered heads. Their wretched bed is on the wet puddle of the floor.

This farm, with those wretched people belongs to Captain Bateson, M.P. who voted the other day against the out-door relief clause of the New Poor Law. It adjoins Cahermoyle. The farm is valued for poor-rates at £1:1s. per acre; the rate is 10d. in the 20s. per annum.

Cahermoyle demesne, consisting of 150 acres, is valued at £185 for rates, and rented by Mr Massey for about £2 per acre for grazing. Wages paid upon that about £2 per annum and diet for one person.

Mr O'Brien's house and garden, and 14 acres of plantation, are valued for poor-rate at £70; the rate 10d. in the pound.

Mr Condin's farm, belonging Mr O'Brien, of 55 acres, is rated at £66. This, and a quantity of other land not on Mr O'Brien's estate, employs at present one youth at 10s. per quarter and diet.

Mr Magner's farm of 150 acres, rated at £190, is connected with other land not Mr O'Brien's. It has two persons employed.

The men usually employed on all of those farms at this season of the year are on the public works. The farmers say that none of the men are worth their 'keep' at present, 'keep is so dear.'

Mr Robert O'Brien, brother to the member for Limerick, gave evidence before the Devon Commission. The reader will understand the force of it after reading the state of those grazing farms, and I have given a picture of them considerably within the truth. Mr Robert O'Brien is agent for his brother, Sir Lucius O'Brien, in Clare; for his brother, William Smith O'Brien, Esq. M.P. of Cahermoyle; for their mother, Lady O'Brien; and for himself and other proprietors in Limerick and Clare. He states, Devon Blue Book, Part II. page 810:—

'If a pasture farm is converted into tillage, it may be taken as a sign that the tenant is going down in the world.'

The tillage farms, it seems, are carried on without capital; the grazing farms must have *some* capital. Whitefield farm barely afforded a living to its tenant and £200 of rent to its landlord when the working capital was only £3:2:7 per acre, and the wages of labour, part of it for a thrasher, was only £75 per annum. Now, exclusive of all wages for draining, building, and road-making, the sum of £312 per annum is paid in wages, though there is machinery for thrashing, for regular weekly hands, and the working capital is £19 per acre.

Mr Morton is a political economist, and as such pays 12s. per week to his men, though the current wages of the district are 8s. and 9s. He gets *better men* and *cheaper labour* by paying 12s. This is political economy.

Mr Smith O'Brien is not a political economist. No portion of his estate measuring 240 acres (the size of Whitefield) pays more than £20 per annum; and the capital per acre is under £3. Instead of trying to get better men, or to *make better men*, in order to have *cheaper labour*, by paying higher wages than the wages of the neighbourhood, as a sound economist would do, he pays one-fourth less than the government pays.

Mr Morton was an advocate for the repeal of the corn-laws, to enable him to carry on his farming with more economy and profit. Mr Smith O'Brien used all the power he possessed to preserve the corn-laws.

It was one of the commonest arguments used on his side of the question that land would go out of cultivation and become pastures if protection was taken away. In Limerick, and on his own estate, it is deemed a sign of a 'farmer going down in the world' when he brings his farm into tillage.

Mr O'Brien demands a repeal of the union, in order that Ireland may keep her produce and her wealth at home. He and his tenants send their cattle to England for sale; and they keep none of their produce at home for the people to consume, nor allow the people to obtain the means of consuming it.

Yet I was told, in the vicinity of Cahermoyle, that if all landlords were like Mr Smith O'Brien, Ireland would have no famine. Ireland would have no complaints; 'Sure everything would be kept at home. Sure it is more of Smith O'Brien's sort that would do Ireland good.'

In short Mr Smith O'Brien is expected to be able to bring 'the repeal' to them, but what the repeal is or will be they cannot tell.

Postscript, 29th March

The Board of Works is now reducing the number of men and the wages, in accordance with the last Treasury order. In all parts the wages are to be less on relief works than the current wages paid in the neighbourhood, to induce men to leave the relief works, and seek employment on the farms. The 'patriots' (Heaven save Ireland from such patriots!) exclaim against this cruelty of the imperial government, and they tell the people how differently an Irish parliament would have acted. It does not seem to occur to them that if they had raised the standard of wages in the neighbourhood, or if they raised them now, the relief wages would follow.

22

NEWCASTLE, COUNTY LIMERICK

This place contains about 3000 inhabitants in its streets, and probably 1000 more closely adjacent in clay huts; the huts standing in crooked rows, and huddled in some parts hut behind hut three deep, with only a narrow passage, filled with filth between them. Behind those huts are fields of grass, as fresh in March and as green as many English fields are in May.

Approaching the town from the direction of Limerick on the east, and from Cahermoyle and Ardagh on the north, the buildings look new, some of them handsome. The rows of huts have been cleared away; the small farms have been made into larger ones; the narrow lanes of the town have been widened into spacious thoroughfares; and a beautiful rivulet comes through the town, falling over ledges of limestone rock, fall succeeding fall, for the space of half a mile; while for a whole mile it is shaded by trees, the trees having the castle among them, and some smaller places of genteel residence.

This stream is beautiful to look upon. But it is large enough to make one feel pained that it is not something more than beautiful. It has no mill upon it to grind meal; all meal must be ground at a distance of ten or twelve miles from hence. Its water falls from ledge to ledge, gathering into broad deep pools, whirling and playing below the shadows of the trees, and starting away again, as if calling for those who look idly on to come and catch it; and again it falls; but the people only look at it; they do not respond to its invitation and go to catch it. This little river, called the Arra, goes on to the Deel, which is a river of magnitude, a mile and a half below Newcastle, and with the Deel it reaches the Shannon by a course of about twenty miles.

Newcastle had once a linen trade of small extent, and it still keeps a few looms going in coarse woollens. It had a bleach-field also for linen woven here and elsewhere, but that has disappeared. Its disappearance is spoken of bitterly. 'England took the linen trade from us, as she took everything else. She takes our corn and cattle, and she has our linen trade.' Thus did I hear consequential persons in Newcastle speak. 'Belfast and the counties in the north of Ireland have your linen trade,' I answered; 'they would take that river Arra from you also if they could convey it there; and depend on it, that if Belfast had those waterfalls which you have, she would make more linen than she does. As to England taking your corn and cattle, there is William Smith O'Brien, your popular member, and, next to Lord Devon, your principal landlord; *he sends* the cattle to England. As to corn, the same thing may be said; it is sold for rent. You have not even thought it worth while to erect a mill to grind corn, though possessing all that water-power to drive the mill. So far from the English people desiring to take your corn from you and leave you to starve, they sought to buy corn in other countries of the world to supply themselves, and struggled hard for many years for leave to do so, but Mr Smith O'Brien did all he could to prevent them, lest they might get enough elsewhere without taking it from you.'

'By gar! his honour is spaking like a gentleman. There is truth in that same about Smith O'Brien and the corn bill.'

'And do not you see, that with all his complaints about the government starving the people in these hard times, that he has been paying working men one-fourth less than the government has been paying them? Do not you see that his farms of 150 acres do not each give employment to more than one slip of a boy, at 10s. per quarter and diet—yellow meal now, potatoes and milk when there were potatoes—while the rent from the same land is nearly £200?'

'By gar! that is the truth, every word of it; and never a word of a lie.'

'Well, the English merchants, despite of Smith O'Brien and the monopolist landlords of both countries, obtained leave to look abroad for corn, and if they had had leave to try abroad for it much sooner, they would have been able to bring much more of it to England, and to

Ireland too, than they have done. But, as it is, they are fetching corn from all the world to Ireland, and Smith O'Brien and his rich tenants are sending their cattle to be sold and eaten in England. Cattle are the only products of his land.'

'And butter and pigs, and a few acres of potatoes afore the disease took them.'

'Very well, butter and pigs; they and the cattle go to England, not by the English forcing them from Smith O'Brien, but by his own free will. He does not allow you to get houses on his land, nor to get the land, nor to work upon it for wages, nor to eat its produce; and yet you say that if all the landlords and members of parliament were like him, you would soon be right enough; that Ireland would soon have her own. Do you mean her own landlords? for, if you do, the Earl of Devon, as an Englishman, who allows the small tenantry to have houses and holdings on his estate, will at least bear comparison with Smith O'Brien, who does not. His Lordship inherited the estate overwhelmed in debt, as you all know. The stewards upon it, of whom some of you have had reason to complain, were the stewards of the trustees. Since his Lordship got the property into his own hands, he has erected a tile manufactory to make drain tiles, and has begun to drain and improve the land by employing labour on it. He has gone but a small way compared with what should be done; but he has, at all events, done more than Smith O'Brien. Now the greater the number of landlords you have in your country who, with their servants, horses, and dogs, consume food and produce none, the poorer do they make your country.'

'But it is the parliament, your honour; the Irish parliament we are looking for to do us good.'

'If you are promised great and good things from the Irish parliament by those who bid you look for it and in whom you put your faith and trust as leaders, it is natural that you should expect the Irish parliament to be indispensable to your well-being. But, in the first place, your parliament, if you had it, would be entirely composed of landlords and lawyers, neither of whom have as yet done you any good service, but much mischief. The imperial parliament was until recently comprised of the same materials. The English commercial classes have, after long struggles, succeeded in changing the current of imperial legislation, a change vastly more important than changing the seat of parliament from one city to another. The representation in parliament of trade, intelligence, and toleration is now beginning to have the ascendancy in England. Feudalism and territorial representation is on the decline. It will decline more and more in England every year; but you would restore it in Ireland by an Irish parliament of landlords and law-jobbers. You

have no middle class to control them. It is to the new current of
legislation from the commercial classes of England that you must look for
real substantial benefits to Ireland.'

'Sure the English manufacturers are jealous of Ireland; they would not
let her wave one yard of cloth or make a shoe for her own foot, if they
could prevent her.'

'Not true, my friends; it is the converse of true. The old suicidal
system of protection by which the feudal representatives legislated
proceeded to bolster up the trade of one place at the expense of another.
Lord George Bentinck for England, and Mr Smith O'Brien for Ireland,
are the representatives of that barbarous system of legislation now. And
you confess that if you had an Irish parliament you would protect
yourselves from the manufacturers of England. By so protecting yourselves you could only make yourselves poorer. England is all the poorer
for her barbarous legislation, having once attempted to protect her
manufactures against those of Ireland. Such a system is one of mutual
robbery in the first instance, and mutual suicide at last. If every man and
woman in Ireland wore a fresh change of Irish linen every day; if they
had as many new garments in a year as they have holes in the old ones; if
they made leather and boots and shoes to walk, and iron and railways to
ride, and manufactured as largely for themselves in Ireland as the people
of Lancashire and Yorkshire do, England would transact business with
Ireland to an extent immeasurably greater than she can now do when
Ireland is poor. English ships from India and America, instead of putting
into Kinsale or the Cove of Cork in passing, for water only, or for
shelter, would put in to deliver cargoes of sugar, tea, silks, and other
things, rich and rare, rich over all the world, rare in Ireland, and they
would reload with Irish manufactured goods.'

'But what if Ireland had ships of her own?'

'All the better; the more ships the more trade; ships create trade.
Ships are to commerce what ploughs are to agriculture; if you had Irish
ships ploughing the ocean, and Irish ploughs ploughing Smith O'Brien's
land, both Ireland and England, and you and Smith O'Brien, would be in
better circumstances than you have yet been in. As to jealousy, you
might as well suppose that England and Scotland would be jealous. As to
ships, you might as well think that if Glasgow had none, and no trade,
that Liverpool would have more ships and more trade. But Liverpool
would suffer greatly if Glasgow ceased to have ships and trade. In like
manner, Liverpool would be greatly benefitted if Ireland was covered
with manufactures, and had her shores swarming with ships. That
narrow policy of protection is now powerless; its office was never
anything but mischief; the English trading classes have overthrown it in

defiance of such territorial legislators as Mr Smith O'Brien. England repudiates the assertion of the Irish repeal politicians, that she was ever benefitted by the barbarous legislation which sought to protect her manufactures against Ireland. She and Ireland were mutually injured. England asks Ireland to protect herself against such bad legislators as the feudal owner of Cahermoyle. The condition of his own estate should be a warning to people who would trust him with the remodelling of a nation.'

Such is the substance of a conversation held in Newcastle, in the county of Limerick; other topics were included, for which I have not space here. I have only space to say, that the estate of the Earl of Devon here is part of the great territorial possessions once belonging to the Irish Earl of Desmond. For an Irishman, as such, to lament that an English Earl should have been substituted for an Irish Earl, is natural enough. It was a wrong policy of that faction in England which has always held the government—the landed faction—to do so; but now that the deed has been effected for some centuries, and it is seen that the ancient race of landlords do no more for their land than the new race, it becomes the Irish people to look to something else for redemption than to landlord-ism.

23

NEWCASTLE, COUNTY LIMERICK

I have written a letter from this place already; but as the subject of this one is somewhat diversified, I send it too. I got a man named Michael Hearn to go with me one day on a pedestrian ramble among the farmers and poor cottiers, over the plain and up the mountain, and I shall here relate what we saw. First, however, of Michael Hearn, as he was a type of a very large class.

He rented about twelve statute acres under a Major Campbell of Scotland, whose property here lies intermingled with the Earl of Devon's and Mr Smith O'Brien's. He had been all the winter working on the public works; but was discharged when the New Relief Act came into operation on the 20th of March, he being a farmer. He had sown two and a half acres of his land with oats, and, having no more seed, had sublet the remainder of the ground for the season. He had a wife and eight children. She and seven of the children were in the workhouse and the fever hospital. His eldest daughter, aged seventeen, remained with him on the farm, but also lay ill of fever and dysentery. He said he had two sisters in London, and did not know what to do unless he put the bed and bedding in pawn, locked up the house, and took his daughter with him, when she recovered, to her aunt's in London, and put over the summer that way, at such work as he could get in England, leaving his family in the workhouse until he returned, and his farm, a rich fertile loam on limestone subsoil, to the care of the person who had the crops for the present year.

He showed me, as we passed along, a field where evictions took place twenty-two years ago, in reference to which the threatening letters signed 'Captain Rock' were first issued. Then he told of a murder that followed; and shewed me where five persons were all hanged in a row at once for that murder.

We next called upon, and were accompanied by, Cornelius O'Donnell, over his little farm of about fifteen statute acres. He is a tenant under Lord Devon, and has his farm in much better order than those of his neighbours, large or small. He drained it with sod drains three feet deep, some of it twenty years ago, some of it recently. The sod drains of twenty years ago were running as freely as new tile or stone drains, which I was surprised to see, but I doubt of all sod drains lasting so long.

One of the new roads of the Board of Works had gone through his farm; it was left unfinished, and he seemed much aggrieved at not having proper fences put up where his pasture field was divided by the new road.

We next proceeded over Cloghdeen farm, of ninety-four Irish acres, which are about equal to 153 statute acres. One of the new roads runs partly through this farm, and continues on one side of it for about half a mile, the farm being long and narrow. The land is almost wholly in pasture, very wet, and full of rushes. It is gently sloping, and could be easily drained in every part. A stream runs through the centre of it, laying bare the limestone rock at the general depth of six or eight feet. On this stream there was once a mill, alleged by Michael Hearn to be 900 years old, and erected by the Danes. It had been laid in ruins and covered up. Part of the water-wheel was dug out of the ruins not long ago. It is of hard oak, and is preserved as a curiosity. The stream does nothing now but wimple over its blue stones, wash the ankles of the bare-footed maidens while they wade in it after their cows, and carry away the farm-yard manure. The farm belongs to Mr Smith O'Brien, and does not give employment to any person but the farmer, a 'slip of a boy,' and a female who makes butter. The soil is a calcareous loam of the best quality, but everywhere undrained and overrun with foul vegetation.

At the west end of it, by the side of the rivulet, is a circular mound of earth said to be the remains of a Danish fort. The Danish water-wheel was found about a mile from this fort, and many human bones, supposed to be the remains of Danish soldiers, have been found.

Cloghdeen farm remains undelved and untouched by spade or shovel; not so this fort. It had the reputation of holding crocks of gold somewhere in its earth works, and many a spade and pick have been at work digging for the gold. Near a tree on the east side, Michael Hearn pointed to a place where the people went in great numbers to dig two or three years ago, in consequence of 'a boy, named Hugh Ward, draming he seen the gold there. He lived in Newcastle then, he is now gone to London. Sure the drame was true and had to do with it, for the people got the tokens, when they dug wid their spades, that the boy seen in his drame. It was a horse shoe and four nails he seen. By gar! they dug, and sure enough there wor the shoe and the four nails; the tokens wor found anyway; but they dug down and down, and all back here, but they did not get the gold. Ah, sure it was God's will, praise be to his name, they wor not to get it.'

The reverence with which these poor flesh-worn peasants speak of sacred things is very remarkable. Michael's hand was instantly at his old hat, and the hat lifted as he spoke the last sentence. Sometimes I talk with a dozen or a score of poor creatures in some wretched cabin, where, seeing me enter, they soon gather together to ask questions. No question is more frequently put to me than this, 'Now, your honour, is the potato gone entirely do you think? Will it ever come back to us to grow as it done before?' To which I usually say, 'I have no fear but we shall have sound potatoes again; every law of nature or ordinance of God known to us justifies that expectation.' The moment they hear me speak the sacred name every hand is lifted to the old hats, and when the sentence is concluded, they say in a low, solemn tone, 'Glory to his name!'

Leaving the Danish fort on Smith O'Brien's estate (the people pronounce this name as if written *O'Breyne*) we proceeded through other farms, all in a state of nature and waste. The only sign of a landowning hand upon the property for any good purpose was a school-house conspicuous from its situation and white-washed walls, built by Lady O'Brien, the mother of the member for Limerick county.

A cross section of hills was half a mile before us, running from south to north, our faces being to the west. In a wooded ravine or recess in the hills was a white house of genteel appearance occupied by a Mr Lake, who holds a number of good sized farms on leases for ever, from a family of Maunsels who again hold them under some other chief. The farms are sublet by Mr Lake, and hardly one furrow had been at that time turned up. The tenants of ninety acres had been working on the relief works up to the 20th of March.

Having expressed much interest on the subject of digging in the earth for gold, I was shewn, at a distance, a place in the wood on the face of the hill fronting us, near Mr Lake's house, where people had dug for gold. The last time any one had tried it, he said, an awful noise was heard in the wood, like a bull roaring, and the wind rushed and made a noise in the trees different from any noise ever made by the wind before that anybody had heard. They left off digging and came away, and the noises ceased.

At another place to which he pointed there was a round spot on which snow never lay in winter, and which never had dew on it when dew was on the grass around; the people went there to dig for gold, but the fumes of sulphur came up out of the ground and they took warning in time and left off.

There is a stratum of coal found in that hilly ridge, containing a great deal of sulphur. Probably the gas escapes from it through the earth at this spot, where snow melts and dew never lies.

But there was still another place where they had gone to dig for gold. Here is Michael's account of it.

'A man in the north of Ireland had a drame that he had seen the gold at this place, (Ballygule), just nine miles beyont there. He came all the way from the north of Ireland in a carriage, and at once knew the place when he seen it, from the drame he had. He offered to find the gold if the man the land belonged to would let him have whatever share he chose to take of it. The man the land belonged to in his turn would not let the man from the north of Ireland have any share more than just what he would think fit to give him; and, by gar! without ever pointing out the place where the gold was hid, the man from the north of Ireland, when he seen the other so hard with him, put his two feet in his carriage and drove away, and has never been seen again at Ballygule, and nobody knows who he wor.'

I told Michael and some of his neighbours that I knew better than any of them seemed to do how to find gold by digging for it; which, with my persevering inquiries as to the localities of iron and coal, and the boundaries of estates, led them to understand me literally. In the sequel I found the supposed profession of that knowledge of gold finding in the soil, by digging for it, troublesome. 'The man who owned the land at Balygule,' and who would not make a fair bargain with 'the man from the north of Ireland,' came all the way to Newcastle to know if I really was a gold finder. Michael Hearn and his neighbours had spread the report so industriously, that several came every day during my stay at the Courtenay Arms. Smith O'Brien's tenant, Mr Sheehy, who occupies the farm containing the Danish fort, so foul and wet though fertile soil, had seen me writing down the particulars told about the fort, and 'Hugh Ward's drame, and the horse shoe and the four nails'; and he also came to me at Newcastle, 'to know did I think I could find the gold.' He was followed by others; and I thought it time to tell all of them that it was in draining, trenching, delving, squaring, manuring and cropping such land as Mr Sheehy's farm that the gold would be found.

From an elevation approaching to the most learned dignity, I instantly fell to the level of the commonest of themselves. Any of them knew that, they said; but how could a poor farmer do all that I said should be done to the land.

I replied that Mr Sheehy was not a poor man, he had a large farm and had the reputation of being rich. He very promptly told me that though he had a few cows more than his neighbours, he was only a yearly tenant. I could not expect him to sell his cows to get money to pay for digging and draining the land, when he might be turned out of the farm as soon as it was drained.

'Mr Smith O'Brien will not do that,' said I, 'will he?' 'I do not say he would,' replied Mr Sheehy; 'but it is the common thing for landlords to put out a man from his land, or put up his rent, whenever he sees him doing the land or himself any good. It is the rent the landlords look for entirely, and nothing else.'

There was no argumentative reply to that position. 'And so,' I responded, 'your landlords not only prevent you from digging for gold, and from finding it in the only hiding places in which it can be found, but in addition to this, they kill your goose that lays the golden eggs— rob the farm yards of the farm stock, turning the farmer out a pauper on the roads, they knowing that, from the excessive competition for land, they can immediately get another tenant with another goose to be killed for its golden eggs!' To which some of them responded, 'Be dad! that same is the truth his honour is telling yez.'

Going up the hill, another place was pointed out by Michael Hearn where gold has been dug for, 'And the crocks that held it wor found; there were three of them; but all full of worms. The gold had been excommunicated, and it was turned to worms.'

Crossing an upland stubble field, I found the son of the tenant of ninety acres, already alluded to, at the plough. He had been at the public works up to the previous week, and was only now beginning to plough the oat stubble, which had carried two crops without manure, to sow oats again. The liquid manure of the cows and yards on this farm, and most of the solid washed by the rain, was running to the streams and rivers. The young man left the plough and the horses standing in the middle of the field, and went up the hill-side with me, where the Board of Works had been making a road in the slaty rock winding up to the turf bogs four or five miles. His purpose in going with me seemed to be to shew how deceptive the slatey rocks were which they had been cutting down at so much a yard, there being hard places where they had not been able to make half as good wages by the yard as the men working by the day.

His father held the land under a tenant who held from a Mr Massey. The lease was thirty-one years and some lives. All the years had expired and all the lives save one. That life was now old. He said if that life was out he would get a new lease, and he hoped a new under-landlord. His father would offer double the rent he now paid, which was about 12s. per statute acre, on condition of getting the land drained. But at present neither the tenant under Mr Massey nor Mr Massey would do anything 'until that old life was out.'

Higher on the hill sides we found smaller holdings and a more numerous population. The measure of land there was a 'cow's grass'. The extent of land called a cow's grass differed according to quality. Its rent was £3:10s. A man named Thomas Killaheel and two children, boy and girl, were digging oat stubble. He held two cows' grass under Mr Lake. He had only two pecks of oats for seed. This man was tall; his children were tall for their age; all three looked like spectres with spades in their hands. I have seen other such sights, but none worse. Their purpose was to dig for life, but they looked as if breaking ground for their own burial, and as if a very shallow grave would serve them, they were so thin. The poor man shook his head when I spoke about his getting seed from his landlord. 'There were too many landlords above his little piece of ground,' he said, 'all trying to get something out of it; none of them would *give*; they would only *take*.'

We left him and went to the top of the hilly range to see the turf bogs, and have a view from thence of the great plain of Limerick and the distant waters of the broad Shannon, lying on the green plain, in colour and shape as if all womankind had been washing and had chosen the plains of Limerick, Clare, and Kerry, to spread down their linen to dry.

I looked behind me, and there stood the phantom farmer, Thomas Killaheel, who had followed us up. He said nothing, but looked—oh! such looks, and thin jaws!

We went on through intricate passes in the bogs; and my attention was directed by Hearn to the district of iron and coals, the latter within a mile of us, the iron supposed to be everywhere through fifty miles of hilly country. I turned round to take the measure of those mountains of

treasure with my eyes, and there again stood the lean hungry man. He caught at my words when I said a mountain of iron was worth more than a mountain of gold, and said, 'Sure the gold will buy more bread than the iron would?' 'But,' said I, 'the iron would make better spades and ploughs to till the ground and make corn grow, and corn must grow and bread be made from it, before it can be purchased with gold.'

The lean man looked as if his spirit, starved in his own thin flesh, would leave him and take up its abode with me. I even felt it going through me as if looking into the innermost pores of my body for food to eat and for seed oats. It moved through the veins with the blood, and finding no seed oats there, nor food, searched through every pocket to the bottom, and returned again and searched the flesh and blood to the very heart; the poor man all the while gazing on me as if to see what the lean spirit might find; and it searched the more keenly that he spoke not a word.

On our return, half way down the hill side to his field, his two spectre children still stood leaning on their spades, which spades being long and narrow—only four inches broad, with handles six feet long—looked like spades made for spectres to dig with. His piece of land *is* sown.

We went into one of the numerous clay huts on the hill side to rest after a very long walk. An old woman was spinning flax. She was aged about fourscore, and could only speak Irish; yet by the aid of Michael, my interpreter, we held a discourse which she seemed well pleased with, so far as I could tell her what she desired to know about the Queen and London. She had two grand-daughters with her, young women, one of them a beauty, both barefooted and very meanly dressed, poor things.

But in respect of beauty in a clay hut, I saw it in another house where Michael took me to get a drink of milk. One of the finest looking women of the English aristocracy is a duchess whose portrait has appeared often in the fashionable annuals. In this clay hut, with a baby four weeks old at her breast, on a stone at the turf fire, sat a young woman, wife and mother, a fac-simile in features and shape of head of that duchess, but younger by sixteen or eighteen years. She was considered to be comfortably married, as her husband and his people had some substance. The milk which I got bore evidence that they had a cow, as did the cow's stall on that side of the floor, two yards behind the beautiful young mother. A horse, which stood on the opposite side, with his hind feet two yards and a half from the hearth-stone, and his head haltered to the wall at the window, was another symptom that they were not the poorest of people. There would have been a pig had there been potatoes. An elderly woman, Michael's sister and the husband's mother, said, speaking of the baby, 'He has come to us in hard times; but may the times be better before he knows them, an it plase God.' To which Michael lifted his hat reverently and said, 'Glory to his name.' And the beautiful young mother, sitting on the stone among the ashes, turned her lustrous eyes to the low black roof of the hut and said, 'Glory be to his name,' and then kissed her baby. Her mother-in-law followed both by the word 'Amen!'

24

CASTLE ISLAND, COUNTY KERRY

This is a small town which we reach, and feel glad to rest at, after traversing the mountain district which unites the counties of Kerry and Limerick.

Kerry contains within it the lakes of Killarney and the mountains which raise their heads to the clouds, to the ceiling of a roof almost too low for them to throw their shadows down into the lakes. I saw one of those mountains a short while ago with his head through a cloud which seemed only an old hat to him. Carran-tual is the name of that mountain. He is 3414 feet high. On the ocean coast other mountains rise hardly inferior in height. Glens and valleys lie between them, and in some parts the Atlantic Ocean has washed away, or, in that everlasting hunger which knows no filling, has eaten away the glens and valleys for many miles inland, and made seas where once there was land, leaving the higher and harder mountain ranges for other times.

Kerry, with its western front to the Atlantic, is bounded on the south by Cork county, on the east by Limerick and Cork, and on the north by the ever-glorious Shannon. From east to west the length is fifty-eight miles, and from south to north the breadth is fifty-four miles. The surface contains 1,186,126 acres, of which 414,614 are arable; 726,775 uncultivated; 11,169 in plantations; 807 in towns, and 32,761 under water.

The subsoil is slate and red sandstone in the higher, and limestone in the lower districts. Copper and lead are found in several places; iron ore abounds in most parts of the county.

In 1841 the county contained 18,332 horses, 103,366 horned cattle, 93,703 sheep, 52,914 pigs, 314,567 head of poultry, and 3304 asses; all estimated at £1,004,419.

The population in 1841 was, rural, 269,406; town, 24,474; total,

293,880. The occupations are, dairy farming, tillage, and fishing; the chief crops, previous to the potato failure, were potatoes and oats. Green crops have in a few, very few instances, been grown; but the universal practice is to let all manure run to the rivers and the sea. The chief towns in Kerry are Tralee, Caherciveen, Dingle, Kenmore, Killarney, and Listowel. Some of these are only large, ill-shapen villages, which have outgrown their best houses as their individual inhabitants outgrow or outlive their clothes, and fall into a state of rags. This village of Castle Island became so worn out a few years ago, that its proprietor was at last ashamed of it, and gave it some new houses.

That proprietor is one of the Herbert family, sprung from the Herbert of Queen Elizabeth's time, who obtained this village, castle, and country, and most of the district about Killarney, including Muckross Abbey. One of the Herberts of the present day was foreman of the Kerry grand jury two or three weeks ago, and introduced and carried the same resolutions to address parliament on the present crisis of the country which originated with the Limerick grand jury. The last of the resolutions stated that the parliament being more immediately connected with England, English interests flourished under its fostering care, while Irish interests were neglected.

Now, if there is one error of Irish opinion more palpable and unjustifiable by any act or ground than another it is the error of supposing that English agriculture flourishes by something which the parliament does for it. Mr Herbert has copied the English form of leases to his tenantry with the covenants set forth in Woodfall's book; those covenants have not one redeeming element of common sense in them. They are adopted or imitated in Galway and Roscommon by Lord Clancarty, the most practical landlord in Ireland; and yet his leases, as do those of Lord Palmerston in the county of Sligo, read like a sarcastic chapter from *Punch*, the only thing about them to make you feel that they are not from *Punch* is their great length and absolute want of meaning. The law-jargon of those leases is hopelessly unintelligible.

Such are they which Mr Herbert's land-agent calls, in his evidence before the Devon Commission, 'the simple leases of England.' They have adopted at Castle Island and Killarney those 'simple' leases of England for a number of years: yet still their agriculture languishes and rents are not well paid; while in England, *they say*, agriculture flourishes and rents are well paid. This, they think, must be because the English farms are nearer to parliament, and parliament must, by that proximity, do something good to them, which, from its distance, it cannot come to Kerry to do.

The fact is, that in so far as the English agriculture exceeds that of

Kerry, it is in defiance of those most stupid and pernicious covenants in the leases, or in the yearly agreements. The agent of Mr Herbert of Kerry was questioned pointedly about the covenant requiring the tenants to preserve the game, and he said no ill effect had arisen from that covenant; that it was not peculiar to Mr Herbert, but was copied from the English leases, where agriculture flourishes.

Now, it so happens that England has a Mr Herbert for a landlord; he too is an Irish landlord. He will be England's next Earl of Pembroke, if he lives till the present Earl dies. He is a member of parliament at present; an agricultural member, the representative of Wiltshire, recently a member of the cabinet, a gentleman of more than ordinary talent, and able and willing, one may suppose, to do those good offices to the English tenantry which the Kerry grand jury and the Kerry Mr Herbert in particular, supposes parliament to do. Here is, however, what Mr Sidney Herbert of England really does for Wiltshire agriculture. I know every tenant and acre of ground in the district of his residence at Wilton, and happen to have with me some letters written by and on behalf of the Wilton tenantry. This is an extract:—

'Mr John Williams of Ugford had the damage done to his crops in 1844 by Mr Herbert's game valued by three professional valuators, and they set the damage down at £70. This occurred on 140 acres of ground. Mr Herbert's agent offered £30 for the damage, which was at first refused, but ultimately accepted. In 1845, the damage to barley by the birds, and to the turnips and clover by the hares, was valued at £100; Mr Herbert paid no compensation.'

It would be out of place to give such extracts at length here. But to any person thoroughly acquainted with English agriculture it is notorious that the farmers are debarred from adventuring in good cultivation by the absurd covenants in their leases, or in their yearly agreements. To any one thoroughly acquainted with the sources of English industry and wealth, it is a fact, clear as the lakes of Killarney, that all industry has thriven best which has been least interfered with by parliament. Agriculture lingers behind every other industrial science in England, and in many counties it has advanced not one step since the days of Elizabeth, who sent the Herberts to Kerry. It is only more profitable than Kerry with heavier taxes on the cultivators and their landlords than Kerry bears, because two-thirds of the population of England give value by their industry to something else than agriculture, and obtain thereby the means of buying the farm produce from and remunerating the agriculturists. It is not by parliament or by the fostering care of their landlords, but in opposition to the cumbrous enactments, erroneous policy, and frivolous pleasures of the parliament and the landlords that the tenant-farmers of England pay the national taxes, heavy poor-rates, and heavy rents. The iron ore of England, and the copper and the lead, do not lie in the earth to be sung about only by poets, or at most talked of by politicians not less dreamy than the poets, as in the mountains of Kerry.

One of the landlords of this county is Pierce Mahony, Esq. the Dublin solicitor engaged for the defendants in the great state trials of 1843 and 1844. Being aware that Mr Mahony was professionally engaged to bring before the Devon Commission evidence of the comparative superiority of Scottish agriculture over that of Ireland, together with the cause of that superiority, I have looked into his statements with some attention. The chief cause which he finds for the prosperity of Scottish agriculture, as might have been expected, is 'the expenditure in Scotland of public money.' The Caledonian Canal and the Highland roads and bridges are his instances. Now the agriculture of Scotland would have just been what it is if all the money expended on the Caledonian Canal had been sunk in the sea. The same cannot be said of *all* the Highland roads and bridges, but of very nearly all. The agriculture of Scotland is not within the range or influence of those communications. The best cultivated shires of Scotland never had a shilling of public money even lent to them, far less granted as a gift. The commissioners of supply, equivalent to the Irish grand jurors, so far as roads are concerned, borrowed money to make the roads, but they borrowed from banks or from private capitalists. The security given was the tolls and their own estates, at least to the extent of one third of their life interests in the estates. The Scottish landowners in making roads rendered *themselves* liable for money expended. The Irish grand jurors expended the money of the cess-payers in making roads, but not their own money, nor in any case are they liable in person or property for the road debts.

But even in grants of public money for roads the few grants made to Ireland far exceed what has ever been granted to Scotland, including all the folly of the Caledonian Canal and the roads made for the exclusive use of a few Highland estates; and this is allowing for the larger extent of Ireland.

As to the mere expenditure of the money in the country, which seems to be the aim and end of the Irish gentlemen, it may be doubted if it does any good at all compared with the mischief it does, if expended in only enabling a part of the population to consume the necessaries of human life without enabling them at the same time to produce them. It is profitable industry which pays taxes and rent; if taxes and rent be used to enable a number of people to consume much without producing anything, the national effect is loss, though the local effect, where the taxes and rent are spent, may be gain.

The expenditure of public money in Scotland was confined to a limited locality; and even there the greater part of it was, is, and ever will be unproductive.

Kerry has had all its roads and bridges made by grants and government loans. They have been and are now under the control of the Board of Works. Kerry alone has had more free grants of public money spent on *useful roads* than the whole of Scotland has. But Kerry has not made a good use of them. No lead, copper, nor iron ore is opened to the reach of industry by the Highland roads and bridges of Scotland; little else than grouse and red deer for the sportsman. Had the iron ore of Kerry been in Argyle or Inverness, it would have made its own roads by this time.

Here is a striking passage in Mr Mahony's statement to the commissioners; let the reader carry forward in his mind the lines in *italics*:—

'I may mention to the commissioners one fact *which has lately come to my knowledge, which demonstrates neglect and a want of due investigation into the wants of Ireland.* An application under the Drainage Act has been made for the drainage of a river called the Woodford River, which runs into Lough Erne from the county of Leitrim; and on its survey for drainage it has been ascertained by Mr Mulvaney, an engineer for the Board of Works, that if, in addition to the sum which the proprietors are willing to give for the drainage (willing to borrow under the Drainage Act he should have said) £40,000 be added, it may be also made a useful navigation; and that if eight miles of canal are added to it, the Shannon can be united by it to Lough Erne, so as to make a complete inland navigation between Limerick, Dublin, Waterford, Clonmel, Newry, and Belfast.

'The commissioners will be surprised as I have been, if they examine a map of Ireland and note the important effects of such an improvement as I now suggest; *and yet, instead of that resulting from a judicious inquiry into the wants of Ireland* through the Board of Works or the Ordnance survey, *it has come to my knowledge by mere accident.*'

Mr Mahony began the statement of which this is nearly the conclusion, by saying:—

'I am a solicitor in Dublin, and have been in most extensive practice in the management of trust and other estates of great value, for thirty years. I am also a landed proprietor in the counties of Kerry, Cork, Limerick, Wicklow, &c.

Whatever Mr Mahony may think, the Englishmen and Scotchmen who are in the habit of exploring, not only the whole surface of England and Scotland, and going down into the depths of the earth and through the waters under the earth at their own expense, to look for the raw materials of industry, will think it remarkable that Leitrim, where the richest and most abundant of the mineral treasures of Ireland lie, should be so easily reached by navigation, and that fact only became known to Mr Mahony after thirty years' practice in the management of all kinds of Irish property, and at last only 'by accident.'

But if the smile which one feels on the face were a smile of mirth and not pity, were there a joke in so grave and lamentable a matter, the best part of that joke would be that Ireland has been surveyed over and over again, its mountains measured, its lakes sounded, its strata pierced, its minerals analyzed, its fertility estimated, its very poultry counted; every conceivable thing which engineer and statist can do to tell what Ireland's resources are has been done, and by government; and more was being done by government in that very survey for drainage, which became an accident to Mr Pierce Mahony, and which was the result of deliberate loan of one million sterling by government, for the drainage of Irish estates on river banks; all this while that gentleman is complaining of its being an instance of the neglect of the government towards Ireland's wants and conveniences. Ireland has vast capabilities for industrial wealth; but she has Pierce Mahonys who live on the industrial capabilities and eat them in the bud. Every germ of industry that shews itself in Ireland is eaten up by landlords and lawyers. Even the Arigna mines, in Leitrim, the only iron mines yet worked in that county, which swells with mineral wealth, with iron and with coals, have been stopped by lawyers and disputatious landlords. An English company with capital to work the iron and the coal were there, and found both plentiful—the iron ore equal in quality to the ore of Sweden. But for eight years, during which England has been calling for more iron to make railways and engines to run on the railways, and has been sending her voice to the bottom of her mines for her miners to send up the iron faster; while Ireland, too, has been calling to England to make railways for her; all those eight years that iron of Leitrim has been lying dead, a prey to rust and law; and neither that company of English capitalists nor any other dares, for the law, to touch the iron of Leitrim. When five and a half of those eight years were past, the 'patriotic' Pierce Mahony heard, 'by accident,' that Leitrim may be connected with other towns by navigation. Two years and a half more have passed, and still the law and the rust eat the iron of Leitrim; and no patriot steps forth to brush either or both away. And in Kerry, though the iron ore may not be eaten by law, for it has not yet been brought to daylight for law to see it and get at it, the agriculture which is in the daylight is almost entirely the prey of lawyers and law; what they leave the potato disease has taken. And now famine is on all Kerry, not only for this year, but for years to come. Little progress, so little that it can hardly be named, is making towards seed sowing. Mr Mahony's estates are no exception. The work people have been all the spring on the public works, the best of the tenants saying they cannot afford to employ them; and now those who are not on the public works are on the soup kitchens or on the public allowance of a pound and a-half of bread per day; the land lying untilled, and the landlord doing as much to it as the man of the moon.

25

O'BRIEN'S BRIDGE, COUNTY CLARE, 12th April 1847

The letters from the county of Limerick, in which the uncultivated estates of Mr Smith O'Brien and his neighbours are described, require that I should now say something of capital required for cultivation. I am now thirty-five miles from Smith O'Brien's property; but this little town, and its long bridge, were built by one of his ancestors, a king of Munster; and at the distance of four or five miles from here, by a road which I have just travelled over, lives his brother, Mr Robert O'Brien, whose experience as a land-agent is large, and whose evidence before the commissioner inquiring into the 'Law and practice of the occupation of land in Ireland' is comprehensive and practical. I may therefore pause at this place on my journey to the north, and take pen in hand once more to write of the land of the O'Briens.

On capital, Mr Robert O'Brien says:—

'There appears to be a great deal of unnecessary outcry on the subject of capital, as there exists sufficient in the country for its agricultural purposes, if it was applied with skill, and it would then become reproductive, instead of lying nearly idle in the funds and banks. A great deal of money belonging to the agricultural classes in this country is lying in bankers' hands, bearing a very low interest, which, if applied on the almost neglected land of the same farmers, would yield large returns; nor can any difference be discovered in the conduct of such persons, arising from their having leases or no leases.'

Because the leases are encumbered with law, and so full of reservations for the proprietors, and of penalties on the tenants, that they cannot cultivate wisely and well. Let them move spade or plough, let them move hands or feet, for the reclamation of their land from waste, the law is at them. To go into the strata of limestone rock under their farms, and

quarry it to make lime of it in a kiln to lay on their farms, they might as well go into a den of animals with tusks which eat men alive, or into the limekiln itself, the lawyers are instantly or ultimately at them, and consume them with law.

I stand now on the north side of the Shannon, where it is approaching the falls of Castle Connell, and opposite to me is the farm of Mr James M'Nab, a Scotchman. The years are yet few in number, only about fifteen, when all that farm had from twelve to twenty feet of bog moss on it. The grass, corn, and root crops which now grow on those farm fields, enlarging the supply of human food, grow where the moss has been removed. The moss has been removed on a scale of greatness and precision of system which only an enterprising man of capital could undertake. The bog which only fed a few wild ducks and snipes was manufactured into fuel for the supply of Limerick city, giving the comfort of household fires to more people at a cheaper rate than they ever had such comfort before. Wages were paid to several hundreds of people, not employed before, in cutting the moss, and at a rate above the usual wages of the county. I see sixty people at work on the farm now at 8s. per week, while ordinary farmers and gentlemen employees pay only 5s. and 6s. per week. Canals are cut, and boats enter from the Shannon, go through the farm where the land is reclaimed, to those parts where it is in process of reclamation, and are loaded with the dry fuel to go to Limerick. Some of the workmen said to me to-day, as I passed them near the road, 'God bless Mr M'Nab and all his sort! he makes farm land where a snipe could not live, and pays such wages as never were paid here before. Pray God, Sir Richard gets the worst of the law, and does not succeed in turning Mr M'Nab out.'

This Sir Richard is the owner of vast possessions measured only by miles, which only fed snipes. He employs himself in feeding horses and dogs, and in hunting foxes. His whole employment is amusement. He has a residence near Mallow, in Cork, and another at Castleconnell, in Limerick. Horses and dogs to hunt and eat corn and meal; idle servants to eat bread and meat; a river, like a sea broken out of bounds, rolling and roaring through his demesne, with water-power equal to the mill-wheels of a world—is also kept idle: those are the signs of what Sir Richard de Burgho does or is likely to do, with the exception that he is at law with Mr James M'Nab, endeavouring to eject him from the farm on some informality in the lease. A similar lease under which Mr Watson, another tenant, held, has been abrogated, owing to the legal technicalities not being complied with, and it is generally feared that Mr M'Nab's lease will be broken in the same way.

Had he taken the bog on lease, and kept it to breed snipes and frogs, miasmatic fevers and famine, he might have held it without his lease being questioned. But to have cattle and corn, and healthy farm fields, and to have much to sell to a population who require much, and the profit going into his pocket, strikes the mind of the De Burgho, chief of an ancient race, as an injustice to him, and he must try to get a share to help him to maintain his dignity, his hounds, horses, and idle servants. The lawyers tell him how to get, not only a share, but the whole; and so he goes to law.

The more honest, and I shall venture to say the more honourable and dignified way of getting possession of such farm fields as those brought from beneath the barren moss by James M'Nab, to beautify a country and feed its people, is for Sir Richard de Burgho to go to work and clear a bog for himself. He has many more to begin upon. Hundreds of people in Castleconnell and O'Brien's Bridge are without work and food; the corn and meal, and bread, and meat which he feeds idle horses, dogs, and servants upon, would afford them wages and food to begin work upon.

At all events, his success in taking Mr Watson's property from him and his attempt to take that of Mr M'Nab, though both held on lease, will not encourage other men of capital and enterprise to try to create fertility and fullness out of barrenness and famine. And, if he succeeds, one other warning will be given to agriculturists to put their money in the bank, even at a low per centage, rather than risk it in the cultivation of land, as Mr Robert O'Brien says they do.

This gentleman proceeds to say—

'The tillage is carried on with a very small amount of capital by the 'free crop' system. And if they do purchase manure, they consume the crop in such a way as to yield little return to the capital, and, by their crops, take out of the land rather more than they put into it. Hence the frequent failures in the overworked soil.'

The term 'free crop' is thus explained:—

'The labourer, not having land of his own, gathers during the year, heaps of manure, and in spring applies to the farmers who have land and not manure, who suffer him to put the manure on the land and cultivate a crop of potatoes; and, according to the quality of the land, sometimes a sum of money is paid, varying from 4s. to £1 per quarter of an Irish acre, in addition to the manure, by the labourer.'

It is always on very poor land where this 'free crop' of the labourer is permitted. Much of his own time and all the time of his family is employed in collecting this manure on the roads, while, strange to say, the very farmer on whose farm it is to be applied—on land exhausted by three, four, or five crops without manure—is allowing the streamlets and rivers to carry away the natural riches of his cow sheds, stables, and farm yard. This waste of manure is universal; but the free crop system is not universal.

Having explained the meaning of that term, Mr O'Brien proceeds to say that no attempt to establish agricultural societies has succeeded, because the only parties having an interest in tillage or a desire to see it extended, are the poorest of the farmers, not able to support agricultural societies; and—

'The gentry generally hold rich lands, which are kept for pasture, and do not as a class feel so direct a sympathy with those who occupy the waste and poor lands. A farmer, with little or no capital, through the medium of conacre and free crops, can sufficiently manage to hold a tillage farm; but he must have capital to hold it as a pasture farm. The consequence of such tillage tends to the impoverishment of the land, and it is for this reason that so many landlords have inserted covenants in their leases against breaking pasture land.'

Mr Smith O'Brien is one of those who do so, while he amuses himself with crying for a repeal of the union as if *it* would repeal the covenants between him and his tenants. If he would do his part as a landlord towards providing that food for Ireland which he blames the government for not providing, he will repeal those covenants, and set himself to teach his tenants how to make their farms productive of food; he will build habitable houses for them and for the cattle, and contrive to drain the meadow springs into the rivulets, instead of allowing the rivulets to take the farm-yard manure.

Mr Robert O'Brien continues—

'Generally, it may be established as a rule, that it is only the poor lands which have been cottiered, (tilled by a cottier tenantry;) for, while the population is very large and poor on the hilly lands, you may find but a comparatively small population on the rich lands.'

This has arisen from the clearance system. Under the old forty shilling freeholds, previous to 1829, the people, if cleared from the rich lands on the levels, were set to the mountains to farm there, for the sake of their votes. Many of the hills were occupied by those people rent free, for the sake of their votes; but when they were disfranchised they were called upon to pay rent, and ejected wherever the land was worth taking possession of, if they did not pay rent. If thus cleared away there, they swelled the measure of pauperism in the towns; if left there, they became the parents of pauper families on the hills. All that the landlords of the levels did or cared for was to keep them either on the hills or in the towns, or to get them off to England or America, or anywhere, so as they did not come down to take the grass from the horned cattle which were feeding to go to England for rent.

Mr O'Brien proceeds thus, in corroboration of similar statements made by me in previous letters, before I knew that I had such a valuable witness—

'The consolidation of arms is generally that of a number of small farms in tillage, giving subsistence and labour to whole families, into large pasture farms *not requiring any labour*; for a single herdsman, who receives no money wages, will be able to do all the labour required on a large farm, which, if kept in tillage, would employ a great many hands.'

Yet on the farms of Cahermoyle, belonging to Mr Smith O'Brien, and on others near them, even the herdsmen have been all the winter and spring on the relief lists of the Board of Works, the farmers, to save the herdsman's diet in the farm-houses, consenting to let some sister, or aunt, or mother, do the herding, that the herdsman might go and earn one shilling and fourpence per day on the relief works, an amount of wages never paid, never heard of, never dreamt of in that part of the country before—wages which even Mr Smith O'Brien, while railing at the government for not paying enough, would not come within fourpence of to his labourers in Cahermoyle demesne.

Relative to the increase of pauper gentry, Mr Robert O'Brien says—

'The great value of land during the war induced many who were of a respectable farming class to sublet their lands, and set up to be gentlemen; and one frequently meets with people who say their father had £100, £200 &c. a-year out of such and such lands.'

This is another testimony against war, and against any policy of government, peaceful or warlike, which shall force consumption faster than production. Armies are paid out of taxes upon industry, and hundreds of thousands of working men and women are drawn from employment nationally profitable to supply the armies with food and clothing which is nationally unprofitable. It is another testimony against forcing money into circulation in greater amount than the industry of the nation requires to keep it in motion. A large supply of money let loose, or forced into circulation, does not necessarily give an impulse to industry and to the production of real national wealth. Its good or evil effects depend on the currents it gets into—whether it sets people to consume without producing something that is useful to others, or sets them to produce more than they consume. In the time of the war it not only excited a vast consumption but from the universal ignorance of industrial economy which then prevailed—and which though not universal, still prevails—the occupiers of land, when the flood-tide of an over-high circulation made eddies at their doors, ceased to work, and ceased to direct the money which flowed to their doors to the farm fields to pay for more labour, to produce more corn; they took the money and retired with it to eat corn without working; they set themselves up as consumers, ceased to be producers, withdrew the national capital from production, and turned the current into a wrong channel.

The Irish members of Parliament, in crying for money to be poured into Ireland, and also seeking to have a larger number of idle consumers compelled to reside in the country—the absentee landlords, horses, hounds, and non-producing servants—do not seem to know that more consumption without more production will only make the country poorer. Mr Smith O'Brien who proposed a few weeks ago to enforce the residence of landowners, under a penalty of a tax of ten per cent on their incomes, is himself an instance of a landlord who takes rent, buys food, clothes, and personal service with the rent, and adds no value to his land or to anything on the land.

Even those who get together a few thousand pounds by trade in Limerick, or in other Irish towns, with the exception probably of Belfast, set up as gentry. A tradesman with £10,000 in the bank, thinks it time to retire from business, and hunt, and keep a carriage and servants. The English manufacturers and merchants do not withdraw from business, to keep a retinue of servants and animals to consume food and clothing, and produce nothing, as soon as they have the means of retiring to be gentry out of business. They add the profits of one year to the capital of the year before, and do more business, create a greater amount of the necessaries and comforts of human requirements, and enable a greater number of human creatures to obtain them.

26

ON THE VALUE OF SMALL FARMS

Small farms are a favourite theme with certain parties in England. To relieve the competition for labour they would introduce a competition for land. Let us glance at the results of competition for land in Ireland, and the evidence shewing how many acres are required in different counties to maintain a small farmer and his family.

ANTRIM:—Mr John O'Hara, a farmer who follows an improved style of agriculture, was asked:—'Can you state the smallest quantity of land upon which, in your opinion a farmer could support himself without extraneous assistance, such as manufactures or anything else?'

'I would not say less than ten or twelve acres, (Irish equivalent to sixteen or nineteen English,) from the mode of farming which is at present practised.'

He gives the details of the cultivation of 8 acres, 15 perches, 26¼ yards English measure, under a rotation of crops, and shews, at the end of the statement, 'Balance for the labourer and his family, £14: 8s.'

I do not find any other witness in Antrim giving evidence on the same subject.

ARMAGH.—Mr Blacker, land-agent:—'It is considered in England that twelve acres are fully sufficient for the support of a family, but in Sussex five acres have been found sufficient. According to the ordinary methods of culture it would require a great deal more, but in the case alluded to in Sussex the improved method of culture is carried into effect; the house-feeding and tanks have produced their effect.'

CARLOW.—No evidence on this subject.

CAVAN.—None.

CLARE.—Rev. Mr Corbett, parish priest:—'Six or seven acres (nine and a half to eleven English) are sufficient to support a family on an improved system of agriculture.'

Mr Gibson, farmer:—'The smallest farm upon which a family can support themselves is from thirteen to sixteen English acres of medium land.'

Mr Keane, land-agent:—'From seven to ten English acres are sufficient to support a family.'

It is necessary to observe, however, that the support of a family is reckoned from the standard of diet common to Ireland. In the succeeding quotations I have rendered the Irish acres into English to avoid the repetition of both measures.

CORK.—Mr Barry, farmer:—'The smallest farm sufficient to support a farmer and family is thirty-two acres.'

Mr Biggs, farmer and land proprietor:—'Less than thirty-two acres of average land is insufficient to support a family.'

Mr Burke, land proprietor:—'Less than thirteen or sixteen acres is not sufficient to maintain a farmer and family.'

Mr De la Cour, land-agent:—'Thirty-two acres are capable of supporting a family.'

Mr Hunt, land-agent:—'Farms of from thirty-two to forty-eight acres requisite to support families.'

DONEGAL.—No direct evidence is tendered on this subject in Donegal. But on the estate of Lord George Hill, at Gweedore, which has attracted much public notice, the farms vary in size from four and three-quarter acres to sixteen. By a new system of culture those farms were supposed to be performing a great social revolution among the rural population.

Lord George Hill published 'Facts from Gweedore;' and the persons engaged in the effort of dividing all the land of Great Britain into farms of two, three, and four acres, republished the 'facts' to strengthen them in their efforts in Worcestershire and Hertfordshire. But it is also a fact that the tenants of Gweedore are without food, and would have died on their farms but for the corn which commerce has brought from foreign shores to supply them, and but for the funds which the commercial strength of England has supplied to buy that corn.

DOWN.—Mr Sharman Crawford, land proprietor and M.P.:—'I think that the portion of land which a *labouring man* should have would in some degree depend on *the extent of employment which he could get*; if he has constant employment by hired labour, or anything approaching to it, he would require less land. If he is to be dependent for his subsistence on the land he holds he would require more. But I am of opinion that a man wholly dependent on the land he holds for support, could support himself and his family comfortably having six statute acres of land, and be capable of paying a fair rent, provided he applied it in the best manner to the production of food.'

Mr Crawford goes on to say that two acres may be made to grow the food for a family, if that family has employment elsewhere than on those two acres to earn wages. There need be no question about that; the question arises upon the getting of the wages. If it were possible for all the working men of Lancashire to have two acres and their workshop wages, the small farm system would be an excellent thing. But they cannot live upon two acres in Worcestershire and work in the workshops of Lancashire.

DUBLIN.—No evidence. Nor would it be applicable if there was. The county of Dublin is small, and the produce of the miniature farms is sold in the city, and shipped to England to people engaged in trade. According to Mr O'Connor's book on Small Farms, the intention is to divide Great Britain, for the direct purpose of destroying the manufacturing system. Yet he calculates all the prices to be received for farm produce sold and consumed off the farm to be the same as the prices of 1843, the year when the book was written.

FERMANAGH.—Mr Mair and Mr Mylne:—'We are both agriculturists, brought from Scotland by Lord Erne, to instruct the farmers in improved cultivation. House feeding has been much introduced since we came here among the small farmers. They are feeling the benefit of the improved system very much. (Mr Mylne)—Ten acres is small enough for any farmer. (Mr Mair)—I think if he has nobody but himself, five is enough for him to work by the spade. It will take two men to labour ten acres by the spade.'

'You think a man could maintain himself on five acres?'—'Yes; if they have large families they could go out to service.'

But if each family in the kingdom had five acres, and there were no manufactures and commerce, existing exclusively as such, where would be the service to go to? And when there was no service to go to, nor commercial cities, nor manufacturing districts, where would be the farms of five acres? They would be divided among the children as they grew up, as the case is now in Ireland and France, and reduced to perches and farm ridges measured only by the yard. If not so divided, the children would have to go to try their hands at trade again; make an effort to establish manufactures and commerce again. Would it not be as well to let them remain, and let every working man endeavour to raise himself, and help to raise those around him, above his present social level, by the acquisition of property which he can hold, and still retain his employment in the places of manufactures and commerce?

GALWAY.—Reverend Mr Griffin, parish priest:—'Farms of four and three quarters acres of good land, near the sea, for manure, are sufficient to maintain a family, if employed in the fisheries.'

KERRY.—Mr Holme, land-agent:—'Farms of fourteen and sixteen acres are sufficient, if cultivated by spade, to support and supply labour to a family.'

KILDARE.—Mr Wilson, farmer and agent:—'Competition for small farms very great.'

KILKENNY.—Mr Reade, land proprietor:—'The size of farms is becoming smaller from the increase of population. Less than sixteen acres not sufficient to support a farmer.'

KING'S COUNTY.—Mr Lacy, farmer:—'A farm of sixteen acres is the least which can support a family.'

Mr J. H. Walsh, land proprietor, of King's County, and intimately connected with the parish of Drum, in Roscommon, presented a statement carefully drawn up, setting forth the number of acres occupied by three classes of occupants, their rents and social condition. The most important portions are here quoted; but it must not be forgotten that the dietary of the farmers and families refers to 1844 and years of ordinary prosperity, when dependent on their acres of land, and not, as in 1847, when the commerce of England is feeding them from foreign shores.

'Total small farms, 838. Of these there are, first class, 146; in second class, 484; in third class, 208. The average acres of the holdings is ten English acres; rent, £6:15:8 each farm. (The precise measure of each seems to be omitted.)

'Diet—Class 1.—Potatoes and milk in abundance; oatmeal butter, and eggs, four months; meat six or eight times in the years.

'Class II.—Potatoes; milk half the year; butter, eggs, and meal occasionally; meat twice a-year.

'Class III.—Potatoes insufficient; milk none; eggs and meal rarely; meat perhaps twice a-year.'

LEITRIM.—Reverend Mr Evers, parish priest:—'The average size of farms is six or eight acres; many from two to four acres. It requires a farm to contain from eight to twelve acres to support a family.'

LIMERICK.—Mr Roche, farmer:—'A farm of sixteen acres sufficient to support a family comfortably.'

Mr Monsell, land proprietor, states that there is no class of labourers in Limerick county who depend entirely on money wages. He pays some of his labourers by giving them land, they paying the rent in labour; and to others he gives conacre, potato ground for one crop only. He says he endeavours to regulate the wages in some degree according to the size of the families, by giving one shilling in summer and tenpence in winter; 'no other person in the county,' he says, 'giving more than eightpence.'

In the letter dated from Rathkeale, which gave an account of the county as seen from the road between Limerick and that place, the agriculture was probably made to appear better than it really is. I mentioned the village of Patrick's Well. Mr Monsell, speaking of his attendance at the petty sessions as a magistrate at that place, says, on the 26th of Aug. 1844—

'It is decidedly desirable to have my labourers holding their ground immediately from myself. There was a curious instance occurred at the petty sessions at Patrick's Well on Friday last; there was a man who appeared before us, and it came out in the course of his examination that he paid *thirty days' work for four perches of ground, and he built a house upon the ground himself.* The person he held from held eight acres and a-half, and he paid £3:8:5 per acre, the outside value of the land being about £2 the acre. He held it from a middleman, and that middleman from another, and he held it again from the head landlord; and I should say such cases are not rare.'

Here we have the competition for land producing five graduations of tenant misery, the lowest tenant paying for four perches of land, the work of thirty days, and building his hovel besides. Yet with those appalling facts known to him, Mr Feargus O'Connor, himself an Irish middleman once, and deriving whatever knowledge he has of agriculture from his experience as a middleman who lived on the rents of a wretched under tenancy, attempts to introduce his pernicious competition for land in England, by parcelling the English soil into two acre, three acre, and four acre farms to begin with. At least he attempts to make the working-men of England believe that they would be independent of the wages of labour and the competition in wages if they had the land.

Mr Monsell proceeds:—

'Subletting and dividing of farms still continues; chiefly in the way of people endeavouring to divide even very small farms for the sake of allocating portions to their children.'

Would not all England, if divided, as propounded by Mr Feargus O'Connor, into small farms of four acres, have to be divided again to allocate portions to chartist children? Listen to the questions and answers which expose the poverty of those parts of Ireland where the population in desperation are still able to get some of the land to divide:—

'What, in your opinion, is the general effect of the system?'

—'The general effect is to produce wretchedness and misery beyond description. The condition of the labourers who do not receive constant employment is very miserable indeed. I have had occasion to make a list of the persons in my parish, in which there is a good deal of employment given to the poor, and they are a good deal looked after, and I find the people are in general in a very destitute state. Out of 600 or 700, there are 158 in a state of very great destitution; they are in a state of great poverty, because they are only partly employed.'

Yet those people have, on an average, more than the breadth of land to each family that is to be allotted to the chartist prizeholders in England; and it is better land than that at O'Connorville, or any other in the county of Hertford. It may be alleged that the rent in Ireland eats up the produce and the profit, and that the chartist prizeholders would be differently circumstanced, having no rent to pay. But their liabilities are equal to a heavy rent at the very outset; while the absence of rent does not save the occupiers from destitution when the land is minutely subdivided. Mr Monsell continues:

'There is one spot in the parish where the proprietor allowed people to settle and charged them no rent, and the state of absolute destitution in which those people are it is impossible to describe.' (This was in 1844).

'Are those people, generally speaking, willing to work if they can get it!'—'Yes, perfectly willing.'

One source of the delusion under which working men in England have been induced to become shareholders in Feargus O'Connor's land company is the fictitious quantity of produce alleged by him to be derivable from the land.

But I shall not at present pursue the subject further. The English working population have neither been so well cared for, nor have they cared so well for themselves, as should have been and as will be; but it is not by a system of general pauperism upon minute portions of land that they are to make a change for the better—they must go forward, not turn back.

27

JOURNEY FROM BANAGHER TO BIRR, KING'S COUNTY

I found myself a few days ago seated on one of Bianconi's cars with a clergyman of the Established Church. Our conversation turned upon topics of common interest, which I have not before written of in this series of letters. It is therefore repeated here.

Whistler—Why is this arch broken down half the width of the road? It seems dangerous to drive here, even in daylight; it must be worse at night; why is the arch broken?

Clergyman—It was broken by the people, in the night time, three months ago, under the impression, silly creatures, that they would prevent the transport of meal from Birr to the Shannon. The mills at Birr grind meal, and it is taken by this road to Shannon harbour, and from thence by canal to Dublin. The poor ignorant people saw it going, and fearing that none would be left in King's county, they attempted to break down the bridges—this and another between Banagher and Birr. They found the masonry too hard for them to make fast progress, and the police were brought upon them before they got more mischief done than you see. The peasantry here are very ignorant.

Whistler—I am glad to have at last met an Irish gentleman who does not justify such an interference with the free buying, selling and carrying of corn and flour.

Clergyman—What! am I to understand by your saying so, that you have met any person holding a respectable position in society, who has justified such an interference with the conveyance of corn and flour?

Whistler—The county newspaper, the county gentlemen, magistrates, priests, and all the clergy whom I have hitherto met in conversation until I met you, not only have justified such an interference, they have advocated it, and condemned the government in angry words because such violence to the free buying, selling, and transport of food has not been general throughout Ireland. The last time I was in a clergyman's society he said that Lord John Russell was answerable for all the deaths arising from famine in Ireland. He said the government should have interfered to bring down the prices of corn and meal, and to take the trade out of the hands of the merchants.

Clergyman—And so do I say. Indeed I am as forward as any one you will find to say that government is answerable for the starvation of the people. But there is no analogy between that and the poor ignorant people breaking down the bridge to interrupt the traffic of the road, is there?

Whistler—There is. The analogy would be perfect, the ignorance, error, and mischief the same in both cases, were it not that the education and ability to reflect calmly of gentlemen like yourself makes your case worse than that of the ignorant peasantry. You would have government to do violence to the usual channels of commerce, which are as indispensable to the procurance of food and its minute distribution over the kingdom, as those roads and bridges are over the King's county.

Clergyman—Well now, really, upon my word you surprise me—quite surprise me; do you compare and class together a crime of an ignorant and excited mob of people with an act which would have been the glory of an enlightened ministry, if we had been blest with one?

Whistler—But I deny that the ministry which would have undertaken the task of buying corn and grinding and distributing meal to the whole Irish nation would have been a blessing, on the contrary, it would have been a curse to Ireland and to England. The merchants are now bringing corn in such quantities that the prices are falling every day, and will fall. Had the Queen's ministers gone into the corn markets of the world, instead of the merchants, they could not have bought such quantities of corn but at an enormous price, if at all. They must have paid the merchants to buy the corn, and have competed for the freightage of ships. As it is, the merchants buy the corn without being paid by government to do so, and they get ships to carry it without government competing with them and raising the price of freights. And had government not gone into the markets of the world, but passed a law or decree that corn, when brought here by the merchants, should be sold at a certain low price—the merchants, supposing this law to have been applied to them in the autumn of last year, would not have been now pouring in the hundreds of heavily laden corn ships every week into all the ports of the kingdom. We should now have corn high in price, with absolute famine for the whole kingdom which even mercantile enterprise could not subdue. As it is, we have now a fair prospect of corn at a moderate price.

The clergyman remains silent for several minutes. We meet and pass a jaunting car, on which is seated Mr Jones, the engineer of the Board of Works, and another gentleman, and he asks our driver who the other gentleman with Mr Jones is. The driver supposes him to be one of the assistant engineers. We go a quarter of a mile further, and pass some men and women breaking stones for the roads, and an overseer and a check-clerk measuring some of the stone heaps to settle the payment. We go a little farther, and meet a pay-clerk of the Board of Works on a car, with a guard of police over him and the money he carries. At last my reverend companion speaks.

Look there! see what mismanagement, to have all those officials under the Board of Works, drawing the money in salaries which the poor people should receive as relief. The last published return of persons employed and of cash paid by the Board of Works—the return for the week ending on the 20th of March, gives—here it is; I have it in my pocket-book—gives a total of 685,932 persons of whom 664,432 were on the roads, and 20,490 employed on drainage. The cost of the whole was £228,940, of which sum the superintendence costs not less than £22,454. Is it not monstrous that so many persons at such salaries should be employed in the superintendence of those works, and yet with their great absorption of the public money acting most inefficiently, and not giving satisfaction to any one?

Whistler—And not giving satisfaction though well paid. Even good pay does not seem powerful enough to obtain a thoroughly practical staff of working public officers. Time and practice are required before 12,000 men can fully understand their several duties and perform them effi-ciently. But if 12,000 officers are required for these relief works, which are chiefly in digging earth and breaking stones, and are not able, numerous though they be, to keep the people honest in the handling of shovelfuls of earth and barrowfuls of stones, nor quite able to keep all of themselves honest, how many officers do you think would have been required to buy corn over all the world, ship it at foreign ports, land it in Irish ports, hire storehouses for it, send it to the mills to be ground, pay for conveyance and for grinding, sell the meal wholesale at the mills and stores, and retail in every parish and village in Ireland; keeping accounts in ledgers, for the satisfaction of parliament, of every pound weight and half pound of meal sold? Has it been a subject of calculation with you, to try to reach, even at a guess, the number of officials who would have been required to carry on a system of government corn and provision dealing, and book-keeping of that magnitude? They would have to be reckoned, not by thousands, as the engineers and overseers on the relief works are, but by hundreds of thousands. All the clerks, book-keepers and mercantile servants in the United Kingdom would have been called from private employment and would have been still too few in number. A supervision to secure honesty would have been utterly impossible.

Peculation and fraud would have been universal. Merchants would have ceased to engage in the corn trade, and government would have been obliged to engage the merchants as public servants. Supplies of corn would not and could not have poured into the country as they are now pouring in. We should have had one vast mass of famine, fraud, robbery, and ruin.

The Clergyman is again silent. The Whistler, as the car jolts and jingles along, and some more wretched looking people are passed breaking stones on the roadside, pulls from his pocket a small volume and reads. The Clergyman sees the title of it on the back of the boards, and says—

I see you have got the 'Black Prophet,' Carleton's 'Tale of the Irish Famine.' What do you think of Darby Skinadre, the meal-dealer, in that book?

Whistler—He is represented as ill-looking, as a hypocrite, a usurer, a miser, a cheat, and a coward. None of those qualities are amiable; when all are combined they certainly make up a most odious man.

Clergyman—Yet a man sketched from reality. He is only a fair specimen of a griping crew of usurers and misers who horde up meal and sell it in times of distress in Ireland.

Whistler—Do no honest men horde up meal and sell it? The exalted virtue of doing so seems worthy of an honest man!

Clergyman—What! horde up the meal and sell it at an extravagant usurious price! It is hardly like the work of an honest man.

Whistler—As Mr Carleton makes Darby Skinadre the only meal-dealer of his district, and makes all the people obliged to resort to him for meal, what would have become of those people if Darby Skinadre had not had meal to sell to them? Would they not have perished utterly? Instead of being a cruel hard-hearted man, he was a benefactor whom they should have blessed and prayed for.

Clergyman—But the extortion of the man is the point in his character reprobated.

Whistler—Then they should have prayed for more meal-dealers, or have endeavoured to make more meal-dealers, and prices would have been kept down by competition.

Clergyman—They would more probably have been kept up by combination.

Whistler—When there is less food than enough, the prices go up, and no combination can keep them down. When there is more food than enough, no combination can keep them up, nor get them up. But the real question is this:—As a sense of self-preservation—an affection for children, for wife, parents, home, country—as neither duty to neighbours nor duty to God would teach the inhabitants of Darby Skinadre's country to provide meal for themselves, not for an unforeseen famine, but for a frequent occurrence of want regular almost as the return of the summer months, (so we are informed in Mr Carleton's tale, and so also in the great blue books of the Devon Commission,) other human motives operated to provide meal for them—a desire to adventure in speculation and to realize a high profit. When there was less famine, Darby would get less profit; when there was no famine he would get no profit. We may infer that in some years he would have a dead loss, as the farmers who bought from him in time of famine, and who found enough on their own farms in time of plenty, would not in the latter case resort to his shop. To induce him to venture in the trade of meal at all he must have looked for profit, and have got one year of gain to pay the losses of years without gain. Mr Carleton is a forcible writer. In proportion to his literary power is the force of the satire he has written on his humble countrymen, unwittingly, while intending only to satirize the most useful class of men which can exist in the time of famine—men with meal to sell. Had Captain Bligh, with his boat's crew, when deserted by the mutineers of the *Bounty*, not apportioned the small store to the breadth of the ocean before them, he would not have saved that crew. But he had eleven days' allowance to spare when he reached the haven he had sailed for. Had not Darby Skinadre stored up meal, Mave Sullivan could not have been generous, nor could she have lived to be married. Darby is made to look odious in personal appearance because he sells meal in a time of famine. A Galway fox-hunter, according to that style of literary cant—a cant not peculiar to Mr Carleton, but to all our popular novelists—would have been a fine-looking, gallant fellow, generous and worthy of every man's esteem and every lady's love, though he kept half a county in a state of agricultural disorder and waste. A legend of the goose that was killed for the golden eggs is the kind of story which should be written to illustrate an Irish famine. No subject ever probed by novelist's pen abounds with better materials for dramatic situations, pathetic narrative, natural description and sound, healthy sentiment.

Clergyman—Perhaps you will write it?

Whistler—It does not follow that I can, because I say it might be written, yet it is possible that I may try. The corn field and the flowery meadow, the busy workshop and the manufacturing town; the struggle of the sound sentiment with the false; the rise and fall of the men who are apostles of the one or victims of the other; territorial feudalism clinging to the skirts of advancing commerce to hold it back, that it may still be governed by it; the principle of progress struggling for existence and space to advance among the millions of working men, some of whom clear a way for it and help it on, others of whom fell it on the head with sledge hammers. The actors in this mighty drama are of every social degree: Squires, whose office is to halloo the hounds and keep human progress under foot; merchants, whose office it is to gird the earth with brotherhood; manufacturers, whose destiny it is to rise in power and position above the lords of territory; lords of territory who open their eyes and discover that they have been in error, and who join with the rest of mankind, and march on gloriously in the front ranks of progress; lords of territory who will not open their eyes and see that the great tide of time is leaving them; wives, children, hope, love, joy, sorrow, famine, pestilence, self-devotion, fire-sides, with happy children around them; summer corn, green and growing; harvests ripe and plentiful, and human hopes ripening like the corn—those are some of the materials which would readily rise to carry out and diffuse upon society the healthy doctrines of industrial economy. If I do not attempt the task it will rather be that I mistrust my power to do it justice than the possibility of making the subject popular. If I do attempt it, I shall do so in the belief that I am performing for society a service.

28

COLLOONEY, COUNTY SLIGO

The county of Sligo is in most respects similar to Mayo already written of in these letters, by which it is bounded on the west. It has on the south, part of Mayo and Roscommon; on the east Leitrim— the Lancashire of two hundred years ago; and on the west the Atlantic Ocean, which might carry Sligo over all the world, but which only carries it to the river Clyde in Scotland, to sell its butter, eggs, and oatmeal. The people of Glasgow who work in iron, coal, cotton, and other articles of national manufacture, consume and pay for the oats, oatmeal, and butter of Sligo and Mayo. I shall devote the next letter, or part of it, to thoughts on industrial economy suggested by this fact—that the inhabitants of Renfrewshire and Lanarkshire in Scotland, counties not more fertile than Mayo, Sligo, and Leitrim, not better stored with minerals, and less favourably situated for ocean transit, should be the chief wealth givers to Mayo, Sligo, and Leitrim, by paying for their agricultural produce. This letter shall take a general view of the county of Sligo.

It is forty-one miles long from east to west, and thirty-eight miles broad from north to south, measured from its extremities. The town of Sligo is 131 miles north-west of Dublin. Its extent in acres is 461,753, of which 290,696 are set down as arable, 151,723 uncultivated, 6134 in plantations, 460 in towns, and 12,740 under water. The soil is variable, some of it on mountains, much of it level; some of it a light sandy loam which the wind makes sport of; other parts, and they are extensive, a deep loam of generous fertility. Bogs are interspersed. Limestone is the subsoil on the levels. It has several lakes and short rivers, but the rivers are strong though short, and they are not all idle as some of the great rivers are in other counties. They drive water-wheels and grind meal, and perform other offices to help men to work. The falls on those streams unite the qualities of utility and beauty.

The population in 1841 was 180,886; their occupations are agricultural; oats, potatoes, and butter being the chief products. There is also some wheat grown, and the soil is suited to grow much more; but the climate is probably too moist for wheat; the moisture, however, would be favourable to green crops and stall-feeding, by which system only can manure be got and applied profitably to agriculture. But Sligo has no farm-buildings suitable for such a system, and few landlords if any willing or able to undertake their erection.

The county contained, in 1841, 7969 horses, 45,839 horned cattle, 32,708 sheep, 12,805 pigs, 164,372 head of poultry, and 3846 asses, all being of the estimated value of £424,146.

The town of Ballina being mostly in Mayo, though partly in Sligo, the latter county has no town containing more than 2000 inhabitants, save that which gives the shire its name. The population of Sligo town is 12,272; they are a busy, industrious people, and by their industry disprove, so far as they are concerned, that general but doubtful assertion, that a Celtic population is not constitutionally fitted for commerce and industrial enterprise.

We once used to hear that it was the Catholic religion which disqualified the Irish for industrial enterprise. The people of Belgium, who are all Catholics, and at the same time marching in the front ranks of industry and civilisation, disprove that assertion; and we seldom hear of it now. But we hear now of the inferiority of the Celtic race to the Saxon. The leaders in Irish politics are, in some measure, to blame for provoking this odious comparison, at least for keeping it in activity. I, as a Saxon, do not believe in the natural incapacity of the Celts for becoming a commercial people. We have Saxons in England as inapt for commerce, and seemingly as ill able to search for and understand the true sources of all wealth, as any Connaught peasant; I allude to the mis-educated landed aristocracy. Suppose we look to the Celt, and see him affectionate to excess; full of love for the land of his birth; trustful in leaders who appeal to his generous confidence; faithful to the chieftains of the land; reverential of traditional authority; a natural-born Conservative; all of which qualities are in themselves positive virtues; may we not see that his faithfulness to territorial chieftainship, his belief with the mis-educated chieftains of territory that the land is the source of all wealth, has retained him on the land, and made him its serf and its pauper?

To those qualities of constitution we may add his hardihood in bearing fatigue and hunger; we may even add his contentedness with misery, which is a virtue of high quality degenerated into a vice, taken advantage of and abused by the objects of his social veneration, the landed chiefs of society. None of those qualities singly, nor all put together, afford a reason for believing the Celt disqualified by nature for commercial enterprise. But they afford a reason for his adherence to the land, and for his trustfulness in the landed chieftains, while *their* prejudices and contempt for the commercial spirit and industrial adventurers of their country is a sufficient reason why the Celt living on their land, clothed with tradition, bound with it, should not readily forsake them and seek subsistence elsewhere. It is at this point that the virtue of endurance and willing fellowship with misery ceases to be a virtue.

The Saxon has, in some countries, but only in some, emancipated himself from this bondage to acres of land and the owners of acres; and his race when once emancipated and free to taste the sweets of personal wealth, the excitement of commercial enterprise goes fast forward. The Saxons of America never knew the bondage; had it not been broken in England, their forefathers would never have peopled America. But the time is still recent when the English people lived in social wretchedness as deep as that of the Irish now, with nothing but landlords above them, nothing but land below them, and very little but famine and pestilence on each side. And the time is still more recent when the Scotch were in that condition.

The Saxon race, as represented by the English and lowland Scotch, would seem to have more aptitude for self-emancipation than the Celtic race as represented in Ireland; or rather, more impatience under servitude, out of which arises the aptitude for commercial enterprise, which practised through many generations, becomes the Saxon inheritance, and would become the inheritance of any race if that race were fairly set in motion.

This view of the subject might be followed up by many proofs from the Irish in America, and from instances becoming more and more common in Ireland itself. Sligo, with a Celtic population, is one of the instances. But that town also affords a proof of the suicidal policy of landlordism. The grand jurors of the county, instead of rejoicing to see a rising town of commerce, to make a market for their farm produce; instead of helping that town to grow and become strong with a healthy trade, they see in it only a strength upon which they may lay a burthen. The expense of making county roads, of maintaining the county police, which are almost exclusively made and maintained for the benefit of the landed interests, has been laid upon the town, while, for the thorough-fares of the town itself, the county cess is withheld.

The county of Sligo affords an instance of the feebleness of the 'agricultural mind,' even when turned in a right direction, which is worth relating; the more so as it is one of those cases sometimes referred to, to shew the impossibility of improving the Celtic population:—

The Rev. Lewis Porter, rector of Drumard, went before the Land Commissioners in 1844, on behalf of Edward Joshua Cooper, Esq., of Markree Castle in Sligo, owner of large estates, and at that time a member of parliament. He laid four documents before the commission-ers, one of which was a letter from Mr Cooper, written in 1841, stating that he would establish an industrial school on the estate, with workshops to clothe the people, and give them furniture and a model farm, to teach them agriculture. The second was a set of formal resolutions passed by certain gentlemen who called a meeting to thank Mr Cooper for his intentions; the third was a letter written in very extravagant terms of praise, also thanking Mr Cooper for his intentions; and the fourth was a set of rules for the school and workshops. Four apprentices were to be taken and made tailors, four shoemakers, four smiths, and four carpen-ters. They were to be taught trades at Mr Cooper's expense. So his letter stated; but it also stated that they were to be lodged, and dieted, and provided 'with decent clothing' by their parents. They were to be bound to Mr Cooper for five years, but to be discharged sooner if found to be competent workmen. The agricultural pupils were also to be apprenticed five years. Only two pupils applied for admission to the school of agriculture, one of whom is somewhere in Clare, the rector says, and the other in Scotland, where he went to work as a labourer, having got a small sum of money to carry him there. The farm and school did not pay their expenses, and were given up in two years and a half from the date of commencement. There were plenty of applications to the trades to be apprenticed; one shop had its full complement of four, the second had three, the third had three, and the fourth had two. But the tailors' shop was set on fire, and none of the shops were 'encouraged by the people and the gentry, and the tenants,' says the rector, as was expected. The people, it seems, who had tailors and shoemakers elsewhere did not all leave those tailors and shoemakers and go to Mr Cooper's workshops and buy clothes and shoes. The scheme did not pay, and was abandoned, as the agricultural school was, in two years and a half. There was no religious nor political opposition to it, only the people would not buy the goods made in the shops in sufficient quantity to make the scheme pay. Mr Cooper, disgusted with their ingratitude, disheartened, and his patience worn out, chose rather to lose £1000, which the whole buildings, tools, fixtures, and masters had cost him, than go on longer and lose more. So, returning to Brighton from whence his first letter was dated, to tell them how ungrateful and impracticable the Celtic Irish are, he sent the rector of the parish also to tell the Devon Commissioners that it was of no use to try to elevate the Irish. He, Mr Cooper, had tried shoemaking, tailoring, carpentering and smith work in general, for two years and a half, and though his apprentices were bound for five years, he had to give up business in disgust, because they had not learned their trades in half the time, and because the people did not buy the things they made fast enough to make the scheme a paying one. The rector also speaks of the people's insensibility to this 'charity' of their landlord, who thus laid out £1000 for their benefit, which they did not repay by their purchases.

A tradesman on his own account would have had to endure a longer trial than Mr Cooper did, and keep his apprentices to the end of their time. Perhaps the last half of the five years would have found the apprentices more expert and their work more saleable. But if not, what right had Mr Cooper to expect that he would get all the trade from other tailors and shoemakers, to his shops, for work sold at full price and done by apprentices, 'lodged and dieted, and provided with decent clothes by their parents?'

And the failure of this scheme, prematurely closed through the landlord's ill-humour, is adduced as an instance of the opposition of the Celtic population to improvement! It would be interesting to hear the rector tell what he thinks would have been the conduct of the Saxons under such circumstances.

I have alluded to the religion of the Irish people, and said that the Belgians are Catholics and hold a front-rank place in the progress of civilisation; yet it is true that the adherence of the Irish to the Catholic faith has been a barrier to their advancement in agriculture and the industrial sciences; not, however, in the manner alleged by those who use this argument against Catholicism; but by the opposite party debarring the Catholics from the rights and privileges of free citizens by the penal laws.

The penal laws directed by political Protestants against the Irish

Catholics were various, one of them forbade that any Roman Catholic should *purchase* land under any circumstances; or hold land upon any lease, not even to build a house upon it, for more than thirty-one years. But the Catholic could not even hold the land, on which he might build, for thirty-one years; his lease was void if the land produced him more profit than one-third of the rent paid by him under the lease. He was not likely to build good houses on such land, nor to exercise much skill and industry in its cultivation; for if the crops were of more value than one-third of the rent above the rent contracted for in the lease, the lease in like manner became waste paper.

The Catholic people were pressed into the deepest degradation by these laws, and became occupiers only. The head landlords were in most cases political servants, not the most exalted in character, of the English sovereigns. They obtained the Irish estates as rewards, and sent men of desperate fortunes, not disqualified by law, to hold the estates as leaseholders, which leaseholders became middlemen, by parcelling out the land among the Catholics who were disqualified to hold it on lease. Hence arose the pernicious system of middlemen, not entirely overcome yet, though gradually on the decline. Hence arose the custom of the landlord and the middleman taking everything from the occupiers of the land, and giving nothing, no house to live in, barn, stable, shed, road, ditch, gate, or bridge. Hence arose the custom of having all houses, barns, stables, sheds, roads, ditches, gates, and bridges of the worst kind, the occupiers being called upon to make them and pay for them, and being afraid to make the land look as if it were valuable, a custom still existing save in respect of roads and bridges, which the landed gentry have had constructed under their own direction, as grand jurors of counties, the occupiers still being called upon to pay for them.

The widest divergencies of governments from the principles of political economy have always given birth to the most widely spread human ills, and have incurred the heaviest retribution. Wars and religious persecutions are the widest divergencies from political economy. The Catholics persecuted the Protestants, and the Protestants persecuted the Catholics; terrible has been the retribution to both. The State Protestants in Ireland, and the landed proprietors as a class, have been the most recently engaged in persecution, and they seem, as a class, to be marked out by the economic laws of nature for ultimate and immediate punishment.

There is no mystery in the operation of those laws of cause and effect called political economy. Nor is there hardship or cruelty in them. To fall from the branch of a tree too weak to bear our weight, and be bruised with the fall, is a hardship; but it originated in our hardihood, or blindness, and not in the force of gravity—the immutable law of nature—which brought us to the ground.

It does not follow, however, that everything is correct which writers have chosen to call political economy, the doctrine of Malthus about population, and some other of his doctrines, are diametrically opposed to political economy, though he is called one of its writers.

The granting of leases to make forty shilling freeholds for political purposes; their subsequent abolition for political purposes in 1829—they being abolished to qualify Catholic emancipation—and the granting and withholding of the £10 leases, since these, according to the political views of the landlords, are all economic errors returning upon the landowners of Ireland with retribution, bringing them diminished rents on one side, and new bills for poor rates on the other.

In Sligo, the tenants are placed, displaced, and replaced, under political considerations as elsewhere. In Sligo, a large proportion of the land is in the hands of lawyers as elsewhere. Not far from the town there is an estate now belonging to a lawyer, who was engaged upon it professionally, and whose costs in law business relating to it were so great, that, on the property being offered for sale, nobody would have it with the attorney's costs on it. The attorney bode for it, and got it himself in payment of his costs. His first step was to make political capital of the land. He ejected the old tenants. Some of them put up rushes and sods in the ditches by the sides of the roads and slept under them, and he brought actions at law against them for so doing, under the name of regaining forcible possession.

29

SLIGO

However defective the agriculture of the west of Ireland may be now, it has, so the general testimony says, been worse. The erections of mills at Sligo, Westport, Galway, Belmullet, and other sea-coast places, to grind the oats into meal, and the settlement there of merchants to buy the oats and meal, has had the effect of gradually bringing oats to the markets in greater bulk, and in bringing land into cultivation within reach of the markets to supply the oats.

It is worthy of notice that Glasgow, Liverpool, and London are the chief places where the farm produce of Sligo and Mayo is shipped to, finally sold at, and consumed. More of it goes to Glasgow than to any of the other ports of the united kingdom. The great population, whose industrious hands in the shires of Lanark and Renfrew, in and around Glasgow, give value to the coals and iron natural to those shires and to the cotton imported there, not only pay for and eat the farm produce of Lanark and Renfrew, and other shires in the west of Scotland, they buy fat bullocks, and eat beef from Stirling and Perth, northward, and from the south-eastern counties of Haddington, Berwick, and Roxburgh; while they at the same time put their hands in their pockets and pull out money and pay for the oats, oatmeal, butter, and pork of the west of Ireland.

Lancashire, in like manner, but to a greater extent, pays for and consumes the farm produce of the east and south of Ireland, of the adjoining counties of England and Wales, and a considerable proportion of the bullocks and fat wethers, and the wheat of the English counties east and north of Manchester. The prices paid for such produce go to pay agricultural wages and agricultural rents. The nearer the position of the one to the other, or the freer the communication between the factory shires which eat and pay for their eating, and the farm-yard shires which produce food to eat and receive the payment for it, the higher are the agricultural wages and the agricultural rents.

'A truism,' you may exclaim in Manchester; 'we know all this: tell us something new.' Were this paper only to be read in Manchester, or within fifty miles of it, what has just been said, and what is about to be said, would probably be omitted. But there are still a great many people who do not understand the true sources of agricultural wages and rents, and possibly some of them may read this. I write for them.

Let us suppose that some of them are Galway fox-hunters. I have been several times with the Galway hounds and hunters within those few weeks bygone, and I can answer for it, that finer horses, bolder horse-men, more awful leaps, better hounds, and more cunning foxes are seldom to be seen, perhaps never to be seen; let us therefore suppose that this letter is addressed to a Galway fox-hunter, or the men of the stable and the kennel who adore the fox-hunter because he hunts in Galway and does not live in England; or the men of the Galway hovels and farm-yards, who look upon the men of the stables and kennels who serve and adore the fox-hunters, and upon the fox-hunters, as the true patrons of Galway agriculture. Those last say that, if every owner of land in Galway, Mayo, and Sligo would stay at home and keep horses and hounds, and hunt, and consume the produce of the farms, and spend the rents at home, it would be well for all of them. 'See!' they exclaim 'the numbers of grooms and helpers in the stables whom they would have; see the tradesmen they would employ by spending their rents here. See how easy it would be for the Galway, Mayo, and Sligo farmers to pay their rents if rent was spent at home. See how much employment they could give to labourers then; everybody would be well employed!'

As the fox-hunter of Galway has a supreme contempt for all such mean men as engage in trade, we shall believe for a minute or two, as he certainly believes every day of his life, and as all his family race believe through every generation, that to consume oats and hay with horses, oatmeal with hounds, and the flesh of cattle, and sheep, and pigs, with men who assist him in living a pleasant life, is the best way of spending rent. Let us suppose that neither Galway, Westport, Belmullet, Newport, Sligo, nor any other port is permitted to send away a barrel of oats or oatmeal, a firkin of butter, a pig, sheep, or horned beast, dead or alive, that everything produced in Galway, Mayo, and Sligo is consumed there. Let us suppose that two divisions of the people are made, one division to hunt foxes and consume the farm produce and spend the rents, the other division to labour on the farms, provide corn and cattle, and pay the rents, and what do we see before us? I think there is a wall before us that 'even a Galway fox-hunter would stand at.

What rent would the consuming division *have* to expend for the benefit of the producing division? If the consuming power of both divisions be just equal to the producing power of the division which works, they cannot have more than food; they cannot advance in comforts; they may retrograde, but they will not advance. The rent which the producers will pay can only be the corn and hay of the horses, oatmeal of the hounds, beef and bread and beer of the fox-hunters and servants. The latter, consuming all the rent, will have none to pay for whips to the whipmakers, boots to the bootmakers, scarlet coats to the tailors.

If they be, as a division, possessed of greater consuming powers than the ability to produce of the other division, they will get less than enough of corn and hay, beef, bread, and beer, and will be still farther from paying for whips, boots, and scarlet coats.

If, however, they consume less than the producing divisions can furnish, some oats and hay, bread, beef, and beer will be left in the hands of the producers, who will sell it, pay the price of it to the fox-hunters as rent, who, in their turn, will pay the whipmaker, bootmaker, and tailor. It is clear that the greater the number of persons who merely consume without producing, the poorer must all be.

The fox-hunter's tailor, boot and whip maker, may think, and they do think, that fox-hunting is good for trade. So far as they may be individually and immediately concerned, they reason aright. They are employed in adding by their skill and labour a greater value to cloth and leather than cloth or leather possessed before. But if they were employed in adding value to cloth and leather for the benefit of a person engaged in adding value to timber and iron, they would be adding more to the world's wealth than they do by making boots and scarlet coats for fox-hunters who consume and produce nothing.

The men who give additional value to timber and iron, whether they fell the trees and quarry the ironstone, or stand by the right hand of Robert Stephenson and help that right hand to execute a new creation, are all, with a compound interest of industry, adding value to value, wealth to wealth. The owner of accumulated capital, who spreads the sails of commerce on the oceans of the world, to bring together materials for their workmanship, is one of them. So is the owner of accumulated spindles, looms, hammers, anvils, and workshops. The more which one man can do himself by his labour, or by his skill, or by his enterprise, or by his savings of industry, or by his inheritance of another's savings, to add value to something which again produces value; and the larger the number of other persons which he can assist in adding value to something useful, the more useful to the world is he himself. He is the employer of producers. Good as it is to produce by one's own labour, it is a more valuable performance to give the power of production to a number of persons who would not otherwise have it.

Some eyes see no difference between the fox-hunting squire who gives employment and wages to whipmakers, spurmakers, bootmakers, saddlers, tailors, and upholsterers, and the mill working manufacturer, who employs and pays wages to mechanics, spinners, weavers, dyers, clerks, brokers, and so forth. But the difference is, that the first makes every one work inwards for himself—the unit, the one atom of nine hundred millions; while the latter makes every one work outwards to the markets of the world, to reach as many of the nine hundred millions as possible, them all if he can.

An owner of money may withdraw his own labour and skill and enterprise from the world, and yet leave his capital in business to help others to make the raw matter of the world more valuable. The world, by his retirement, possesses less than it possessed before, by the amount of his personal labour, skill, or enterprise. If he betakes himself to a country mansion and keeps horses to eat corn and hay; servants who only minister to his pleasure, and who eat bread and meat; if he buys whips and scarlet coats, and top-boots, and hounds, and feeds the hounds, and rides after them fifty miles a-day, over fences and through fields, where ewes in lamb and cows in calf run from him and his hounds in terror, he may do some harm, but cannot do good beyond the pleasure he gives himself. Still, as his money which purchases that pleasure comes to his hand as profit upon capital working in the world for the world, he may be said to produce the purchase money of his profitless consumption of pleasure. In this he differs, and it is a great difference, from the fox-hunter of Galway who produces nothing, gives value to nothing, but consumes the produce of the land in personal pleasure.

Some persons may say, and some do say, that the land is to him what the capital of the retired merchant is in the last paragraph. Not so. The retired merchant has, as it were, a streamlet of commerce which flows and runs over; and he gathers the drops carefully and fills his cup of pleasure with what runs over. The main stream runs untouched. The Galway squire dips into the main stream; and being a stream so frequently dipped into, it becomes small, and often stops, in which case, rather than restrain himself, he goes to the spring head, the tenant's farm yard, and dips in there.

But such a squire is not confined to Galway nor to Ireland, though in Ireland it is more common than in England to find a gentleman eating golden eggs to his breakfast, having killed the goose the day before. Anywhere, in England or in Ireland, the mere consumer, wear what colour of coat he may, is a fugitive from usefulness.

Those remarks, extending by no means to the end of the subject, have been suggested by the fact that the oats and oatmeal, and butter and pork, of the west of Ireland, which are sold to get money to pay rent, are carried to the west of Scotland, and paid for and consumed there by a population whose industrious hands are engaged in manufacturing human comforts for themselves and for all the people of the world who will or can buy from them. If a part, or a very considerable portion of the rent, which is the price of the oats, butter, and pigs, be sent to the landowners who do not live in Ireland, to England it may be, the loss is doubtless felt in Mayo. Those exports of farm produce and of farm rents give rise to some well founded complaints, but also to many errors. An argument for the repeal of the union is founded on the exportation of farm produce and of farm rent. And England, which is supposed to seduce those gentlemen of the west from their hounds, horses, bugle-horns, and native hills, has a great deal of scolding to hear and bear for keeping them from home. All which Henry the Second and Elizabeth and Cromwell did in Ireland is mixed up with the charge of having seduced from his home the fox-hunter of Galway and Sligo. If Henry, and Elizabeth, and Cromwell were now alive, they might very properly be spoken to on the subject of making war on Ireland; but the persons who now eat Irish butter, pork, beef, eggs, poultry, and meal, and who *pay* for it all, have no interest whatever in, or from, anything done by the King, Queen, and Republican aforesaid. All the wars of those sovereigns and their servants were mischievous to England as to Ireland. War, like fox-hunting, consumes without producing wealth. Nor is it of any benefit to England as a nation that the Irish squires choose to go and live idly there. Whatever they or their servants may eat in a day, that day passing without their adding some value to something of usefulness in England, is national loss, though it may not be a local loss in London.

At all events, they do not live in Glasgow, nor does Glasgow care the value of one peck of meal whether they ever do or not. She does not even question the place of residence of her own landowners. Nor had Glasgow or Scotland any share in the union of England and Ireland. Yet Glasgow receives more of the oats, oatmeal, butter, and pork, of Mayo and Sligo than London does. But she pays for them. And, hard as the case of Mayo and Sligo is, obliged to sell their farm produce in Glasgow to obtain money to send to their landowners elsewhere, there is a possibility of their being in a case still worse. As it is, there are mills to grind the oats and millers who are paid wages for adding value to the oats by reducing them to meal. There are ships, warehouses, wharves, roads, sailors, porters, carmen on the roads, road-makers, and others, all giving greater value to oats and to meal; to cows, butter, poultry, eggs, hogs, horses, and the provender of all of these. Now the worst conditions which it is possible to be in is that of having all the landowners and their families at home *to eat food and still be idle,* with no market beyond their own shores; and still, as now, nobody among themselves employed otherwise than in working on the surface of the land.

To work at something which shall become of greater worth, and to work in such aggregation or in such division of numbers as shall give the work the greatest worth in the shortest time, is the way to make national wealth; and the greater proportion of the people of a nation so employed, otherwise than on the land, the more wealth will they have to exchange for agricultural produce, and the richer will agriculture be the sooner that this is understood in Ireland, and in some other places which might be named, the sooner will Ireland rise out of destitution.

The following passages in the evidence of Mr M'Donnell, a corn-merchant of Westport in Mayo, given in July 1844, are worth notice at the present time:—

'Has the use of wheaten flour at all spread among the farmers?' 'No, they do not use it themselves, they sell it. I have never known them use it by any means in this country except when they could not dispose of it. In the year of scarcity, in 1831, when we got money from the benevolent people in England, we were then, from the want of oatmeal, obliged to bring wheat from different parts of the country; but the people never make use of wheaten flour except when they cannot get oatmeal. The poor man uses oatmeal for meat and drink, when reasonable in price. He has thin oat gruel and oaten bread, and he takes it out with him to the fields. The price of labour has been very low. During the winter there were not more than twenty men in this neighbourhood working, and they at 7d. and 8d. per day. When the potato crop has been injured by blasts from the sea, the people have suffered very much. In the year 1821, we suffered very severely in that way, and also in 1822. We had to import food from other countries.'

'Was there no oats in the country?—'Yes, there had been oats, but they had been exported previously. In truth, the vessels had met each other going out and coming in. A man may have engaged his vessels for two months before, and he must go on with his business, no matter what the consequences may be. I have imported wheat into this country, and the vessels taking out oats have actually met the vessels bringing in the wheat.'

This was the case in 1846 and the year before; and even in 1847, oats have been sent from Westport to England, where they are in demand, at high prices, for horses; and Indian corn, coming to Westport, has met them in other ships. To those who have an interest in understanding the self-adjusting principles of commercial exchanges, those passages will be instructive. To those who feel desirous of knowing the chief evidence of all the witnesses examined by the Land Commission in Mayo and Sligo, and who cannot read all that was deposed to, I may say that the burthen of it was, destitution among the mass of the population every year; misery at the best of times, absolute famine often; and I may add that my belief is that the bulk of the west of Ireland population is better provided for now by government than they used to provide for themselves; that they, never having parted with rent, but when money or produce, often the latter, was forced from them, they will not be readily induced to work on their land now for rent, when they see food given to them from some where else than from their own country.

EXTRACTS FROM IRISH LETTERS

To conclude this account of the condition of Ireland in the year of famine and pestilence 1847, and to conclude this volume, I shall here give some passages from letters written by me on the state of Ireland in 1843. Copies of those letters were given to the leading members of parliament. At the beginning of the session of 1844, Lord John Russell, in the famous debate on the condition of Ireland, referred to them, but said the facts detailed therein were almost too horrible for belief, and he would not read them to the house. Sir Robert Peel, in the same debate, referred to the letters as mentioned by the noble Lord, and said he had read the pamphlet in which they were contained; the statements were indeed horrible, but he feared too true. The Marquis of Normandy, in the House of Lords, quoted the pamphlet soon after as an authority, and, about the same time, the *Dublin Review* had an article on the subject of these letters, and said that the facts were known to the writer of the article to be as truly horrible as I had given them. Indeed, as regards Sir Robert Peel's belief in the facts, he, as prime minister, had taken the best possible means of inquiring into the truth. He sent a private and confidential agent to the locality of these landlordly crimes, after my first reports were sent to London and privately laid before government, upon whose report, confirmatory of mine, the Devon Commission was issued, to inquire into the whole subject of landlord and tenant in the whole of Ireland.

Thus much, by way of introduction to the passages of the Irish letters which I now append, is deemed necessary, lest readers, innocent of knowing much about Ireland, might lift their hands and heads in wonder, and let this book fall, and cry, 'Impossible! we shall not take up that book again!'—They must take it up again; at any rate the subject of these letters must be taken up again and again.

In different parts of the country of Kilkenny, in several directions from the town, there were what is usually called 'disturbed districts.' In one place a murder had been committed, and in several others there had been attempts at murder—at all events, there had been accusations against certain parties of attempting to murder; but we shall see by-and-bye, from the trials at assizes and from other evidence, that it is no unusual thing in Ireland, and especially in a 'disturbed district,' to get up accusations of attempted murder for purposes which, when we come to the facts, will be easily understood.

The cases of ejectment now about to be particularized were not the cases of tenants-at-will, nor of an under tenantry who held their land from some one subordinate to the landlord; they were leaseholders, holding direct from the landlord himself, under covenants as indisputably legal as any lease in Scotland or in England. The landlord never attempted to dispute the validity of the leases; he knew that most of them had been granted by his immediate predecessor, and some by the predecessor's father. He knew that he could not eject any one of the tenants by disputing about the lease, but he knew that the law gave him power to eject if the tenant did not pay his rent. But here he encountered a difficulty. The very fact which excited him to a war with his tenantry operated to defeat him. The farms were generally held at about 30s. an acre, and from that to 40s.; he knew the land could be let for more; for in some cases, where farms on the same estate were not let on lease, he had raised the rent to 60s. and 70s. an acre; and found that the people would rather pay that than renounce their holdings. Thus, because the farms were let at a moderate rent to the leaseholders, he sought to get them into his own hand, and he might re-let them at higher rents; but, because they were cheap, the tenants kept clear of arrears, and he having no means of breaking through the leases, was at a considerable loss to know how to act; but he did act; and a history of his proceedings will not only exemplify the condition of landlord and tenant in Ireland, but will, at the same time, shew how the laws in Ireland can be set at defiance by a man who has money and is a staunch adherent of the dominant party. This last fact is most necessary to be borne in mind, because the landlord now under notice has been defended by the press of the dominant party as one of the best though worst used of churchmen. He has been heard of through the government newspapers over the world as a martyr and a Christian. How far he is entitled to the honour of either will become apparent in the sequel. Suffice it now to say, by way of preface, in addition to what is already explained, that my authority for the following statements rests, first, on the narratives of the tenantry themselves; second, on the account given me by Mr Coyne, a gentleman of respectability, who for two years acted as the agent of this landlord, but, who at last, threw up his situation, out of sheer disgust at the odious work he was called on to perform; third, on the testimony of several magistrates and other gentlemen in the towns of Kilkenny and Thomastown; fourth, on the information, very comprehensive and valuable, afforded me by the solicitor who has been engaged in defence of most of the tenants in the numerous lawsuits which have arisen during the last three years; fifth, on evidence given in various cases tried at the sessions and assizes, part of which has been published in the local papers, all of which has been recorded by official persons who furnished me with matters of importance not published; and, sixth, from what I heard with my own ears from the witnesses in the assize court.

The district in which this estate is situated, it may be proper to say, was, until three years ago, a peaceable one; agrarian crime was unknown; the people industrious and moral; and there were no constabulary in the neighbourhood, nor any need of them. It is only four years since the present landlord came to the estate, since which he has had upwards of 250 lawsuits with his tenantry, has erected a police barrack on his property, and obtained from government a detachment of armed police to remain there continually. The military, both cavalry and foot, have been greatly augmented in the district in the same time. Several men have been tried for their lives—some transported, and some hanged. The tenantry amount to between seventy and eighty, and the estate occupies a beautiful situation on each side of the Nore at Bennet's Bridge.

CASE OF JOHN RYAN

John Ryan had been a road contractor as well as a farmer. The landlord alleged a debt against him, and threw him into prison. While there his contract was unperformed, and he lost it, and sacrificed his security to perform it. It was satisfactorily proved, in a court of law, that the debt never existed; that it was brought forward by the landlord at the expense of forgery and false swearing; upon which John Ryan brought an action for false imprisonment. Had the defendant not been a landlord, the plaintiff might have prosecuted him criminally; but being a landlord, there was no chance of succeeding against him. Even in the action of damages there was little hope for John Ryan; but the case was so very bad, and the judge, in summing up, made such severe comments on the conduct of the landlord, that the jury gave a verdict for plaintiff. I was present at the trial, and I quote both from my notes and from the report of the trial as published in the local papers, in giving the following words as a portion of the judge's summary:—

'Gentlemen—If you believe that the defendant fraudulently alleged this debt against plaintiff, that he might put him in prison and ruin him, you will give a verdict accordingly. In that case you will make him worse than the man who goes boldly to the highway and robs openly. You will weigh well the evidence you have heard, and if you are satisfied that plaintiff has been injured, you will give damages accordingly. Do not give overwhelming damages; still you must teach defendant that, though he is a gentleman of rank and property, he is not to trample on a poorer man than himself with impunity.'

To this the jury gave a verdict for plaintiff—damages £100.

The landlord, out of about 250 actions at law, of various kinds in less than three years, has been defeated in four-fifths of them—and though he had thirteen cases at last quarter sessions, and was defeated in all—he still triumphs. He appeals to higher courts. He does not pay the £100 damages to Ryan. He makes an appeal which will not be settled until some time next year. Meantime, Ryan, by being in prison and by being involved in litigation, of which this is but a mere sample—by losing his contract for the roads, having all his implements and farming stock seized and sold while in prison—was unable to cultivate his land so as to enable him to pay his last Michaelmas rent. The rent being less than £100, which the landlord owed him in damages, it might have been supposed that this £100 would be a set-off for the rent. But no, a letter to me on the 8th of November says—'And he (the landlord) canted John Ryan to the potatoes, and did not leave his family one bit that would eat.' This John Ryan, it must be borne in mind, was a leaseholder, and never owed a farthing of rent until those proceedings were taken against him to compel him into arrears which would justify an ejectment. His case, from first to last—from the time that he was an independent man, with as happy a family around him as lived in the Queen's dominions, living in a house of his own building, with a farm-steading erected at his own expense, which are equal to any cottage or farm-steading of the same extent in England or Scotland for cleanliness, order, and substantiality— I saw them with my own eyes, and judged for myself; from the time that John Ryan was an independent man in that farm to the present, when he and his family are potatoless and penniless, and to the point of being ejected, the proceedings against him have been of the most extraordinary kind and almost beyond belief.

CASE OF WILLIAM RING

William Ring is also a leaseholding tenant on the estate, and is uncle to Patrick Ring. He is considered a man of substance, and was never known to owe any man sixpence unreasonably, being at all times scrupulously punctual. He has a limekiln on his farm, and makes and sells lime. On one occasion eighteen or twenty months ago the landlord had lime from him to the amount of £9. William Ring sent in his account, but the landlord, through his steward, taunted him with having assisted Patrick Ring to plough and sow his land at a time when the landlord had seized and carried off Patrick Ring's implements, (these were carried off, as afterwards appeared by the decision of the jury, when no rent nor debt of any kind was due; they were carried off that Patrick Ring might be unable to cultivate his land and pay his rent. Patrick went to law and got damages against the landlord. He also got assistance from three of his neighbours to plough and sow his fields; all the other neighbours, though willing to help him, being afraid of the landlord, save these three, one of whom was his uncle, William Ring, whose case about the lime I am now relating.) The landlord refused to pay the £9 for the lime, saying, through the steward, that as William Ring had thought fit to set himself against him by helping Patrick Ring to plough and sow his fields, he, the landlord, would set himself against William Ring; he would not pay the £9 for the lime—he would let him do his best.

William Ring might have let it remain to be deducted from the next payment of rent, some one will say. But this would not do in Ireland, at least with a landlord such as his, who hesitated not to seize on tenants who owed nothing. He knew that an immediate seizure would be made on the day the rent was due if this £9 was deducted from it, because it had become common on this estate, and is yet, as shewn by the reports of the trials at the last sessions, to proceed to distrain on the day following term day. Seizures in some cases had been made at one o'clock for rent due at twelve; and in one case, that of Mathew Dormer, brother-in-law of Patrick Ring, a distraint was made at ten o'clock of the rent-day; therefore William Ring did not let his claim for the price of his lime stand over to be deducted from the rent. He summoned the landlord, and in due course got a decree against him. The landlord had to pay; but on the same day he did so, he got a party of the armed constabulary, who are located on the estate for the purpose of carrying on the war, and with them, and a carpenter, and his steward, he proceeded to William Ring's farm. The farmhouse and haggard (garden, &c.) were sheltered and ornamented by trees and bushes which had been planted by the tenant and his forefathers, and which were highly prized by the farmer and his family. In law they were the property of the landlord; and the landlord, the carpenter, the steward, and the police, set to work, cut them all down, and carried them home to the landlord's residence.

CASES OF MATHEW DORMER AND JAMES MULLINS

Mathew Dormer, the brother-in-law of Patrick Ring, is a leaseholding tenant, but holds only a small field of about three acres. The other farms are from twenty to fifty acres. Dormer does not depend on his land further than for potatoes to his family and for keep to his horse, with which and a cart he does jobbing work. He had assisted Patrick Ring in time of trouble, and thus brought on himself the power of the landlord. His field can only be approached by either of two roads through other farms from the village where Dormer lives. Having paid all rent, the landlord had no power on him but by shutting him out of his field. The tenants who occupied the land through which Dormer had to pass were served with notices that, if they allowed him ingress with a cart or horse they would be ejected. I went and saw the field, and was told by Dormer and his neighbours the whole case. He had planted his potatoes without manure, and, though it was August when I saw them, they were not six inches above the ground, nor did they shew symptoms of at any time being more; and this because Dormer was not allowed to carry the manure, of which he had abundance, to his field. He was told by the lawyers that he had a good case, and would be sure to gain a suit at law; but while that is pending the potato season has passed over with almost no crop, and winter has come without a potato for his family; worst of all, his barley, which occupied, I think, about two-thirds of the ground, (I saw it when nearly ripe in August,) and from which he hoped to pay his rent and get provender for his horse, was still in the field rotting on the 8th of October. Thus Mathew Dormer will be unable to pay his November rent, and a process of ejectment will of course issue and take effect.

Another case which may be mentioned now is brief and characteristic. A tenant who held on lease went with his rent to the landlord last spring on the day it was due. Says the landlord, 'Mr Mullins, you need not be so particular about paying your rent, you are always very punctual and you may perhaps want the money for some other purpose. I should advise you now to buy some cattle and sheep at the fair, and depasture your grass fields instead of making hay this year; but, even if you do make hay, you have not enough of stock.' To which Mr. M. replied, 'I am exceedingly obliged to you; I would have bought stock had it not been for my rent; but if you forego it for the present, I will do as you suggest; and, if you have no objection I will hire another field for the season as well, and put cattle in it.' 'An excellent thought,' said the landlord; 'buy all the cattle your money will afford; you will, no doubt, be able to hire pasturage for them.' And Mr M. did as his landlord advised. But what was his astonishment when, in less than a week, indeed within three days, the landlord distrained on the whole, and sold all the cattle, and all the farm implements as well, for his rent. This, of course, gave rise to litigation, which will only end in the ruin and ejectment of the tenant, with the re-letting of the farm at a higher rent, an object not far from being accomplished.

Since these remarks about Dormer were written, the *Kilkenny Journal* has been received, containing a report of the cases at petty sessions on the 18th November. Of ten cases which occupied the attention of the court, seven arose out of the disputes between the landlord and his tenants in the disturbed district already described. Five of those cases were at the instance of the landlord against the tenant Mathew Dormer, who had been excluded from his field, and whose corn, as stated in a letter which I quoted, was standing rotting on the ground up to the 8th of October. It does not appear by the report of the cases decided at petty sessions whether the corn is yet in the field or carried home; but it appears to have been in the field on the 15th of November. On that day Dormer proceeded to make a gap in a stone wall, the gates being shut against him, to get into his field. For making this gap three actions were brought against him by the landlord, and two by persons whom the landlord put forward as prosecutors. It seems the first time the gap was attempted was on the 13th of October. The field through which Dormer then attempted to pass to his own field was in the occupation of the landlord himself; and the landlord now prosecuted under the Malicious Trespass Act; but the magistrate dismissed the case because it was not *malicious*. His remarks give a better exemplification of what law is in Ireland than any description of mine could do. The case is thus reported:—The steward of the landlord called 'deposed that he saw the defendant levelling a wall, the property of the plaintiff; he was making a gap in it.'

Cross-examined: 'I live with Mr Shee. The defendant said he would not be prevented till the law prevented him, and that he must get a passage, *and that if he got a passage he would build up the gap at his own expense.* There was no other passage to his field than that. There was formerly a passage to the farm through a field of one Ring, but Dormer was since prevented.'

The attorney for the defence then addressed the bench; stated that Mathew Dormer owed nothing to the landlord, and had a legal right to a road to his farm. He had followed the way which had been formerly used, namely, through another tenant's ground; but at the instance of the landlord this tenant had been compelled to prosecute, and Dormer had been fined for trespass by this bench. He then attempted to make this gap and have a passage, as complained of to-day, through a field in the occupation of his landlord, who was bound to give him a passage to that farm, the rent of which Dormer would be compelled to pay as soon as it became due. What, therefore, could the poor man do? His corn was rotting in the field at that time, the middle of October.

To which the magistrate, in giving his decision, replied, 'It was a hard case; but he thought Mathew Dormer had no right to break Mr Shee's wall or commit the trespass. It certainly was not malicious; and if Mr Quin (the defendant's attorney) insisted on it, the bench must dismiss the summons; but another summons might be brought for common trespass, and the case would have to be heard *de novo*. Why did not Dormer bring his action?'

The Attorney—'And so he will.'

'The magistrate, after some farther discussion agreed to dismiss the complaint, Mr Quin undertaking to prove, should another summons be brought for common trespass, that Dormer had a right to break the gap.'

The point, of all others, which the English public should look at here, is the question of the magistrate, 'Why does not Dormer bring his action?' The magistrate knows well that in this case Dormer would succeed in an action against the landlord; that is to say, if the jury should not be entirely a landlord's jury. But the action could not be tried before next spring or summer assizes; and the landlord might, as he has done in similar cases already, make an affidavit that he was not ready to go to trial even then. And if this was overruled, and the case proceeded with and decided against him—as it would be, provided always the jury was not one formed of men of his own rank, politics, and religion—he could appeal to a higher court. Meantime Dormer is ruined. He could not plant his potatoes last spring without committing a trespass by walking on another man's land—not the land bearing or preparing for a crop, but the footpath at the bottom of it. He planted his potatoes, however, and was fined for this trespass. But he planted them without manure, for he could not get an entrance at which to carry it in, and the crop was worthless. 'Why does not Dormer bring his action?' asks the magistrate. No doubt he can bring an action, and ultimately carry it too'; but his crop is rendered worthless in the meantime, and the same magistrate fines him for walking on the footpath which leads to it. 'Why does not Dormer bring his action?' The magistrate who has fined him for going to his land without having first brought his action, which would occupy probably one or two years, asks this question on the 18th of November, knowing that Dormer's crop of barley was still rotting on the field, or had been so as late as the 15th three day's before! No doubt the magistrate administers the law as it stands; but it is the law as it stands of which such men as Dormer complain. The object of the landlord is to render the payment of rent impossible, and a consequent ejectment certain. This is the policy by which a leaseholder is overcome in Ireland.

But the prosecution did not end by the magistrate dismissing the first summons at the petty sessions. Another prosecutor was ready. A man had been sent by the landlord to watch Dormer in case he made a gap in the wall; and on the 13th of October, when he began to make the gap, this man, who is a mere minion of the landlord—fit for any kind of work—went to prevent him. Wherever Dormer attempted to lay the stones, this man put himself in the way, that the stones might fall upon him, and that a case of assault might be got up at the same time as that of malicious trespass. This case, however, did not succeed, Dormer having taken care not to hurt him, although he put himself in the way of the stones for the purpose. The summons was dismissed. The following is a portion of the cross-examination of this witness:—

'He was in England last summer twelvemonths. He was there also at the time of the Whitefeet; is not aware that the neighbours ever said he used to be out with his face blackened. Was up in Cork lately; saw Mr Shee, who gave him travelling charges to the amount of £1:5s. Had no conversation with him then about Mathew Dormer. Had a conversation with Mr Shee lately about him at Blackwell Lodge.'

The Attorney—'On your solemn oath, did Mr Shee (the landlord) say he would give you anything in the world if you would transport Dormer?'

'The witness,' says the *Kilkenny Journal*, 'was silent amidst the sensation of the court, and the question was again and again repeated, and he was still silent. At length he muttered an evasive answer.'

It may be proper here to remark that Dormer is a man bearing the very best moral character. He was several years in the police, and saved some money. I saw and read the certificates of character which he held, and they bore out the good report of his moral character. Moreover, in his very appearance he carries respectability of behaviour. He is a tall man, about forty years of age, and has a wife and several young children.

The next prosecutor against him, for making a gap in the wall to get to his field and crop, was a man who alleged that the field over which Dormer trespassed was in his occupation, and not in that of the landlord. This man produced a lease, signed the 16th of November, in which he appeared to be the tenant of the field. It was argued that Dormer made the gap previous to that lease being completed. It was a gap in the same wall at the same place as that of the 13th of October, that having been, it seems, built up. The court in this case decided against Dormer, and fined him a shilling, and cautioned him against a repetition of the offence. Two other cases of trespass came on in which the landlord was plaintiff and Dormer defendant. They were dismissed through an informality in the summonses.

These cases, though they are as innocence itself compared with some others in which the landlord has been engaged, will shew how powerless the law is to protect a tenant in Ireland, even where a magistrate inclines to mercy. But perhaps the most remarkable fact of law in connection with these cases is, that while the wages of a working man in the district is 6d. a-day, with many not able to get employment even at that, the expense of doing any work for which the law allows payment is fully as high, in some cases much higher, than similar work costs in London. The expense of building up the gap which Dormer made (not being allowed to build it himself) is 10s. It is only a *dry*-stone wall, between three and four feet high. Now, supposing the gap wide enough to admit a cart, any labouring man could rebuild it in three or four hours at the very utmost.

In the matter of seizures the charges are similar. In London, a broker who distrains can only put one man in possession, and charge for him 2s. 6d. a-day. In Ireland a landlord puts what men he chooses in possession, and charges for them from 2s. to 2s. 6d. a-day. The landlord now spoken of has, as law papers proved to me when I inspected them, seized on a man's potatoes who was working for 8d. a-day, the current wages, and put two men on as 'keepers' for a week, and allowed them (the law allows him to do so) 2s. 4d. a-day.

The following extract of a letter from Patrick Ring, whose case (just ended with his utter ruin and beggary) I shall relate at length, will give some information of the high wages allowed by the law, even where men are willing to work for 6d. a-day:—

'I got my crop valued by two farmers, and they valued it at £30. He (the landlord) then takes and puts three keepers on it to run up expenses, and canted it (sold it) for £17:10s., and out of that, keepers' fees and expenses were £6:10s.'

It may also be stated that a landlord in Ireland can call on any one of his servants or labourers to act as auctioneer. If he wants to buy a bargain himself, or to ruin the tenant to have him ejected, he can give this domestic auctioneer orders to knock an article down at a price far below its value. The landlord under notice has, in many cases, bought the effects of his tenants himself though an agent.

Case of Patrick Ring

Patrick Ring held three small fields, amounting in all to about eighteen acres. He had a lease of thirty-one years and his own life. He had succeeded his father in the occupancy of the farm, who had also been on the estate for many years. Ring's mother, an aged woman now bordering on eighty, was born on the farm so long held by her husband and son; and thus there was doubtless a strong attachment to the place on the part of the whole family. Previous to the accession of the present landlord they had been on the best of terms with those to whom they paid their rent; and, having the land at a moderate rate, they had never fallen into arrears. They are Catholics—the present landlord is a Protestant. But whether it was that he wished to serve his party by substituting a Protestant tenantry for a Catholic tenantry, Protestant jurymen for Catholic jurymen; whether it was merely to have the leases broken and the farms re-let at a higher rent; or whether it was to accomplish both objects at once, is not clear, nor is it a matter of great importance; the landlord, and those who support him in all he does, are welcome to excuse themselves on any ground they choose to take as excusable. It is sufficient to say that the ejection of Patrick Ring and many more was resolved upon.

As he owed no rent, and as no possible reason for getting rid of him as a tenant could be assigned, nor was ever offered until long after proceedings had begun, a bold stroke to make a beginning was absolutely requisite, and it was struck. The lease specified a certain day in May and in November as that on which the half-yearly rent would fall due. Those days had been strictly adhered to, and no one knew this better than the landlord. But in 1841 he obtained a warrant of distraint, and seized on Ring on the 26th of March for rent alleged to be due on 25th. It might have been a hard enough misfortune to be distrained on the day following that of the rent being due in any case, especially in spring, when the cattle and implements of labour, as also the seed-corn and potatoes, the articles distrained, are required for the peculiar duties of that most important season, seed-time. But when such distraint was made in such articles so indispensable in their uses, even for a day, to say nothing of weeks, and no rent nor debt of any kind owing, the case is peculiarly a hard one on the tenant.

Patrick Ring caused a replevin to be entered with the sheriff, that is, he gave security that he would pay the rent, if rent was due, as soon as a trial at quarter-sessions or assizes could be had, that he might in the meantime have the use of the property upon which the distraint lay. He accordingly proved by his lease that he owed nothing—that no rent was due until May. But before that was done May had come, and the rent was due. He paid it punctually, and proceeded against the landlord for damages, or rather for the costs to which he had been exposed. This, being opposed, occupied much time, and before it was settled the landlord once more distrained for rent alleged to be due on the 29th of September. Again Patrick Ring replevined, and proved his rent-day to be in November and May, and not in September and March. The case of costs and trespass came to trial in respect of both seizures, and was decided in Ring's favour. Thus a jury and a judge certified by their decision that the tenant was right and the landlord was wrong. The damages awarded were very moderate, only £12 and costs; but the tenant looked on the verdict as most important in respect of its setting, as he thought, the validity of his lease and the period of his rent-days at rest. But that the damages were too moderate as regarded the landlord was manifest from the fact that he again distrained in March for rent not due until May.

He now, it being again seed-time, took a more effectual way of crippling the tenant than before. He seized on the farm implements and stock, of which the dunghill was in his eyes the most important. He had it, without a legal sale, carried away to his own farm-yard, even to the very rakings and sweepings of the road and the yard near which it lay. This he did that Ring might have no manure for his potato ground, knowing that crops so planted would not easily afford the rent; and that, when no rent was forthcoming, an ejectment would soon follow. Other things, a plough and a horse, and some furniture, were sold, and Ring was once more involved in litigation. These things were bought in with his own money, save the dung heap, which the landlord would not give him a chance of buying in; and thus Ring was obliged to pay his rent before it was due, with all the expenses of a distraint and sale—the most expensively conducted of any distraints and sales under the British crown. He thought to recover damages for all this loss, but he was not able to pay his rent in addition to all this when it became due; and thus, by some hocus pocus of the law, the two cases became so mingled together as to be inextricable.

It would be too tedious to give a detailed account of every lawsuit that now followed; but from that time, the summer of 1842, up to the summer assizes of 1843, the landlord proceeded in the courts for a warrant of ejectment against Ring nine times. On the first eight cases he was defeated, but he succeeded on the ninth. He had thirteen other lawsuits of various kinds with the same defendant, during which he sold his furniture five times and his horse twice. In all, he had twenty auctions of sale previous to midsummer of this year. Part of the furniture was in several of these instances only bought back by the agent Mr James Coyne, handing money privately to Ring to pay for it. This is the agent formerly spoken of, who at last gave up his situation out of sheer disgust at the odious work he was called on to perform.

The crop of 1842 was seized on and sold at seven different times. It was much more than sufficient to pay the rent, even though the manure was carried away in the spring by the landlord; but those seven different seizures, with seven different sales, with a number of men receiving at each of the seven seizures 2s. 4d. a-day as keepers to watch the crop from the day of distraint to the day of sale—those seven seizures on a crop which might have been all seized and sold at one time, with only one set of expenses—resulted, as they were intended to do, in nearly doubling the rent. Moreover, the crop being distrained on while growing, was cut down by people whom the landlord employed, although the tenant and his family were standing unemployed; and to such work people the landlord can give any wages he chooses, to be deducted from the tenant, up to 2s. 6d. a-day! even though the harvest wages of the district be 8d. or 10d. a-day! even though the tenant, who is thus not allowed to give his own labour on his farm, may, to avoid starvation, be compelled to work to another employer for the fourth part, to wit, 7½ d. a-day, of what the law obliges him to pay for workmen on his own farm.

It will give some proof of the exertions made by the tenant to pay his way when I state that, notwithstanding all the extraordinary expenses of the seizures, and of the protracted and complicated litigation, the rent was paid by the autumn of 1842. There was nothing owing by Ring save a sum of £1 and odds, connected with the expenses of a summons which had been decided against him on some technical point of law.

For the recovery of this debt a decree was obtained against Ring, and orders were given by the landlord to arrest him and put him in gaol. This Ring endeavoured to avoid by keeping out of the reach of the officers, which he did successfully for the space of a month and some odd days. The reason why he was so averse to go to gaol, and why the landlord was so desirous to have him lodged there, is worth relating at full length, as it is characteristic of certain customs in Ireland altogether unknown on this side of the channel.

It is a very rare thing to find a landlord in Ireland building a house or farm-offices for a tenant—the tenant builds them himself. Hence it is that so many mean houses exist in that country; and hence, also, the desperate tenacity with which the Irish peasant or farmer holds to his house when an ejectment comes upon him. If his lease has expired, or if he is ejected for the non-fulfilment of some condition of his lease, say the regular payment of his rent, he must leave the house and barn and stable which he built, the doors and gates he erected, without receiving anything for them. To live in a house which we have ourselves built, or which our father or grandfather built at no expense to a landlord, is to live in a house which we are naturally inclined to consider our own, though in law it may not be ours, and therefore an ejectment is the more distressing. It is thus that we see so many houses in every part of Ireland in ruins; that we see in the county of Kilkenny the walls of stone and lime, substantial and undecayed, but roofless and marked with violence, because the landlords, not having built the houses, nor having any fear of being obliged to rebuild them, hesitate not to unroof a house in order to eject a tenant. It is a remarkable fact, exemplified on almost every estate where the clearing away of a tenantry has been practised, that wherever an ejectment takes place, the legality of which is doubtful, the landlord, or the agent who acts for him, levels the house and farm buildings with the ground the moment the holder is forced out, lest he should come in again.

This is particularly the case on the estate where the unfortunate Pat Ring held his farm; and Ring had seen that the landlord did not always wait for an ejectment of the tenant before he pulled down the house. In one case, that of a tenant named Bushe, of whom, with many other sufferers, I have not yet spoken, the landlord resolved on an ejectment; but Bushe owing no rent, he could only proceed as he had done against Pat Ring, or by some other process of a like kind. He took a shorter one.

It so happened that, though Bushe had paid his rent in order to keep the house above his head—a very good house it was, to judge from the size and worth of the substantial walls which, in most parts, were still standing when I was there—he had not paid every man in the county to whom he was indebted. He owed one person, residing at a distance, a sum of money, more, as it soon appeared, than he could pay at once. This man the landlord found out, through some of his agents appointed for such purposes, and purchased from him the debt which Bushe owed him. This account being legally conveyed to the landlord, he at once proceeded against his tenant, the debtor, threw him into prison, and as soon as he got him there, went and took the roof off his house, turning out his wife and six young children upon the open highway. There they remained without shelter and without food until some of the people of the adjoining village assisted them. The father was in prison, and could neither resist the spoliation of the house which he himself had built, nor could he do anything, by work or otherwise, for his family's subsistence. In every respect, the proceeding was illegal on the part of the landlord; but, though the lawyers urged Bushe to prosecute, and assured him of ultimate success, he was too far gone to listen to them. He was heart-broken. He had no confidence in any redress the law might give; he had seen a rich man set the law at defiance; and the ruin of his roofless house—every piece of timber from which, and every handful of thatch, as also the doors and windows, had been carried away by order of the landlord, and by the assistance of the constabulary, who are located on the estate at the express request of the landlord, and by sanction of the government—the ruin of his roofless house, and the utter beggary of himself and family, so overwhelmed Bushe, that he would trust nothing more to law. He was heart-broken, and rather than stay among people who had known him happy in mind and comfortable in circumstances, he would leave that part of the country altogether, and be a beggar, now that he was compelled to be one, where he was not known. A less sensitive man than he was might have done differently. There have been cases in Ireland, many of them, and in that county, even in that district of the county, where fathers of families so treated have taken the law of vengeance into their own hands, and have afforded the newspapers and the police *Hue-and-Cry* the materials for publishing to the world para-graphs and advertisements of offered rewards, headed '*Un*provoked assault!' 'Barbarous outrage!' 'Frightful state of Kilkenny—the fruit of unchecked political agitation!' 'Attempted murder of the excellent Prot-estant landlord, Richard Shee, Esq. of Blackwell Lodge!'

Such paragraphs are by no means rare; and many people in England believe that Tipperary and Kilkenny are filled with criminals who take a savage delight in assaulting landlords and land-agents without any provocation. Others, who do not believe that every assault is so entirely '*un*provoked' as the newspapers would make appear, have an opinion that the Irish do not allow the oppressor to escape with impunity; but the case of Bushe is one of the many of the vast majority of such cases that prove the contrary. We hear of those tenants who, feeling or fancying a grievous wrong, avenge themselves and their starving families; but we never hear of the many—the far greater number—who submit to die in the ditches and highways quietly; or who, like the spirit-stricken Bushe, wander away with their wretched families, to famish in the Irish towns, or to fill the St Giles's and Peter Streets, the Cowgates and Wynds, the Saltmarkets and Vennels, of London, Edinburgh, Glasgow, and Liverpool.

Now, it was the knowledge that Pat Ring had of such cases of house-demolition by order of landlords, when a tenant was out of the way—lodged safely in prison—that made him so fearful of the officers, who had a decree on which to arrest him for the non-payment of costs due to the landlord by one of the many cases then pending having been decided in the landlord's favour. The amount was not great; but the frequent seizures, with costs of lawsuits and rent, had reduced him to less than his last penny. He had potatoes, a part of the feeble crop grown on the land which in the spring had been defrauded of its manure, and, though there were less of them in his possession than would keep his family over winter, even without feeding a pig, he might have sold some to pay this bill of costs rather than go to gaol, where he could do nothing either for his family or farm. But, though the potatoes were distrained upon, the object of the landlord was not so much the payment of the small debt of costs as the confinement of the tenant in gaol.

For more than a month Ring avoided the officers by crossing the walls and ditches and fields whenever he got notice of their approach. He slept in the fields as well, and in the shelter of limekilns and ruined houses—houses ruined as he feared his would be, and as he feared but too truly. The case came at last to a crisis, thus:—

He was seen to enter his house; the bailiffs followed, but found the door fastened, and therefore could not legally enter; but they kept watch outside, to see that he did not escape. They received orders that, if he did not surrender, they were to remain there night and day, and prevent the introduction of any article whatsoever into the house, food or water. The potato-store being out in the field, and no supply in the house, and the water being also outside the house, it was expected that the family would soon be starved, and that Ring must capitulate. In thus laying seige to the house, the bailiffs might not be acting according to the law of the land, but they were acting according to the law of the landlord, which, on that estate as on many others in Ireland, is of paramount importance compared with the law of the land.

Before the first day of the seige was over, there was neither food nor drink in the house; and there were shut up in it the father, mother, and five young children. Next day the children cried for food and for drink, but got none. Some of the neighbours and relatives of Pat Ring would have supplied them, but they were sternly told that, if they attempted to do so, they would not only be prevented, but that the landlord would cause them to regret it. Again and again, through night and through day, did the cry for water come from that famishing family. It was not the case of a shipwrecked crew at sea, with no hand to help, with 'water, water everywhere, and not a drop to drink!' with no probability of being relieved but by reaching some unknown land in some unknown ocean, or by meeting a ship—blessed though rare chance—whose mariners would joyfully share their own scanty water for the relief of those perishing with thirst. It was not a case of this kind, where men in their desperation will drink salt water, and go mad from so doing; but, having done so, do not always all die, but sometimes live to tell us of the pangs they endured, until our breasts burn with pity and our hair rises on end with horror at what they did. This was not a case like theirs. This was the captivity of a family in their own house; foodless for days, though they had a potato-store in the field; waterless and unquenched by any liquid, though they had a well within a minute's walk; and all this by the mandate of a man who lived at the distance of half-a-mile, in the enjoyment of every luxury which wealth could procure and voluptuous-ness desire. The mother had a sucking infant, and in her attempt to save all her children from starvation by admitting them to the privilege of infancy, she but augmented their distress and her own. She saw her infant famishing, for, when she would have divided her own milk, there was none to divide; she was herself starving, and to her infant she was without nourishment.

It was the third day, and hunger and thirst in the house were so manifest to the bailiffs outside, by the pitiful cries of the children, and the wailings of the mother—who begged for water from their own well, and for potatoes from their own store—that hopes were entertained of a speedy surrender. Reports of the symptoms of extremity were conveyed at intervals to the landlord, who, as he heard of the increasing cries for water and food, gave orders afresh to the bailiffs to persevere, to keep watch and prevent all supplies from getting in, being assured that as the pangs of hunger and thirst became more poignant, the sooner would the beleagured family capitulate.

Mrs Dormer, the wife of the tenant who is shut out of his land, and whose crop of barley is rotting on the field in November, though he owes nothing to the landlord—this woman, who has herself a family of young children, and who is the sister of Pat Ring, went many times to the beleagured house to offer relief, but was not permitted to approach it with anything in her hand. She was allowed to approach the window when she carried nothing, that she might hear the sufferings within and so urge her brother to surrender.

She listened to the sickly wailings of the mother and children, and at last on the fourth day heard the horrible fact from the mother that the children in desperation had drank their own urine. At this moment she seized a dish of some sort which lay in the yard, and filling it quickly from a pool of stagnant water in the yard, broke the window with her hand, before she could be prevented by the officers, and gave the unwholesome water to the family, which they drank greedily. Perhaps she would have done more, but she was compelled by the officers to desist. The landlord was informed of what she had done, and he promised that she would live to repent it. The crop of Dormer rotting in the field in November, and his potatoes poor and meagre for the want of manure, because he is not allowed a road to his field, tell whether the landlord forgets his promises.

The sufferings of the family and of himself now worked on the father until he could hold out no longer. He opened the door. He had a pitchfork in his hand, and he shewed it to the bailiffs. He bade them keep off—said he would not touch them if they did not touch him—but that the hunger of himself and family had made him desperate—that he had potatoes in his store in the field, and potatoes he would have; and he bade them prevent him at their peril.

They did not offer to prevent him; they waited until they saw him take the potatoes, and then they informed the landlord. On that instant a criminal warrant was sent for from Kilkenny. It arrived; so did also a party of the armed constabulary, who occupy the barrack built by the landlord on the estate, and the door was at once forced open, and Pat Ring was taken and lodged in gaol on a charge of robbery accompanied with threats of violence. He had stolen his own potatoes, they being under distraint, and he was in due course of time tried at Kilkenny for the felony. The jury refused to convict for a crime committed under such circumstances, and he was acquitted.

This case has now reached the month of July 1843. At that time he was once more in prison for the non-payment of costs incurred in defending himself against the landlord.

These were paid, and a new decree for some other costs was got against him. There was also a warrant for his ejectment obtained. At this time his family were ill of typhus fever, and had been for several weeks. The sheriff refused to execute the ejectment while they so suffered. The landlord was exceedingly anxious to eject as early as possible, because (let the English reader mark this peculiarity of Irish tenures) a tenant, though ejected, may recover possession; the law says he may redeem within six months. Now Ring had an action for damages pending against the landlord, a very simple action which could have been easily tried, and in which a jury could not have hesitated to award ample damages. To this, at the summer assizes, the landlord, through his law agents, pleaded that he was not ready to go to trial; consequently it was put off until next assizes, to wit, March 1844. If, therefore, Ring could have been ejected in July, or early in August 1843, the six months in which he could redeem possession of his land would have expired before the trial of the case postponed to March 1844—a case which promised to put Ring in a condition to redeem his land by payment of his debt to the landlord.

We need not proceed farther with those cases of injustice. The landlord now under notice has proceeded in litigation and expenses until he is no longer in the management of his estate. Others in Ireland, less tyrannical than him, but not more wise in the management of their estates, have brought Ireland to a condition unparalleled in the history of nations. It would be vain to speculate on what the future may be, we can only say that the present (end of 1847 and beginning of 1848) is deplorable. Law set at defiance, rates uncollected; and rents unpaid.

APPENDIX

JOURNEY FROM NAVAN TO TRIM.—VISIT TO THE BIRTHPLACE OF THE DUKE OF WELLINGTON IN 1843

We left Navan on the 16th of August, the day after the Tara meeting. Having hired a car to Trim, distant towards the south about nine English miles, we had a pleasant journey, on one of the loveliest days with which Heaven ever blessed a fruitful earth. My object in that direction was chiefly to visit Dangan Castle, the birthplace of the late Marquis Wellesley, eldest son, and of the Duke of Wellington, sixth son, of the Earl and Countess of Mornington; also the birthplace of another distinguished individual, Feargus O'Connor, chief of our English chartists. It is not a matter of undoubted certainty, but it is extremely probable, that the Wellesleys and the O'Connors were born in the same chamber; at all events, they were born in the same house.

We had a fine rich soil, wretchedly cultivated, on each side of us, journeying from Navan to Trim. I saw some dozens of able-bodied men in Navan standing idle in the streets, seeking employment, and no one asking their price. I saw others at Trim similarly situated, and was told at both places that had it not been fine weather, and the hay-harvest just at its height, I would have seen hundreds where I only saw dozens. I spoke to several of those men, and found them eager to be engaged at eightpence and ninepence a-day. In Kilkenny I had seen several hundreds of able-bodied men seeking work at sixpence a-day; but in Meath the wages were higher, many of those employed at haymaking having tenpence. Passing between Navan and Trim, those whom I saw at work near the road, and within reach of conversation, were receiving eightpence and ninepence, few as much as tenpence. Others, again, had threepence and fourpence a-day and their diet, which diet consisted of potatoes and butter-milk twice a-day; if oatmeal was used, once; if the latter was omitted the potatoes were used thrice; but many families could only afford one meal a-day. With a superabundance of labourers at such wages, a soil, equal to Northumberland, or the richest parts of Berwickshire, was lying with its crops overpowered by the rank ripening weeds; docks overtopping the corn; thistles contending with the docks in the cornfields, and literally subduing the hay and pastures; rushes displacing both thistles and grass, and proclaiming in the face of bountiful Heaven that they had the best right to a wet soil, when that soil, though rich, was too wet to grow anything else. Potato-fields, too, struggled with foulness, and they struggled feebly; for the ill-managed farms of Meath do not produce the necessary manures to make crops profitable. Waste ridges lay at each end of the fields, and frequently a piece of the enclosure, the very richest piece, lay worthless and idle, because ten men for a-week were not employed to make a cut through some rise to admit of this being drained, which, after being drained, would have been profitable to its owner for ever.

But however applicable these remarks may be to the country between Navan and Trim, they are still more so to the country lying between Trim and Dublin. I saw farms in that district which, in luxuriant foulness, exceeded anything seen elsewhere. The reader who has travelled by railway through Staffordshire and Cheshire to Manchester must have remarked the many miles of country in which every second or third field is yet in the state it was in on the landing of the first Roman on British soil; he must have noticed the stagnant mires and rushes and all manner of *home-grown* aquatic weeds, on the low wet ground; and the thistles, and docks, and charlock, that occupy the drier soils on the higher ground. But no part of Staffordshire is worse cultivated than many miles of the county of Meath lying south and east of Trim; while there is this to be said against the landowners of Meath, that their soil is richer, kindlier, far more fertile than Cheshire, Lancashire, or Stafford. The very rankness of the Meath weeds proclaims the richness of the soil. But there are occasionally fields of grain seen, which, happening to be cultivated by persons who dare to cultivate well, they being protected from ejectment, show us what the soil can produce. Yet even such tenants as these go unskilfully to work; none of them that I have seen or heard of can produce a good crop of wheat without wasting an entire season in fallowing the soil.

Everywhere in Ireland, so far as I have yet seen, the land is comparatively profitless for the want of labour. And I find, in talking with the small tenantry, particularly about Kilkenny, that they are not ignorant of this fact; but even where they have this knowledge, and have in their own families a sufficiency of labourers, they choose to let their land assume an appearance of poverty which it should never wear. They have no security of tenure, and sad experience tells them that to enrich the soil is to invite an ejectment. Many of them in that county have leases, but even a lease in Ireland is no security. A landlord has only to make a profession of a wish to exchange a Catholic tenantry for Protestants, and, under cover of such a pretence, he may commit, *and does in this very year*, 1843, *commit* the most damnable and detestable robberies. He has only to assume the profession of political protestantism, and he becomes the defended and rewarded of the leaders of that party; all his sins are covered by the cloak of his political religion through the newspapers; and if aught be said against him on the other side—if he be only called a 'notorious landlord'. he prosecutes; and by moving the venue to some county where the dependant may not be known, he gets there—or, if he chooses, he may have the same in his own county—a jury of political Protestant landlords—men of his own station, of his own feelings, of his own character; he may have such a jury to try his cause, and give him a verdict.

Such is the present state of domestic affairs in Ireland. The landlord can do anything. The press of the dominant party protects and adopts him; and if the newspapers of the prostrate party expose him, or take but a step thereto—breathing but a whisper—he has the law and the jury of his own class ready to shield him.

I press these facts on the notice of the public, because the soil of Ireland is capable of producing crops far beyond anything yet common to agriculture, because her people are easily induced to adopt new theories and modes of working if their confidence in the experimenter or employer be first secured, and because, at the present time, in their own country, they regard with extreme jealousy any new doctrine in agriculture, and any new specimen or lesson from a new comer, seeing, as they have invariably seen, that such doctrines, and specimens, and injunctions to improve, were only preparatory to their being sacrificed and their land seized. And in a country almost devoid of trade and manufactures, to be turned out of a holding of land is a calamity falling on a family like a death stroke. There are people in England who have insanely said—and they are only worth referring to because they are not yet shut up in madhouses—that England would be as rich and powerful a country as she is were all her factories and factory towns hurled into the sea, and the sites they occupy furrowed by the plough. These people also allege another untruth, though its fallacy is not generally so apparent, namely, that a fall in the price of agricultural produce, caused by an influx of foreign grain, would throw a large portion of the soils of England, Ireland, and Scotland, out of cultivation. They assume that if a certain quality of land, at a rent of £2 per acre, each acre producing four quarters, does nothing more for the cultivator than pay its expenses, with wheat at 55s. a quarter, it will cease to afford any rent when wheat falls to 45s. a quarter; and they add, that when wheat falls below that, say to 40s., such land will go out of cultivation altogether.

Now, at first sight, this proposition seems plausible; but practically it is the reverse of true; and, startling as such a declaration may be to mathematical theorists writing pamphlets and leading articles, and making legislative speeches in London, or to well-meaning noblemen and other landowners, too rich or too busy with trifles to look after their own affairs and study their own interests, it is easily, though it cannot be briefly, substantiated. In this article I would be departing too far from my subject—a visit to Dangan Castle—were I to enter closely upon it. I will not, therefore, repeat the arguments and facts hitherto adduced in '*Notes from the Farming Districts*' of England, nor enter upon the still stronger facts tending to the same point which I see in Ireland; these I promise to use on any early occasion, when the proposition here asserted, in contradiction to the theorists, shall be fully proved. Meantime I give them the following truths to ponder over; they are not less at variance with the assumed facts of mathematical politics than the other proposition, and they do not require arguments and proof; they are visible to the eye. Any one travelling through the rural districts of England, Scotland, and Ireland, as I have done, and am now doing, may see the facts to be as I state them; indeed the traveller cannot shut his eyes upon them, for they press upon the sight so unceasingly, stare him in the face so palpably, that he has no choice but to see and believe them. These facts are—

1. That wherever the supply of labour is most plentiful and cheap

(and it is always cheapest where most plentiful) the land is worst cultivated.

2. Wherever the land is naturally richest it is worst cultivated and least profitable to the cultivators.

3. Wherever the expense of cultivation is greatest the comfort of the working people, the profit of the farmer, and the rent of the landowner are highest.

These truths will puzzle the rule-of-three writers as much as the denial of their assertion; but they must see the world as the world is, before they presume to say it moves like clock-work. As seen through our agriculture, the world is a pig driven to market; it gets there by turning its head the other way, or it is like a crab, moving side-ways or back-ways, any way but the way right a-head.

The scenic appearance of the country I have been speaking of, the district of Trim, in Meath, where the soil is so rich, the agriculture so poor, the people so plentiful, wages so low, and so few labourers employed at wages—the scenic appearance of this district is soft, luxurious, and seductive. The country, on a far stretch of the eye, seems level, but it is gently diversified by undulations. The river Boyne winds through the rich green meadows, and the hedge-rows and dotted woods add to the beauty, until variety itself forms a broad unchanging sameness.

The farms are from twenty up to fifty acres; but more of them vary from fifty up to two hundred acres. I saw a fifty acre farm, held by a gentleman tenant, who did not work himself. He kept only two labourers in constant employment, and being in constant work at ninepence a-day—no other perquisites—they were considered well paid by the people who worked in the neighbourhood for less. There was not a good fence on the farm, the land was wet, foul, and most unsightly to an agricultural eye.

The cottages of the poor are poor indeed. They are mostly clay huts, thatched with straw. Some of them are very tidy, whitewashed outside, and, besides having good windows and doors, are ornamentally thatched and decorated. But for one of these there are ten that are neither pleasing outside nor comfortable within. In respect of darkness and dampness, being without windows, having clay floors, and being small and ricketty, they resemble what the dwellings of the farm labourers used to be in Berwickshire, and what on many estates in Northumberland, near Berwick, they are to this day. Coming out of Navan, on the Trim road, I passed between two long rows of miserable hovels; one of the rows so very long and so very miserable, that I at last stopped the car, and went into some of them to see the interior and talk with the people who, from strange choice or unfortunate doom, inhabited them. One of them was four paces wide and five long. I could touch the thatch with my hands. There was no light but what came in by the low doorway. A partition wall of clay, four feet high, parted off an apartment for a pig and a bed occupied by four children. The father and mother and two more children slept in the front apartment. There was no fixed bed; whatever the bed was, it was stowed away during the day. Some articles of crockery were arranged, not without regard to show, on shelves, and a couple of iron pots, a table, a wash-tub, two or three seats, some of which were large stones, completed all the furniture I saw. The father of the family was at work to a farmer; his wages were ninepence a-day. Last year he got tenpence, but this year he had, like others, been reduced. The mother complained of headache, and said her health had been bad for years. All the children had been in fever, and fever was never out of the row of houses. They were the property of the Rev. Mr Hamilton, the Protestant clergyman. The rent paid for that one now described was eightpence a-week. Since wages had been reduced they tried to get house rent reduced, but had not succeeded. Some of the other huts were larger—as large as eight paces by five; but all were equally dark, dirty, and ill furnished. The rents were as high as a shilling a-week; the average being tenpence. The tenants were not suffered to run into arrear; the custom being, both in Navan and in Trim, to eject, by warrant of the magistrate, as soon as a fortnight's rent becomes due and is not paid. This Rev. Mr Hamilton is said to be rich - at least, he holds a good living, he has also landed property, which partakes of the management of other land in those parts.

Having visited some of the remarkable ruins around Trim, chief of which is a vast pile called John's Castle, we hired a car, and at six o'clock in the evening drove off to Dangan Castle, four miles south, or south-east. Arrived at the margin of the domain, we entered a narrow avenue by an iron gate, which was opened by a woman whose house was one of two or three low thatched huts. There were no trees shading the avenue, but a high thorn hedge, bushy, wild, and lofty, skirted it on either side. When we had proceeded three or four hundred yards, the park, that had once been finely wooded, but which, like a bald head, with a tree here and two of three there, and a few more, stunted and denuded of their ornamental branches, beyond, this park, with its fine valleys and finer eminences, once so magnificently wooded, now so shabbily bare, opened upon our view. The road went towards the left and again wheeled to the right. On the brow of a gentle slope stood the castle, like a huge ill-shaped barn—grey, treeless, shelterless, and in most parts roofless. Broken cars, and waggons, and ploughs that were idle, because it was summer, and

harrows idle as the ploughs, lay strewed about, and told of people who
were as idle as any of them, else they would have had them put tidily out
of the way. Cows were lowing in rear of the house to be milked, and
calves were clamorous for their allowance of what the cows were to give.
The gates that crossed the road, at various places, keeping vagrant pigs
and cattle asunder, were kept to their posts by old ropes and stones,
which had to be rolled away ere they could be opened, and rolled back
again ere the pigs could be restrained from accompanying the visitors to
the front of the castle; and even then, a sharp admonition over the snout
was requisite to make them remember they were pigs. The dogs, which
were ready to bite them on the ears, or to bark at the refractory cows and
calves, or at strangers like us, until told to be quiet, were lying on the
dunghills that lay on the roadside; and those who bade them be quiet
were leaning idly on the hay waggon or the stone wall, doing nothing
more than trying to make us think they were not looking at us.

On being spoken to, one came and opened a gate to allow us entrance
to the front of the castle, and another went the back way to carry our
compliments to the inmates and our request to be admitted to the
interior. The front shewed us the windows partly built up and the roof
wholly carried away. It may have been a pleasant house, it occupies a fine
situation, and is surrounded by ground which, if it has not been, might
be made, one of the finest pleasure parks in the world; but at all times
the house must have been plain. A red-painted door, made to fit its place
by a great portion of the doorway being built up to fit it, being opened to
us from the inside, we entered and found the main portion of the
building entirely cleared of its partitions and party walls. It was all open
above; and what had once been the dining-room, parlour, and library
floors, was now a flower garden. During the time the house was occupied
by the O'Connor family, who rented it from the Marquis Wellesley, it
was burned, save in the wing towards the rear, where the present
inhabitants now live. To this wing we proceeded; and the young lady
who kindly led the way, on taking us to what is now a comfortably
furnished parlour, told us that the common belief was, that in this room
the Duke of Wellington and the other members of the Mornington
family were born. There was a spacious bow window looking out upon
the garden and farm-yard, which occupied ground sloping from this to a
streamlet below, distant 100 or 200 yards. Inside the room was a large
circular recess, now shelved round, the shelves filled with articles of
ornament and use—glass, china, and such like. This recess is quite large
enough to have held a large bed; and, as we were told, did hold the
family couch of the Countess of Mornington, and subsequently that of
the mother of Feargus O'Connor.

When about to leave Trim on this visit, I put a few questions to an old gentleman who stood by the doorway of the hotel, such as, 'How far to Dangan Castle?' 'Who lives there now?' and so on. He told me that he was a tailor, still carried on business in Trim, and had made clothes for the young Wellesleys when boys. He made clothes for the Hon. Arthur Wellesley, now Duke of Wellington, when a boy. He also did work for him when he was the Hon. Captain Wellesley, and came to Trim on the recruiting service. He remembered, 'as distinctly as if it had been but yesterday', when the corporation of Trim elected this young officer to be one of their members in the Irish Parliament, when it was alleged that he had not attained his majority. On that occasion the nurse who attended at his birth was brought into the Court House at Trim, and he remembered seeing her, 'as plainly as if it happened but yesterday', put on the witness's table and sworn, and she proved that that very day one-and-twenty years she saw the Hon. Arthur Wellesley born at Dangan Castle.

I found this venerable tradesman intelligent and instructive. His name is Sherlock. He and his brother still conduct a respectable business in Trim.

On leaving Dangan Castle we drove through the park, and returned by a road skirting its exterior. The sun had now gone down, and the marshy hollows wore a thin covering of white fog; which, as we came along, rose gradually thicker, until it seemed to be a sheet which the fields, tired with the heat and labour of the day, had drawn around them on going to bed. Where there was a height to which the fog had not reached, we had only to suppose that the world had gone to bed without a nightcap, and that this was its bare head.

INDEX